Death of a Legend

The Myth and Mystery Surrounding the
Death of Davy Crockett

Bill Groneman

Republic of Texas Press
Plano, Texas

Library of Congress Cataloging-in-Publication Data
Groneman, Bill.
  Death of a legend : the myth and mystery surrounding the death of
  Davy Crockett / Bill Groneman.
      p. cm.
  Includes bibliographical references (p.) and index.
  ISBN 1-55622-688-8 (pbk.)
  1. Alamo (San Antonio, Tex.)—Siege, 1836. 2. Crockett, Davy,
  1786-1836—Death and burial. 3. Peña, José Enrique de la, 1807-1841
  or 2. Reseña y diario de la campaña de Texas. I. Title.
  F390.G845   1999
  976.4'03—dc21   99-28769
                                                      CIP

© 1999, Bill Groneman

Republic of Texas Press is an imprint of Wordware Publishing, Inc.
No part of this book may be reproduced in any form or by
any means without permission in writing from
Wordware Publishing, Inc.

Printed in the United States of America

ISBN 1-55622-688-8
10 9 8 7 6 5 4 3 2 1
9904

All inquiries for volume purchases of this book should be addressed to
Wordware Publishing, Inc., at 2320 Los Rios Boulevard, Plano, Texas 75074.
Telephone inquiries may be made by calling:

(972) 423-0090

iv

Death of a Legend

The Myth and Mystery Surrounding the
Death of Davy Crockett

Bill Groneman

Contents

For my children,
William Francis Groneman IV
and
Katherine Kelly Groneman

(Billy and Katie)

After all, I guess it doesn't matter whether you look down or up—as long as you look.

John Steinbeck, *Sweet Thursday*

"You May Take Our Lives, But You Will Never Take Our Freedom"
by Kirk Stirnweis

Full color prints of the cover art are available from:

Americana Historical Art
34 Sumner Pl.
Ft. Leavenworth, KS 66027
(913) 682-2543
E-mail: germmr@aol.com
website: http://members.xoom.com/aha98

Acknowledgments

I would like to thank and acknowledge all of the following: My wife Kelly, son Billy, daughter Katie, and Dalmatian Glennis. Ma and Mikey Novak. My friends at Republic of Texas Press, Russell and Dianne Stultz, Ginnie Bivona, Beth Kohler, Martha McCuller, and the rest of the fine staff. My friend, mentor, and former editor at Republic of Texas Press, Mary Goldman, for all of her encouragement. Also, Bill and Debbie Chemerka; Don and Terry Griffiths; Cathy Herpich; Clyde Hubbard; Brian Huberman, Ph.D. and Cynthia Wolf; Paul A. Hutton, Ph.D.; Bob Strong; Kirk Stirnweis for the cover artwork and to Dr. Harold Mermelstein for directing me to the artwork; and especially Tom Lindley, Joe Musso, and Rod Timanus for their continued support and assistance; the members of the Alamo Society; and the Western Writers of America. Also the staffs of the Daughters of the Republic of Texas Library at the Alamo, and the Malverne Public Library. And all the institutions, libraries, and archives that allowed me to use their artwork and photos: Maggie Reynolds of Americana Historical Art; The Center for American History, Austin; Daughters of the Republic of Texas Library, San Antonio; Institute of Texan Cultures, San Antonio; New York Historical Society, New York City; Sam Houston Regional Library and Research Center, Liberty, Texas; the Texas State Archives, Austin; and the *San Antonio Express-News*.

"Death of a Legend"
by Don Griffiths

Prints of "Death of a Legend" are available from:

Don Griffiths
2375 Fawn Hill Lane
Auburn, CA 95603
(530) 885-8117

Foreword

In 1994 I published a book with Republic of Texas Press entitled *Defense of a Legend: Crockett and the de la Peña Diary*. Originally the book was to be titled *Death of a Legend*, but my publisher was concerned that some confusion might be caused by an earlier article I had written and given the same title. My intent in writing that book was to bring forth new information relevant to the endless debate over the exact manner of David Crockett's death at the Alamo. The book focused on the alleged "diary" of Lieutenant José Enrique de la Peña (hereafter Peña) of the Mexican army. This "diary" includes an account describing Crockett's execution *after* the battle, dispelling the belief of Crockett's combat death. It has been used as the key bit of evidence to prove that Crockett actually did not die fighting during the legendary battle.

It was not my intent to prove that Crockett died as some Norse god, clubbing away at his enemies with every last ounce of his strength. Such is unprovable. It was not my intention to prove that he was not executed. He may have been. *Defense of a Legend* had more to do with the historical process that allowed an account such as the Peña "diary" to have become the final word on Crockett's death (or any historical subject) without having ever been verified or authenticated.

I had studied the Peña account on and off for years. I could never understand how Peña could have identified Crockett. Peña had been in San Antonio for only two days before the Alamo battle. There is no evidence that he had ever been to the United States or that he had ever heard of Crockett. Yet, according to his alleged account he was able to make a positive identification of the frontier congressman and to relate some background information on him. His "diary" never explains how he came by this information. The account does not describe the man identified as Crockett as having stated anything to Peña or to anyone else. This was knowledge that sprung fully armored from the brow of the writer of the account. This little problem never bothered anyone who used the Peña account as a historical source.

At any rate, I took another look at the account and came to the conclusion that the document in which the account is contained is a modern-day fake—a forgery. I believed that then and I believe that now. However, I am neither a professional historian nor a document expert. I do have a Bachelors degree in history, and some years back I had experience as a criminal investigator. As a fire marshal with the New York City Fire Department I investigated fires and made determinations as to whether the fires were accidentally or intentionally set. New York City fire marshals are police officers by New York State law. Their conclusions determine whether or not certain fires will be investigated as a crime. It is a similar function to that which a medical examiner performs regarding deaths.

Does this background qualify me to make determinations about historical documents? Absolutely not. What I did learn from working in this field of criminal investigation is that certain crimes follow certain patterns and have certain characteristics. The same holds true for document forgeries. They follow certain patterns and have certain characteristics. I cannot state conclusively that the Peña document is a forgery. I *can* state that the "diary" (the physical document and its text) contains a number of characteristics that are indicative of historical fakes. I felt this information was significant enough to be made public. The result was the 1994 *Defense of a Legend*.

I thought the book would be embraced by the professional historian and antiquarian communities. Historians would appreciate it since I was making an unknown known, and the antiquarian community would find it of interest since there was an investigation into forged Texan documents going on at the time. I believed my information would add to the general body of knowledge in this area. This was not necessarily so.

There were a number of problems with the book. I failed to correct some spelling errors, and I gave the incorrect name to an important reference library. Also I had recently reread Tom Wolfe's *The Right Stuff* and was influenced by his somewhat flippant writing style. In an effort to keep the book from being stuffy I also made some facetious remarks and engaged in some self-deprecating humor in places. As a result my presentation was perceived by some to be arrogant and combative.

The book received mixed reviews, mainly due to the nonacademic writing style. The book did create a stir, though. Professor James E. Crisp of North Carolina State University, whom I had met in San Antonio in 1994, was supposed to review the book for the prestigious *Southwestern Historical Quarterly*. Instead he wrote a scathing article ripping the book (and me) to shreds. This began a war of words between Jim and myself, which continues to this day.

Meanwhile, others have been drawn into the fray. Since the publication of *Defense* in 1994, approximately forty articles related to Peña, his "diary," or Crockett's death have been published in a variety of magazines, journals, and newspapers. In addition, the question of Crockett's death has been addressed as chapters in a number of books.

As the time approached for *Defense of a Legend* to reprint, the decision was made to replace it with a completely new and updated book, which would include all of the new developments that had taken place since the writing of *Defense*. The most significant of these was the announcement of the intended auction of the Peña holograph in November of 1998.

I wanted to move on from the question of Crockett's death, which Professor Paul Andrew Hutton of the University of New Mexico calls " . . . [my] favorite hobby horse." On the other hand, I saw this as an opportunity to present a history of the mystery of Crockett's death without primarily focusing on my belief in the Peña "diary" as a fraud. Of course, the Peña "diary" is a major part of the story. For some it is a Rosetta Stone bringing corroboration and understanding to all of the wildly discordant tales of Crockett's alleged execution. To others who have used it as a major source of information and for colorful "sound bites" in their historical writing, it now may be a millstone. They are so attached to this account through their dependency on it in their writings that they cannot detach themselves from it. To many others it is a keystone by which all of the accounts of Crockett's execution either stand or fall. (Okay, to some of us it is getting to be like a kidney stone.) So the Peña "diary" *must* be written about in a book such as this.

This new book gives me the opportunity to present the history and evolution of our beliefs regarding this one brief moment in history. It also gives me the opportunity to adjust the tone of the telling of the story to something less combative than that in *Defense*. I can present readers and reviewers a warmer, more cuddly Bill Groneman—the real me.

The question of the importance of the exact manner of Crockett's or any other person's death is often raised. Many writers have assured us that it is not really important how he died but how he *lived*. Writers usually make this statement after they have gone on for a while about Crockett's death. It is a "feel good" ending to the story. Of course, worlds are not going to turn on how Crockett died. However, the subject is of endless interest, as is evidenced by the many articles and books that have been generated by it. The subject certainly is still important to some students of the Alamo battle. It also may be interesting to people fascinated by historical mysteries. It is probably of interest to the many descendants of Crockett, who have had to endure watching a variety of writers and historians twist Crockett's reputation from that of an impeccable hero to that of a groveling coward. This is an opportunity to look at the question from beginning to end. Maybe the importance rests in the evaluation of how the historical process works, using the subject of Crockett's death as an example.

While I have my own opinions, I do not attempt to tell anyone the exact manner of Davy Crockett's death. I leave that to others. In the recent past some writers have described Crockett's death and even provided information on what he felt, thought, said, tried to do, etc. These detailed descriptions were given in historical books and articles. Novelists have gone further based on the historical descriptions. Jeff Long in his novel about Sam Houston, *Empire of Bones*, opened the book with a well-written, if gratuitous, chapter about Crockett's death by execution. In it Long paints Crockett as a jittery, pathetic buffoon. He also shares with us, in great detail, Crockett's fear-induced gastrointestinal and urinary functions.

Will my book answer all the questions? Probably not. Will it end the controversy? I hope not. Will it add to our body of knowledge about one little part of western Americana? I hope so. At least it may help to put the whole story into perspective. Maybe it will provide the background for those who wish to investigate further.

Introduction

On February 23, 1955 (the 119th anniversary of the beginning of the siege of the Alamo), the Disneyland television show aired the final episode of its series *Davy Crockett, King of the Wild Frontier*. The episode was "Davy Crockett at the Alamo." A giant Texan named Fess Parker portrayed Crockett in this series as a low-keyed, amiable, and always reliable frontiersman. At the end of this final episode the Mexican army overruns the Alamo. Crockett's companions are picked off one by one. Crockett stands alone at the top of a stairway to the battlements, flailing away with his rifle "Old Betsy" as the Mexican troops close in. The camera fades out on this scene and Crockett's image becomes that of the Alamo flag, which then becomes the Texas flag. It was good filmmaking and nice, safe history. Nineteen fifties "Baby Boomers" did not see Crockett die. It was just as well, since no one at the time knew how Crockett died. It was also a good idea in that it did not traumatize a generation with enough trauma ahead of it. *Davy Crockett* became one of the most popular TV shows in history. A marketing campaign of Crockett merchandise was wildly successful. Anything sold as long as it had Davy Crockett's name on it.

I bring this subject up in order to get it out of the way. You cannot speak about the historical Crockett and the circumstances surrounding his death without mentioning this landmark of Crockett myth and legend. I became familiar with it on its many reruns over the years. *Davy Crockett*, along with other Disney shows about historical incidents and figures, sparked my interest in American history. Most of the "Baby Boomers" interested in Davy Crockett and the Alamo today were influenced similarly. I was interested in the Crockett TV show but not obsessed by it, nor am I today. It is important to state this because if you write about Crockett or the Alamo today and do not go along with trendy revisionist views on those subjects, someone invariably points out that you are obsessed with childhood images and heroes. This is not the case, at least regarding me. Yes, I am interested in the subject, but no, I do not feel obligated to defend the reputation of the historical Crockett or any of his cinematic manifestations.

Within one month of the airing of the Alamo episode on TV, a Mexico City numismatist and flea market salesman self-published a book purported to be the diary of a Mexican officer who participated in the Battle of the Alamo. The book contained one passage that described Crockett as being taken alive with six other Alamo defenders at the end of the battle. He and the others are then executed on the orders of Generalissimo Antonio Lopez de Santa Anna. This revelation did not generate any particular interest at the time. It was mentioned in some books and articles but remained virtually dormant for the next twenty years. In 1975 Carmen Perry translated this "diary" and published it with Texas A&M University Press. The news media picked up on the passage describing the executions and had a field day portraying Crockett as something less than our traditional view of him. Then Perry began to be harassed with hate mail and crank calls, and the news fed on this. History gave way to media hype.

Three years later, Dan Kilgore, president of the Texas State Historical Association, published his own book on Crockett's death, also through Texas A&M University Press. The book was developed from a speech he had given before the association. Kilgore was justifiably upset over the harassment that his friend Perry had received. In his book he came to her defense by offering six other, supposedly firsthand, accounts and to the satisfaction of many corroborated the Peña account. Instead of becoming the peacemaker, Kilgore became the target of the threats, harassment, and name-calling. Kilgore's book served the purpose of superficially authenticating the controversial information in Perry's book. The idea of Crockett being executed after the Battle of the Alamo became installed as historical fact.

Fast forward to 1994 and the publishing of *Defense of a Legend* in which I advanced the theory that the Peña "diary" is probably a modern-day fake, and that all of the other accounts used to corroborate it are somewhat less than they seem to be on the surface. This initiated the continuing brouhaha between myself and Jim Crisp, which at times has been bitter and at others comic. There is something irresistible about the argument. Others are drawn in, sides are taken, and alliances are formed. At times the participants seem to be just on the verge of exchanging gunfire. Peacemakers emerge to end the debate with well-thought-out theories of their own. They end up rolling around in the street with everyone else. All of this over the last fifteen minutes of a life that lasted almost fifty years and ended over one hundred and sixty years ago.

As the argument goes on, it shifts and changes and splits off into finer points of contention. Questions are raised and theories put forward on whether Crockett died fighting or was executed; whether he surrendered or was taken captive after an all-out fight (if he was executed); whether he was a hero or a coward; whether or not any particular piece of evidence that supports any particular theory is real, etc.

The history of the American West is a curious blend of myth, legend, fact, fancy, and sometimes fabrication. Legendary events and people abound, as do unanswered questions. The death of a famous (or infamous) person involved in an epic event and shrouded in a little mystery is a natural attraction. There is no better place for this than the West. The deaths (and sometimes reappearances) of a number of figures of the Old West are of enduring interest. Controversy surrounds the deaths of Jesse James, Billy the Kid, George A. Custer, Butch Cassidy and the Sundance Kid, Andrew Bierce, and even John Wilkes Booth, to name just a few. People like to keep their heroes (and villains) alive. This may explain the many stories of some of these figures "reappearing" after having lived incognito many years after their supposed deaths.

Crockett made no such reappearance, although there were rumors that he was made a prisoner and worked as a slave in the mines of Mexico. Some contemporary newspaper stories claimed that he did not die at the Alamo but was off hunting in the Rocky Mountains. The persistent rumors and stories that keep legendary people "alive" long after they are gone serve some psychological need in us. The stories of Crockett's execution seem to serve a similar need. If Crockett is cut down in the din and smoke of battle, then he is gone. It happens in a split second and then he is gone—immediately and forever. If he is taken alive and then executed, it gives us a chance for one more look at him. For his admirers it is a time of poignancy and reflection. They are given an opportunity to see the living legend stand before his executioners with nobility and dignity. They can bid him farewell. It is like the closing scene of the film *Butch Cassidy and the Sundance Kid*. Butch and Sundance charge out. You hear the gunfire of the soldiers, but you do not see Butch and Sundance rendered into bloody messes by the bullets. In freeze frame the scene fades to a sepia-toned photograph, and the outlaw heroes are preserved in our memories as they were in life. So is Crockett preserved before his alleged execution—in noble, if not tragic, dignity before his captors. To Crockett's detractors and those who need him as a symbol of American jingoistic expansionism, his execution serves a similar purpose. They are also given one last look at the frontier hero through a different lens. They see a broken phony humiliated before his enemies. They revel in watching a fear-crazed wretch wriggle and squirm on the hook before his captors execute him in disgust.

It should be pointed out that none of the purported "eyewitness" accounts of Crockett's alleged execution give such a description. This fact has not kept modern writers from extrapolating this exact scenario from what little information actually is given. Unfortunately, this image of a cowardly, degraded Crockett has appeared in "history" books without any background or explanation. Invariably this information makes its way into newspapers for a quick, sensationalistic story, and this is the image impressed on the minds of the public.

As we stand now, the opinions, the arguments, the haggling, and our need for Crockett to be a symbol of something beyond what he was have overshadowed the facts. What follows is our current body of knowledge concerning the last moments of a common man who had the fortune (or misfortune) of becoming a legend in his own lifetime. The ongoing brawl over Crockett's memory is so integrated with the story of his death that it cannot be left out. I will try to point out when something is opinion (my own or someone else's) as opposed to absolute fact.

There is no reason to believe that this book or any other will ever lay Crockett or the battle over his death to rest.

CHAPTER ONE

Davy Crockett and the Alamo

· · · ◆ · · ·

When [Crockett] arrived... everybody wanted to see him, shake hands with him and congratulate him... my childish curiosity, got the better of my politeness... and I turned around and looked at him steadily until with a nod and a smile, he indicated that he was more amused than offended. I have never forgotten his face and that smile on that occasion.
—Dr. S.H. Stout (on a childhood memory
of seeing David Crockett in 1829)

We have been often times asked, "What sort of man is colonel Crockett?" and the general reply was... "just such a one as you would desire to meet with, if any accident or misfortune had happened to you on the high way."
—Niles Weekly Register, 1833[1]

The Hon. David Crockett was seen at all points, animating the men to do their duty.
—William Barret Travis, 1836

THE STORY OF THE BATTLE OF THE ALAMO and the Texas Revolution are complex. Both have been the subjects of books, scholarly articles, dissertations, etc. For the purposes of this book a brief description is necessary. Texas, part of the Mexican state of Coahuila y Tejas, engaged in a revolt against Mexico in the autumn of 1835. The reasons for this revolt were many, but basically Texas was fighting for separate statehood within the Mexican Republic. Most of those involved in the revolt were emigrants to Texas from the United States and Europe. Also involved were some of the native Texans, or Tejanos as they are now called. A Texan military force was assembled hastily. It constantly changed and reorganized itself, but it did have some success in the early stages of the conflict. During 1835 the Texans enjoyed victories in minor engagements at Gonzales, Goliad, Nueces Crossing, and Concepcion. Their most significant victory came in December of 1835 when they defeated the Mexican garrison under General Martin Perfecto de Cos at San Antonio de Bexar. Cos and his men were permitted to leave Texas under parole. This left Texas in the hands of the Texans. It also left the town of San Antonio de Bexar and the former mission San Antonio de Valero (the Alamo) in the hands of a Texan garrison under Colonel James Clinton Neill.

The pressure on the Texans had relaxed with the withdrawal of the Mexican army. The garrison in San Antonio dwindled to as few as eighty men during the winter of 1835-36. Neill had every reason to believe the Mexican army would be back in force during the spring. He began to call on the embryonic Texan government to send him men, supplies, and money. His requests were answered, to a certain extent, with the arrival of several small reinforcements. The most notable of these were a company of Regular Texan cavalry under Lieutenant Colonel William Barret Travis and a volunteer company under Colonel James Bowie.

The Texans at San Antonio in early February 1836 had no way of knowing it, but the Mexican army was only three weeks away. Neill left San Antonio at this time in an effort to hasten on more reinforcements and supplies. He appointed Travis to command in his absence. It was about this time, in early February, that David Crockett and a small band of men he had joined on the road to Texas arrived in San Antonio. A few weeks earlier they had been sworn into the Volunteer Auxiliary Corps of the Texan army. At San Antonio, they joined the garrison.

Crockett was born on August 17, 1786, in what is now Green County, Tennessee. He was the son of John and Rebecca Hawkins Crockett. At age twelve and with a very minimal education he left home on a cattle drive to Virginia. He was gone for two years before returning home and was on his own thereafter. In 1806 Crockett married Polly Finley. They had two sons and a daughter and lived in Lincoln County, Tennessee. He tried farming but usually sustained his family through his hunting skills, which were considerable. In 1813 he enlisted in a militia unit in Winchester, Tennessee, for service in the Creek Indian War. He took part in the massacre of Indians at Tallussahatchee, Alabama, and later served in Florida in pursuit of the Creeks. Crockett resigned from the army with the rank of sergeant after serving two hitches.

Polly Crockett died in 1815. The following year Crockett married Elizabeth Patton, a young widow with two children whose husband was killed in the Creek War. Crockett and Elizabeth had two children of their own, and he raised her children as his own.

Crockett moved his new family west, to the Shoal Creek community where he began to dabble in local politics. He served as magistrate and was elected colonel of the local militia unit. He also tried some business ventures, which were consistent in that they ended in failure. In one instance he tried to transport barrel staves by flatboat down the Mississippi River. The boats sank, his whole cargo was lost, and he managed to just barely escape with his life. In another instance he established a gristmill, powder mill, and distillery that were all washed away in a flood.

In 1821 and 1823 Crockett was elected to the Tennessee legislature, representing a district of eleven western counties of the state. From 1827 to 1831 and 1833 to 1835 he served in the United States Congress. Although his congressional record was not spectacular, Crockett achieved national prominence. The newspapers loved him and kept him in the public eye. In 1831 a popular play *The Lion of the West* premiered, with its main character "Nimrod Wildfire" based on Crockett. In 1834 Crockett's autobiography appeared, and a year later the first of a series of *Crockett Almanacs* were published that elevated Crockett and his exploits to a mythological level. They would continue a run lasting twenty years after Crockett had died.

David Crockett (1786 - 1836)
Watercolor by Anthony Lewis DeRose.
Collection of the New York Historical Society, New York City.

Crockett's pet political projects were squatters' rights and the prevention of the uprooting of the Cherokee and other Southeastern Indian tribes from their traditional lands. His ideals and outspoken opposition to President Andrew Jackson led to his defeat in 1831 and to his formal break with the Jacksonians. He was then embraced by Jackson's opponents, the Whigs, and won a seat in Congress for the final time in 1833. He was finally defeated in 1835. By now Crockett had soured on politics. He told his constituents that if they did not elect him they could go to hell and he would go to Texas. They did not and he did.

Crockett set out for Texas in 1835 with a small group of companions, none of whom would continue on with him to the Alamo. Crockett's fame preceded him, and he was feted at a number of towns along the way. On the route he fell in with another loosely organized group of men. On January 14, 1836, many of these men swore an oath of allegiance to any future government of Texas at the town of Nacogdoches. Crockett balked until they changed the wording to any future republican government. It was here that they were enlisted into the Volunteer Auxiliary Corps of the fledgling Texan army. Crockett and the others may have jocularly referred to themselves as the "Tennessee Mounted Volunteers." It is unlikely that Crockett actually commanded these men. The group traveled together, more or less, from Nacogdoches to San Antonio de Bexar and the Alamo, arriving on or about February 9.

The siege of the Alamo began on February 23, 1836, with the return of the Mexican army. The Mexican force was led by none other than Antonio Lopez de Santa Anna, the president of Mexico. With the approach of Santa Anna and his men, the Texans abandoned San Antonio and took refuge in the fortified Alamo. The Alamo stood across the San Antonio River from the town, with its west wall only about one-half mile from the center of town. With the Texans locked up inside the Alamo, the Mexican army settled down to siege warfare. During the next thirteen days more Mexican troops arrived. Travis also received at least one, but possibly more, small reinforcements. Couriers left and entered the Alamo right up until the final day. The siege culminated in a predawn battle on the morning of March 6.

The Alamo was the former mission San Antonio de Valero, established by the Franciscans in its present location in 1724. The cornerstone of its church was laid in 1744. It had served as a mission and later as the headquarters of a Spanish cavalry company. It had most recently been used by the Mexican army under General Cos as a fort. The Alamo itself was a sprawling complex of walls and buildings roughly resembling a capital "L." Its main plaza ran north to south and comprised the long axis of the "L." On the interior of its west wall were a series of small structures built against the wall. Across the plaza to the east were sturdier two-story buildings known as the "long barracks." The top of the "L" was the Alamo's exposed north wall. The south wall was comprised of a building known as the "low barracks" and included the Alamo's main gate. To the east of the main gate, or along the lower axis of the "L," was a small walled-in courtyard, and to the east of that, the Alamo's most recognizable building, the church. North of the church and courtyard and east of the main plaza were walled-in horse and cattle corrals. The whole complex comprised about three acres. Its west wall faced the town of San Antonio on the opposite bank of the San Antonio River. The walls were from eight to twelve feet high, and the roofless church building had walls twenty-two feet high. It was not much of a fortress. Its major strength lay in the

The Alamo

A. Main entrance of the Alamo fortress.
B. Inner courtyard.
C. Alamo church.
D. Main Plaza.
E. Hospital and barracks.
F. Horse quartel.
G. Wooden palisade.
H. Southwest artillery position.
I. Low barracks.
J. Cattle pen.
K. Conjectural position of wells.
L. West wall with series of small rooms.
M. Long barracks.
N. Low wall.
O. Irrigation ditch.

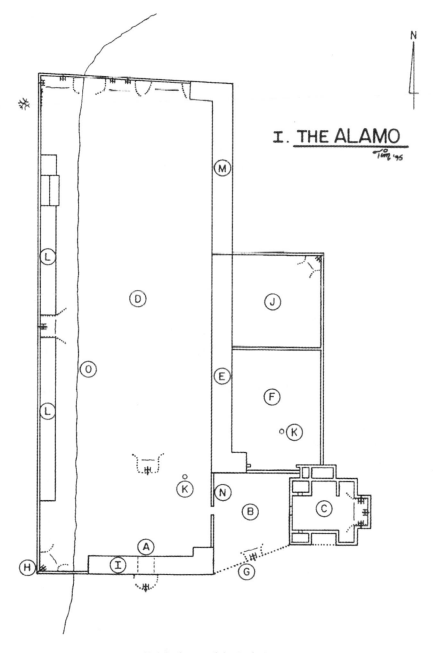

I. THE ALAMO

(Original artwork by Rod Timanus)

fact that it was a walled enclosure with a substantial collection of artillery, numbering anywhere from fourteen to twenty-one pieces, depending on the source. It was located near a fairly large town that also was the local seat of political power. Finally, it was garrisoned by a group of men, although small in number, who were willing to tough it out since they fully expected to be reinforced.

Information on Crockett's role in the siege is scant. There is a longstanding and much quoted account attributed to Texan soldier John Sutherland that describes the opening scenes of the siege. In this account Sutherland accompanies John W. Smith on a scout outside of town after a sentry in the bell tower of the San Fernando church claimed to have spotted the approaching Mexican force. After Smith and Sutherland confirm the arrival of the troops, they ride back to town at breakneck speed to sound the alarm. Sutherland's horse slips in the mud and goes down, injuring Sutherland's knee. Smith helps Sutherland to remount, and they continue to ride into San Antonio. By the time they arrive they find the town abandoned by the Texan troops. Only Crockett and his men remain as a rear guard. Smith leaves to close up his house in town while Crockett accompanies Sutherland to the presence of Travis in the Alamo. Sutherland reports what he has seen to Travis. The commander, recognizing that Sutherland has injured his leg, decides to send him off as a courier rather than use him as a combatant. While Sutherland is conferring with Travis, Crockett hovers in the background. Finally he interrupts, "Colonel, here am I, assign me a position, and I and my twelve boys will try to defend it." Travis assigns him and his "Tennessee boys" to the defense of a low wooden palisade. This wall connects the southwest corner of the Alamo church with the low barracks, the Alamo's south wall. The palisade is considered a weak point in the Alamo's defenses, and its assignment to Crockett bespeaks Travis' trust in Crockett and his men. In later histories it is considered a "post of honor."[2]

Sutherland's account is the dramatic beginning to a dramatic story and has been used in almost every telling of the

Alamo battle since it first appeared in 1896. In recent years, however, the story virtually has been shot down through the research of Thomas Ricks Lindley. He has shown that the Sutherland account first given to John S. Ford by the Sutherland family in 1896 was an expanded and embellished version of a deposition he had given in 1854. His 1854 statement was made in a petition for land based on his service in the Texas Revolution. The earlier and much shorter version makes no mention of Crockett. A still earlier and unsuccessful request for a land bounty by Sutherland contained neither a mention of Crockett nor the story of Sutherland's serving as a scout and courier for Travis. Lindley also shows there is no documentation that places Sutherland at San Antonio on February 23, 1836.[3]

Sutherland's account was important because it gave us a glimpse of a flesh and blood, human Crockett at the beginning of the Alamo siege. It also gave us a location for Crockett inside the Alamo during the siege. This is the area directly in front of the famous Alamo church and the area, according to tradition, that Crockett did defend. Years later several Alamo survivors or alleged survivors placed Crockett (or his body) in this area.[4]

There is only one other reference to Crockett during the Alamo siege. He is mentioned in a letter by Travis of February 25, 1836. Travis wrote of the action of that day in which two or three hundred Mexican soldiers made a foray against the Alamo. He described in glowing terms the fight that lasted two hours. Finally the Mexicans were driven back by the Texan fire of grape and cannister as well as small arms fire. Travis stated that "The Hon. David Crockett was seen at all points, animating the men to do their duty." Crockett was not the only one to receive recognition. Travis also praised Lieutenant [Cleland K]. Simmons, Captains [William R.] Carey, [Almeron] Dickinson, [Samuel] Blair, Charles Despallier, and Robert Brown.[5] Crockett is not mentioned in the two or three letters written by Travis on March 3.

Tom Lindley has presented the idea that Crockett left the Alamo and then returned just prior to the battle. Lindley theorizes that Crockett was sent by Travis to Cibolo Crossing on the Cibolo River to hasten reinforcements on to the Alamo.[6] Since Crockett had a fairly well-known name, at least to those exposed to Tennessee politics and Eastern newspapers, he would certainly have been a logical choice. He probably would not have traveled alone since he was new to the country. Some support for Lindley's theory comes from Alamo survivor Susanna Dickinson. Years later she was quoted as saying, "Col. Crockett was one of the 3 men who came into the Fort during the siege & before the assault. He was killed, she believes."[7]

Travis' letter is the only contemporary description of Crockett's activities during the siege. Several accounts given many years later also describe his activities. Another account by Susanna Dickinson appeared in 1875 in James M. Morphis' *History of Texas from Its First Discovery and Settlement*. In this book she is credited as saying, "I knew Colonels Crockett, Bowie, and Travis well. Col. Crockett was a performer on the violin, and often during the siege took it up and played his favorite tunes."[8] An oft repeated bit of Alamo lore has Crockett engaging in musical duels with Scotsman John McGregor, who played the bagpipes. Crockett's lighthearted demeanor may have faded during the tedious siege. Dickinson went on to say, "I heard him say several times during the eleven [sic] days of the siege 'I think we had better march out and die in the open air. I don't like to be hemmed up.'"[9]

Enrique Esparza was the eight-year-old son of Alamo defender Gregorio Esparza. His family lived in San Antonio, and he along with his mother and siblings accompanied his father into the Alamo after the arrival of Santa Anna. Esparza's role in the Alamo battle went unreported until after the turn of the century. In a 1902 interview the seventy-four-year-old Esparza described his memories of the battle:

> I remember Crockett. He was a tall, slim man,
> with black whiskers. He was always at the head.
> The Mexicans called him Don Benito. The Ameri-
> cans said he was Crockett. He would come to the

fire and warm his hands and say a few words to us in the Spanish language. . . . Don Benito had conferences every day with Santa Anna. Badio [probably Badillo], the interpreter, was a close friend of my father, and I heard him tell my father in the quarters that Santa Anna had offered to let the Americans go with their lives if they would surrender, but the Mexicans would be treated as rebels . . . . Don Benito, or Crockett, as the Americans called him, assembled the men on the last day and told them Santa Anna's terms, but none of them believed that any one who surrendered would get out alive, so they all said as they would have to die any how they would fight it out.[10]

Five years later, in 1907, another newspaper interview with Esparza appeared. In this one he gave a more descriptive picture of Crockett.

Crockett seemed to be the leading spirit. He was everywhere. He went to every exposed point and personally directed the fighting. Travis was chief in command, but he depended more upon the judgment of Crockett and that brave man's intrepidity than upon his own. Bowie, too, was brave and dauntless, but he was ill. Prone upon his cot he was unable to see much that was going on about him and the others were too engrossed to stop and tell him. Although too weak to stand upon his feet, when Travis drew the line with his sword Bowie had those around him bring his cot across the line.

I heard the few Mexicans there call Crockett "Don Benito." Afterward I learned his name was David, but I only knew him as Don Benito.[11]

Andrea Castañon de Villanueva, known as "Madam Candelaria," claimed to have been in the Alamo during the entire siege and battle. She was known as Madam Candelaria due to her marriage to Candelario Villanueva. She claimed she was in the Alamo as a nurse to the ailing James Bowie. In later life she gave a number of interviews and would enthrall visitors with her stories of the Alamo. She offered one of the oddest descriptions of Crockett. "He was one of the strangest-looking men I ever saw. He had the face of a woman and his manner was that of a young girl."[12]

Historians are still undecided about Madam Candelaria's role or her actual presence in the Alamo. In a 1901 article Enrique Esparza is quoted as saying, "...she was not there. She had been in [the Alamo] frequently before it fell...and was there immediately afterward, but was not present when the actual fall of the Alamo and massacre of its patriotic defenders occurred...." In his 1907 interview he tempered his remark somewhat and said, "I do not remember having seen Madam Candalaria [sic] there. She may have been there and I shall not dispute her word. I did not notice the women as closely as I did the men." Another Alamo survivor, Juana Navarro Alsbury, was not able to verify Candelaria's presence but expressed no disbelief in her statement. She added, "There were people in the Alamo I did not see."[13]

One other often-quoted possible description of Crockett comes to us in the writings of James T. DeShields (1861-1948). DeShields quoted Creed Taylor, a "...grizzled old veteran...of the Texas War of Independence" in his book *Tall Men with Long Rifles*. Taylor allegedly obtained this information in Corpus Christi, Texas, at the end of the Mexican War. According to Taylor, the information came from one Captain Rafael Soldana of the Tampico Battalion. Soldana supposedly led a company in the attack on the Alamo. According to DeShields/Taylor/Soldana:

> A tall man, with flowing hair, was seen firing from the same place on the parapet during the entire siege. He wore a buckskin suit and a cap all of a pattern entirely different from those worn by his comrades. This man would kneel or lie down

behind the low parapet, rest his long gun and fire, and we all learned to keep at a good distance when he was seen to make ready to shoot. He rarely missed his mark and when he fired he always rose to his feet and calmly reloaded his gun seemingly indifferent to the shots fired at him by our men. He had a strong, resonant voice and often railed at us, but as we did not understand English we could not comprehend the import of his words further than that they were defiant. This man I later learned was known as "Kwockey."[14]

"Kwockey" is believed by many to have been Crockett. However, this colorful account is not verified by any independent sources. More on the alleged Soldana account will be discussed in a later chapter.

Any accounts given long after the fact are subject to question. Esparza and Dickinson were advanced in years when they made their statements. We really do not know how much their memories had been affected by the trauma they experienced at the Alamo, the passage of time, and the contamination by their exposure to other sources and accounts.

Esparza's descriptions of Crockett have given historians some problems over the years. He described Crockett as a "slim man," but the one full-length portrait of Crockett done from life shows him to have been somewhat stocky.[15] What the portrait tells us is that Crockett was stocky in 1834, at the time the portrait was done. Crockett was still serving as a U.S. Congressman at that time. During his trek from Tennessee to Texas, Crockett was forced to sell his watch (which was later returned to his widow) and trade his rifle for one of lesser quality plus a monetary balance. If things were that bad during his trip to Texas, it is unlikely that he was eating as regularly as he may have become accustomed to in Washington, D.C. It is likely that he would have lost weight on such a journey, so perhaps his description as a "slim man" is accurate.

There are further problems with Esparza's reminiscences, especially with calling Crockett "Benito." In Yale University's Bieneke Rare Book and Manuscript Library there is a letter believed to have been written by James Bowie. The letter is a message to the commander of the invading forces below Bejar [San Antonio de Bexar] and is dated February 23, 1836, the first day of the Alamo siege. The letter inquires as to whether or not a parley had been called for by the Mexican force. The carrier of the message is identified as "Benito" Jameson and is called Bowie's "second aid" [sic]. The Alamo garrison's engineering officer was Green B. Jameson, a Kentucky-born lawyer who came to Texas in 1830 and lived in Brazoria. It is not known if Jameson normally was called "Benito" or if Bowie's message was the only reference to him by that name. Many of the things that Esparza said about Crockett fit Jameson fairly well. Having been in Texas since 1830 it is reasonable that he did acquire the Spanish language, especially if he was plying his trade as a lawyer. This would explain his being used as emissary to the Mexican forces. It would also fit Esparza's description of the person, identified as Crockett, who would come over to the fire and "say a few words . . . in the Spanish language." It is not known if Crockett could speak any Spanish. However, like anyone else who travels to a foreign land, he may have picked up "a few words" along the way. It would have been more likely for Jameson, an officer of the garrison, than Crockett to have acted as an emissary between the Texans and the Mexican army.

It is possible that Esparza, in his old age, confused Jameson for Crockett. It is also possible that he was speaking of Crockett but attributed some of Jameson's actions to him. Perhaps the "Benito" was a generic nickname, like "Johnny" or "Pal," used in lieu of a person's actual first name. Jameson and Crockett both may have been called "Benito."

March 6, 1836

The thirteen-day siege of the Alamo ended in battle in the early morning hours of March 6, 1836. Two days earlier, Santa Anna's First Brigade of Infantry arrived. The brigade included the Aldama and Toluca Battalions and the Engineers and brought the troops up to the number Santa Anna needed to assault the Alamo. Later that day he convened a meeting of his officers and decided on a plan of attack. On the afternoon of March 5 General Juan Valentine Amador issued a directive to all units outlining the plan. Four columns carrying twenty-eight scaling ladders would attack the Alamo at 4 A.M. on the following morning.[16] The directive also specified that weapons "especially bayonets" should be put in top condition. There was no mention of what was to be done with prisoners. Santa Anna's officers should have known that already. In a letter of March 3, Santa Anna wrote to General José Cosme Urrea, commanding the Mexican army's east wing:

[Official] In respect to the prisoners of whom you speak in your last communication, you must not fail to bear in mind the circular of the supreme government, in which it is decreed, that "foreigners invading the republic, and taken with arms in their hands, shall be judged and treated as pirates"; and as, in my view of the matter, every Mexican guilty of the crime of joining these adventurers loses the rights of a citizen by his unnatural conduct, the five Mexican prisoners whom you have taken ought also to suffer as traitors.

[Unofficial] In regard to foreigners who make war, and those unnatural Mexicans who have joined their cause, you will remark that what I have stated to you officially is in accordance with the former provisions of the supreme government. An example is necessary, in order that those adventurers may be duly warned, and the nation be delivered from the ills she is daily doomed to suffer.

In another letter, this one to General Joaquin Ramirez y Sesma, Santa Anna reminded the general that "In this war you know there ought to be no prisoners."

Travis himself wrote in a letter, "The enemy has demanded a surrender at discretion, otherwise, the garrison are to be put to the sword, if the fort is taken."[17]

Actually, this was an accepted policy of siege warfare that dated back to medieval times. This policy dictated that the longer the besieged delayed, the higher the price he paid. Once a breach was opened in the walls of a castle or fort and the besieged did not surrender, the besiegers were no longer obliged to offer quarter. The Alamo is often spoken about as having a breach opened in its north wall prior to the final battle. This may or may not be so. The north wall was a long, freestanding wall unsupported by buildings on the inside. Wooden beams and planking had been used to support it. This is evidenced by the fact that the Mexican attack columns assigned to the north wall were issued axes and crowbars along with their complement of scaling ladders. Perhaps Mexican artillery fire did open up some type of breach. Mexican infantrymen certainly did breach the north wall during the final assault, and the Texans did not surrender. Whether by virtue of a hole blasted in the wall or by the Mexicans scaling the wall, the besiegers were absolved from showing mercy by the accepted practices of the time.[18]

Inside the Alamo the Texans were worn down by twelve days of siege. They still held out hope that reinforcements would arrive. As late as two days earlier Travis had received word from his friend R.M. Williamson, assuring him that help was on the way and urging him to hold out. The Texans worked long into the night shoring up their defenses.[19]

The Battle of the Alamo commenced a little later than planned. At about 5 A.M. on the morning of March 6, 1836, the four Mexican columns advanced on the fort. Travis had been asleep in his quarters when his adjutant John J. Baugh of

Virginia roused him with the alarm. Travis and his slave, Joe, ran to their defensive position on the north wall of the Alamo.

The Texans in the Alamo probably never had any clear-cut strategy. Legend tells us the Texans were buying time in order for Sam Houston to raise an army, or they were trying to cause so many enemy casualties that Santa Anna's victory would be worse for him than defeat. Either seems a pretty thin goal at the expense of losing the lives of all of your men, all of your artillery, and your post. It is more likely Travis was following a tried and true policy of the Texas frontier: When there was trouble, you met it head on, delayed it, and waited until help arrived. This system had worked a number of times against Native American tribes. It also had worked the previous October when Mexican troops were sent to the Texan town of Gonzales to retrieve a cannon on loan to the townspeople. The Mexican force was met and delayed by a small group of settlers, the "Old Eighteen," while a call for help went out. Within days the Texans had grown in number to approximately one hundred fifty. They sent the Mexican force reeling back toward San Antonio.

Now, some of the men who had taken part in the Gonzales skirmish were inside the Alamo. They had every reason to believe help was on the way. In fact, a number of parties of reinforcements were on the way. However, they would not reach the Alamo on time. If Travis had any specific plans or tactics for the defense of the Alamo, it is doubtful he had time to implement them. When he reached the north wall he fired his shotgun over the wall once and was immediately struck in the head by gunfire from without. Joe described Travis as dying on one of the cannon ramps.

Travis' death left the Alamo garrison leaderless. It is recognized that Jim Bowie was seriously ill during the siege and out of the action of the battle. Company officers probably kept their small units together for a while, but with the size of the Alamo compound it is unlikely that any type of organized defense was followed. If the Alamo had any strategic value, it was the fact that it was a walled enclosure armed with a considerable array of cannon. Descriptions of the Alamo's artillery range from four-teen to twenty-one pieces (perhaps not all mounted or serviceable at the time).[20] Also, it was situated right outside of a major town. The Mexican army could not ignore it.

The Texans had done the best they could have during the siege. They had slowed up, somewhat, Santa Anna's incursion into Texas. They did not do this for the traditional reason of buying time for Sam Houston to raise an army. They held Santa Anna in place fully expecting enough reinforcements to arrive to defeat him. As long as the Alamo garrison held on and kept the Mexican army outside of the walls, there was still the slim hope that they could succeed.

The bulk of the Mexican assault converged on the north wall of the Alamo. One smaller column struck the south side, probably as a diversion. The best efforts of the thinly spread, outnumbered defenders could not check the assault. Mexican troops gained a foothold on the north and south walls almost simultaneously. Once this foothold was established, whatever strategic values the Alamo held became irrelevant. The battle became a brawl.

The Texans had fulfilled their duty in setting up the Mexican force for battle for as long as they were able. Once the Mexicans had control of the walls at both ends of the Alamo enclosure, this goal was no longer valid. The Texans no longer had any hope of winning. With Mexican soldiers pouring into the Alamo compound, the loosely organized Texans began to abandon the walls. Some jumped from the walls into the interior of the Alamo. Many others jumped outside the walls. Some sought to escape. Others continued to fight. At this point, any of those who did fight were probably fighting for their lives and those of their comrades rather than for any specific strategic goal.

The Mexican soldiers swept through the Alamo compound and cleared pockets of resistance within the buildings. Here and there they came upon women and children noncombatants. They were spared except in a few isolated cases. Travis' slave, Joe, had taken refuge in one of the Alamo buildings and continued to fire on the Mexicans until his ammunition was exhausted. He was discovered and taken prisoner. His life was spared by a Mexican officer because he was a slave. There is some evidence that other slaves survived the battle.[21]

The Texans who tried their luck outside the walls were met by the Mexican lancers under General Joaquin Ramirez y Sesma. Despite some stiff resistance, these men eventually were cut down. At least one, Henry Warnell, seems to have made it through the Mexican troops. He made it as far as Port Lavaca where he died of his wounds two to three months later. Others may have made it out of the Alamo. If they did, their stories are unrecorded by history. Santa Anna even recognized this as a possibility when he wrote, "...few are those who bore to their associates the tidings of their disaster." In the same letter Santa Anna also wrote, "Among the corpses are those of Bowie and Travis, who styled themselves Colonels, and also that of Crockett...."[22]

Most of those who remained in the fort were not as lucky as Joe. Blood red flags had flown above the Mexican camp since the siege had begun. Their meaning was clear. No prisoners would be taken and no mercy shown. Anyone who gave up the fight, were unable to fight, or attempted to surrender were killed. Even some of the noncombatants became casualties. Years later survivor Juana Navarro Alsbury reported that a sick man named Mitchell tried to protect her from the Mexican soldiers. The soldiers bayonetted him right by her side. She also reported that a young Mexican, pursued by the soldiers, seized her arm and tried to keep her between himself and the soldiers. The soldiers stabbed him with bayonets and shot him four or five times.[23] Joe described a little man named Warner, who was discovered alive when all of the bodies were being removed from the Alamo. He was quoted:

> ...a little weakly body named Warner, was left alive. He, and he only, asked for quarter. He was spared by the soldiery; but on being conducted to

Santa Anna, he ordered him to be shot, which was promptly done.[24]

Enrique Esparza described an American boy who was about Esparza's age but larger. As the Mexican soldiers charged into the room the boy stood up and drew a blanket around his shoulders. He was slain by the soldiers and his body fell over Esparza.[25]

A number of accounts were attributed to Susanna Dickinson in later life. All probably were affected by a certain amount of editorializing by the reporters of the various accounts. As a result, her accounts vary a good deal. Most of Dickinson's accounts mention a man or men being cut down before her eyes. The number of men vary from one to three, and in one account there are two young boys. The stories differ but are not necessarily mutually exclusive. What is consistent in her stories is the fact that no mercy was being shown to defenders, and at least one but probably more were slain in her presence.

The fighting inside the Alamo was chaotic enough that some women and children were killed. Writer Walter Lord attributed this to the capriciousness of war. Most of the women and children survived. Alamo defenders encountered by Mexican soldiers during the heat of battle stood no chance of survival. This is true whether they were fighting, running, surrendering, or helpless. Negro slaves were spared, which saved Joe's life. Had he been discovered while he was still firing on the Mexican troops, it is safe to say he would have been shown no mercy.

Once the battle had died down, the noncombatants were rounded up from different parts of the fort. These were about twenty women and children, families of some of the defenders, and an unverified number of slaves. Along with the noncombatants a small number of defenders were gathered up. Joe reported that one man, Warner, was executed. Dickinson told of five defenders who "for a moment survived their companions." Two of these men were pursued into her room and killed in her presence. One other inmate of the Alamo, Brigido Guerrero, is

Later, letters written from Gonzales expanded on the news by supplying more information from the two messengers. E.N. Gray wrote, "All within the Fort perished. Seven of them were killed by order of Santa Anna when in the act of giving up their arms." On the same day Houston wrote, "After the fort was carried, seven men surrendered, and called for Gen. Santa Anna and quarters. They were murdered by his orders."[29] These communications set into motion the idea that seven men were killed either after the Alamo was conquered or while in the act of giving up their arms.

Years later an account by an uninvolved witness to the battle added some credence to the number seven. Maria de Jesus Buquor (nee Delgado) gave her description of the battle to the *San Antonio Express* in 1907. She was a ten-year-old at the time of the battle. The article states that "She related the death of seven Texans who tried to make [their] escape from the Alamo and were killed on the river bank near her house...."[30] The seven men killed, as reported by Houston and Gray, probably were the same men as reported by Buquor, killed outside the fort.

On March 15, 1836, Benjamin Briggs Goodrich, in Washington-on-the-Brazos, Texas, wrote a letter to his brother Edmund in Nashville, Tennessee. In the letter he reported the death of their brother John C. Goodrich in the Alamo. He also wrote:

> Seven of our brave men, being all that were left alive, called for quarter and to see Santa Anna, but were instantly shot by order of the fiendish tyrant. Col. Bowie was murdered sick in bed. Amoung [sic] the number of your acquaintances, murdered in the Alamo, were Col. David Crocket [sic], Michajah Autry, formerly of Haysborough, John Hays, son of Andrew Hays of Nashville, and my unfortunate brother John C. Goodrich: but they died like men, and posterity will do them justice.

Goodrich's three sentences are important in the reporting of Crockett's death. In the first sentence he reports the story of seven men being killed on Santa Anna's orders. In the following two sentences he mentions five men whose names were known to his brother. There were two distinct thoughts being conveyed, but a quick reading of the letter tends to blend the two. Goodrich's mentioning of the execution and the immediate naming of five individuals give the impression that he was naming five of the seven men executed.[31]

The logical mail route from Washington-on-the-Brazos would have been down the Brazos River to the Gulf of Mexico to New Orleans. At the time, the schooner *Comanche* was plying the waters of the Brazos. On or about March 19 the *Comanche* left the Brazos (or the town of Washington-on-the-Brazos itself). In slightly over one week it arrived at New Orleans with word of the fall of the Alamo. As soon as the *Comanche* arrived at New Orleans, reports on the Alamo began to be influenced by the information it carried. Possibly, that information included the Goodrich letter. The *Louisiana Advertiser* reported "The Alamo has fallen into the hands of the Mexicans under Santa Anna, and its garrison have been massacred in cold blood after their arms were surrendered, Col. David Crockett is among the slain." This gives the impression that Crockett, along with the *entire* garrison surrendered and then were executed, despite the fact that the article later stated that "David Crockett...fell, fighting like a tiger."[32]

The *New Orleans True American* reported:

> The Mexicans fought desperately until daylight, when seven only of the garrison were found alive. We regret to say that Col. David Crockett and his companion Mr. Benton, also the Col. Bonham of South Carolina, were of the number who cried for quarter but were told there was no mercy for them. They then continued fighting until the whole were butchered.[33]

This report helps plant the idea that Crockett was one of those who tried to surrender if one ignores the last line that they "continued fighting until the whole were butchered."

One month later the *Natchez Free Press* published the text of a letter by William Parker. Parker had traveled to Texas seeking information about his son Christopher, who had perished at the Alamo. The letter contained information Parker had obtained from William Hadden of the Texan army. It concerned what Susanna Dickinson had witnessed in the Alamo, and it allegedly was given to Hadden by Dickinson herself. It states:

> ...of the five [Alamo defenders] who, for a moment survived their companions, and threw themselves on the victor's clemency, two were pursued into her room, and subjected in her presence to the most torturing death. They were even raised on the points of the enemy's lances, let down and raised again and again, whilst invoking as a favor, instantaneous death to terminate their anguish, till they were at last too weak to speak, and then expired in convulsion.[34]

For years Alamo historians and writers have wrestled with the question of the different numbers of Alamo defenders executed. Joe said one was executed. The accounts originating after Bárcinas and Vargara reached Gonzales said seven. Then, Dickinson's account said five. Austin researcher Tom Lindley has recently hit on the simple explanation that has eluded all. There were a number of separate incidents during or immediately after the Alamo battle in which defenders were shown no mercy. Since the red flag of no quarter had been flying, the Mexican soldiers necessarily would not have needed a direct order from Santa Anna to cut down any Texans in their paths. When accounts state that a man or men were killed "by order of Santa Anna" it may indicate that the Mexican soldiers involved were following the standing orders of the day.

Most of these incidents probably were not witnessed by Santa Anna. We have attributed the word "executed" to all of these scenes, whereas most of them simply were cases of Mexican soldiers withholding mercy from those who had ceased fighting or were too weak to continue fighting. A formal "execution" denotes a scene involving a little pomp and theatrics. A scene in which beaten defenders are brought before Santa Anna with some formality, are forced to endure a few moments of uncertainty before him, and then are put to death.

So, word went forth about the fall of the Alamo and the execution of one or some of its defenders. The information was passed on verbally, in correspondence, some of which was printed in newspapers, and in newspaper articles reporting the battle. It was a common practice in those days for newspapers to reprint articles from other papers. The news generally spread east and north with the towns of Gonzales and Washington-on-the-Brazos as points of origin and New Orleans and the Mississippi River as its main conduits. The news of the execution of prisoners could follow any of a number of story lines, with different numbers of prisoners, depending on where and with whom the story originated.

Survivors who had been inside the Alamo and would have known Crockett never singled him out by name as one of those executed. They reported seeing his body. In most of the correspondence and articles reporting the Alamo battle, Crockett's name is also mentioned since his was a recognizable name. As the news spread, his name began to be massaged into the report of the executions simply because of the proximity of his name with the executions in the articles and letters.

Following the debacle at the Alamo, there was no official inquest into the battle. Another country, firmly established in the community of nations, probably would have conducted one. A battle had been lost. A large portion of the Texan army had been wiped out. A major outpost had been lost to the enemy. Under normal circumstances reasons would have been determined and appropriate blame leveled. This was not the case.

The Mexican army continued to press northward and eastward through Texas. Santa Anna followed a central route. General Antonio Gaona traveled north and then east. General Urrea took a northerly route between Santa Anna's and the Gulf Coast. Their goal was to capture the government officials of the fledgling Republic of Texas and to destroy those foolish enough to take up arms in its behalf. Of the three columns, only Urrea's saw much action other than that at the Alamo. His men easily rolled over small units of Texans they encountered along the way. In accordance with Santa Anna's policy, no quarter was the order of the day. Texan prisoners of war had very short "shelf lives" after being taken.

On March 12 to 15, Urrea's men overcame the small forces of Lieutenant Colonel William Ward and Captain Amon B. King at Refugio. Most of King's men were executed. Mexican colonel Juan José Holsinger spared six Refugio colonists and two native-born Germans. Ward's men were taken prisoner, but a few were spared to work as boatwrights for the Mexican army. On March 19 to 20, Urrea encountered the force of Colonel James Walker Fannin at Coleto Creek. Fannin was in the process of finally following General Sam Houston's order to fall back from his post at Goliad. Unfortunately he had delayed too long. After being caught in the open with no water for his wounded or to cool his artillery pieces, Fannin was forced to surrender his command of over three hundred men. His men, along with those of Ward, were held prisoner in the cramped church of the Texans' former headquarters at the Presidio La Bahia. Urrea recommended mercy for the prisoners but was ignored by Santa Anna. On March 27 Colonel José Nicholas de la Portilla marched the majority of prisoners from the Presidio under the pretense of transporting them to the United States. A short distance from the Presidio they were executed by the Mexican troops in accordance with Santa Anna's policy. Fannin and others too badly wounded or sick to move were executed in the Presidio. Approximately sixteen, who were doctors or had some medical background, were separated and spared. They were needed to care for the Mexican wounded. Approximately twenty-eight men escaped while the mass killing was in progress. The executions at the Alamo paled by comparison. In this one event, more Texans were executed than the total killed in defense of the Alamo. It would be another month before Sam Houston would defeat Santa Anna at San Jacinto, thus ending the Texas Revolution and setting Texas on the road toward independence.

While the drama of the Texas Revolution was still being played out, the word of the Mexican victory and the executions at the Alamo radiated north and east through Texas and then to the United States. The news traveled by word of mouth, by correspondence, and in newspapers. The news was reported, interpreted, and embellished by people who were not at the Alamo nor were witnesses to the battle. It was not a system conducive to accuracy.

By March 11, 1836, the news of the Alamo's fall had reached Gonzales, Texas; on March 15, Washington-on-the-Brazos. Two weeks later, the news had reached New Orleans and from there spread to the rest of the U.S.

Original artwork by Rod Timanus.

What Happened?

As the word spread, people wanted to know what happened to the defenders of the Alamo, especially those who had relatives or acquaintances in the garrison or with the Texan volunteer army. On March 24 the *Telegraph and Texas Register* published an early story on the battle, including an initial list of those who fell there. A number of people naturally tried to find out what happened to their loved ones.

Davy Crockett was of special interest. He was a fairly well known figure in the United States by virtue of his service in the U.S. Congress and by the outlandish *Crockett Almanacs* that had been publishing fictitious exploits attributed to him since 1835. Crockett was the best known of the Alamo defenders. In a sense he belonged to the whole country. It was already known that he was at the Alamo, so people were anxious to find out what happened to him. Actually there were not many possibilities. Santa Anna did not provide much of a menu for the defenders of the Alamo. A defender was either killed in the battle, killed after the battle, or somehow managed to escape or survive. Susanna Dickinson and Joe reported the fall of the Alamo as early as March 11. Joe included a description of seeing Crockett's body among the dead. These reports did not prevent newspapers from printing a variety of fates for Crockett. One of the earlier versions described Crockett as having survived the battle. The *Morning Courier and New York Enquirer* of March 26, 1836, reported, "Colonel Crockett, as we said when we announced the rumor of his death, is *not* dead, but still alive and grinning." Two days later the *Stamford (Connecticut) Sentinel* printed a similar story, but in this one Crockett was "alive and kicking" instead of "grinning." The article went on to say, "Information has been received from him recently. He had been a Coon hunting among the Rocky Mountains, and is expected home soon." The *Monroe (New York) Democrat* announced:

> Davy Crocket [sic] not dead—We are happy to state on the authority of a letter from Tennessee that the report of the death of the eccentric Davy

Crockett is not true. "He started (says the letter) on a hunting expedition to the Rocky Mountains, and then dropped down into Texas; but we expect him home early in the Spring."[35]

The *Cincinnati Whig* was more descriptive but a little more cautious:

COLONEL CROCKETT, the hero and patriot it is said IS NOT DEAD!! The cheering news is brought by a gentleman now in this city, directly from Texas, and who left the Colonel, as he states, three weeks ago, at the house of his brother-in-law in Texas, where the Colonel was lying quite ill, but gradually though slowly recovering from his wounds.

The gentleman who brings this news is known to a number of our citizens, who believe him to be a man of veracity. He states that Crockett was left upon the battleground of the Alamo covered with wounds, and, as the Mexicans supposed,—dead. That after the Mexicans had abandoned the place, Crockett was discovered by some of his acquaintances to be lying among the slain, still exhibiting signs of life. He was immediately taken care of, and conveyed to comfortable lodgings, as before stated, where his wounds were dressed, and every attention necessary to his recovery paid him. He had received a gash with a tomahawk on the upper part of the forearm, a ball in his left arm, and another one through his thighs, besides several other minor wounds. When the gentleman left his brother-in-law's house, Crockett was doing well.

The *Whig* showed uncharacteristic restraint for newspapers of its time when it went on to say:

Candor compels us to say that there are many improbabilities in relation to the truth of this

report, but the respectable character of the gentleman who says he saw him with his own eyes in the
condition and under the circumstances above
stated, induces us to give it credit. We have, never-
theless, some doubts of its truth. We give the story,
however, as the gentleman represented it, and we
sincerely hope that it may prove entirely authentic.
It is either true, or the man who has detailed to
numerous persons in the city the above statements
is a LYING VILLAIN! It is due him to say, however,
that those persons here that know him, give entire
credit to his statements.[36]

Four years later, in 1840, rumors of Crockett's survival still
appeared. One report stated that Crockett was working as a
slave in a mine in Mexico. The report was compelling enough
that Crockett's son John Wesley Crockett, then a U.S. Congressman, launched an investigation into it. The report originated as
a letter to the editor of the *Austin City Gazette*. The letter stated:

Sir: I was, formerly a citizen of the United
States, and have been living in Mexico for 17 years.
My business in this country is such, and has been,
as to require me to travel much from place to place.
I was not long since, at a mining district in Mexico,
in the neighborhood of Guadalajara, and while
there, a Mexican came to me and said that there
was a man from Texas, working in the Salinas mine,
who had requested of him to ask the first American
he saw, to come and see him, as he wished to send
some word to a family he had left in Tennessee. To
enter a mine in Mexico you have to obtain permission from the worker or owner, and he sends with
you the overseer, who is ordered to keep strict
watch that you take out of the mines no ores or
valuables. I went to the owner, and obtaining permission, went with the overseer, and was taken to

that passage of the mine where the convicts are placed to work. There was some 20 or 25 at work, and amongst them I recognized the manly form of one of my countrymen, who, the owner had told me, was one of the prisoners brought on by a part of Filisola's division, when he retreated from Texas.

The American upon seeing me stepped forward and grasping me by the hand said, "Well, stranger, you are the first American I have seen since I have been in this damned country; and I don't think I would have seen you if I had not made a friend of one of these devils that oversee the mine."

"My unfortunate friend," I replied, "I have been made aware of the circumstances that place you here, and they are such as to debar me from rendering you any assistance more than bearing for you any message you may wish."

"I know that," he returned, "so let us go about it. My name is David Crockett. I am from Tennessee, and have a family there. They think that I am dead, and so does every one else; but they are mistaken. I should have written them, as the overseer told me I might write, if I could get any person to take a letter from me; that was the reason I persuaded the overseer to look out for an American for me. And, thanks be to God, I have got one at last."

He related to me the particulars of his having been taken at Fort Alamo, in Bexar, and sent, with two other men, to Laredo; from which place they had been removed, with a part of the army that moved to Monterey, and when the troops marched from Monterey to Mexico, they were sent to Guadalajara, and placed in the mine by the alcalde, at which place they had been ever since.

He wrote, by me, a letter, to be sent to his wife and children in Tennessee, which I sent from

Matamoras, with directions to mail it in New Orleans, retaining in my possession a copy thereof, for fear, by some mischance, it should miscarry. To Col. D.L. Wood, with whom I met in Laredo, I gave another copy, which he promised to publish, but I have since heard he did not get in safe, which is the reason I send you this by a Mexican going from here to Bastrop and Austin. I have directed him to give it to any American he saw in either place, who would know where to send it.

In great haste, I am,

Your humble servant
Wm. C. White

The newspaper went on to explain:

The letter comes from an unknown source, and may or may not be true...already have letters been written to Mrs. Crockett, and to the Texian Consul in New Orleans, for the purpose of ascertaining whether a letter has ever been received by the unfortunate hero's family...May not the whole be a contrivance of the federalists to gain the assistance of Texas.

Several federalist states of Northern Mexico had declared themselves the independent Republic of the Rio Grande at the time. Crockett's son John Wesley Crockett believed that this story might have been true. He wrote to Secretary of State John Forsyth, asking if an investigation into this matter could be initiated through the U.S. minister to Mexico. It is unknown if any investigation actually was started.[37]

It is not surprising that such unfounded stories made their way into newspapers at that time. Such reporting has happened since and it happens today. Some of the earliest headlines regarding the sinking of the *Titanic* reported:

> "2000 Lives are Saved off wrecked *Titanic*. By Wireless; Vessel is Reported Sinking." (Actually the number was closer to 705.)

> "*Titanic* Passengers Safe on *Carpathia*; Damaged Steamship Reported Sinking." (The *Titanic* was already on the bottom of the Atlantic by the time the *Carpathia* rescued the survivors.)

> "The New *Titanic* Hit by Iceberg." (As opposed to it hitting the berg!)[38]

Newspaper articles and headlines cannot always be relied on as accurate recorders of fact. Nor is it surprising that the subject of these reports were Crockett's alleged survival. Popular, legendary, famous, and infamous people always have a way of staying with us for a while after they have shuffled off this mortal coil. There are many examples. Sometimes they come in the form of sightings. At other times these figures make a reappearance in one form or another after many years. In the 1820s a young daredevil named Sam Patch discovered that people would pay money to see him leap into various bodies of water from incredible heights. His final stunt occurred on Friday the thirteenth of November 1829 when he plunged into the Genesee Falls near Rochester, New York. Patch disappeared into the churning water and never resurfaced. Despite the fact that his body was found four months later, frozen in a block of ice, he was still reported to have been seen in Albany, Canandaigua, and Pittsford. Another story reported that he was found in the China Sea where he had swum, by a New England ship captain.

American journalist Ambrose Bierce disappeared into the interior of Mexico in 1914, never to be seen again. Still, stories kept him alive in England, in his home in California, and in the California State Insane Asylum.

Captain Edward J. Smith of *Titanic* fame was seen, by a crewman, walking onto the bridge of the doomed ship just before it sank. Another crewman who entered the bridge at the same time did not see him there. Yet another crewman last saw him in the water holding a small child. This same crewman also claimed that Smith was pulled onto an overturned lifeboat, only to let go and exclaim, "I will follow the ship" before he disappeared into the black waters. Other people claimed he shot himself before the *Titanic* went down. Three months after the sinking, another ship's captain, Peter Pryal, reported meeting Captain Smith in Baltimore, Maryland, and offered to swear to the truth of his statement since he had known Smith for a long time.[39]

Research into the lives and deaths of Jesse James, Butch Cassidy and the Sundance Kid, Billy the Kid, John Wilkes Booth, and many other legendary figures offer similar tales of sightings, reappearances, and multiple versions of deaths. At least eight Native American warriors were sure that they alone were the ones who dealt Lieutenant Colonel George Armstrong Custer his deathblow. The story of the Alamo offers a number of different versions of James Bowie's death, as well as William B. Travis'. Caution is advised in taking any one of the stories about a legendary person as the final word.[40]

Despite the stories of his survival, Crockett did meet his end at the Alamo. The question that has interested many people since the event itself is *how* he died.

CHAPTER TWO

Execution

· · · ◆ · · ·

*David Crockett made a choice. The Go Ahead man
quit. He did more than quit. He lied. He denied his
role in the fighting.*
   —Jeff Long

*He surrendered at the Alamo.... There is very little
room for doubt that Crockett was captured and executed at the Alamo.*
   —Paul A. Hutton

*There is no conclusive evidence that Crockett surren-
dered, and no stigma has ever been attached to the
capture of an exhausted soldier by an overwhelming
foe.*
   —Dan Kilgore

*The word "surrender" or even "capture" is never used
[in the Peña account].*
   —Carmen Perry

THE QUESTION OF HOW CROCKETT DIED at the Alamo is
important to some, of interest to many, and in my opinion unan-
swerable. The debate basically swirls around two possibilities:

Crockett died in combat; or he was taken alive during the battle and later executed on the direct orders of Santa Anna. Both scenarios are possibilities. The latter also is broken down into finer points: Was he taken alive after becoming exhausted and wounded, unable to fight anymore? Did he merely cease fighting when further resistance became useless? Did he surrender in order to save his own life? Did he behave in a cowardly manner? etc. All of these possibilities have been put forth in recent years. At times they have appeared in novels as fiction. At other times they have appeared in historical books and articles as absolute fact.

Before analyzing the variety of reports on Crockett's manner of death, a look at the statements that identify him as dead in the Alamo are in order. The first of these is a statement attributed to Joe in the weeks after the battle and one by Susanna Dickinson many years afterward. I use the word attributed in regard to Joe, since the manner in which it appeared in various newspapers makes it unclear whether Joe or Dickinson actually was supplying this information.[1]

One of the statements attributed to Joe states "... The Honorable Davy Crockett died like a hero, surrounded by heaps of the enemy's slain." The other states "Crockett, the kind hearted, brave DAVID CROCKETT, and a few of the devoted friends who entered the Fort with him, were found lying together, with 21 of the slain enemy around them."[2]

Dickinson's account states "I recognized Col. Crockett lying dead and mutilated between the church and the two-story barrack building and even remember seeing his peculiar cap lying by his side." Twenty years later elderly Eulalia Yorba claimed that she was one of a number of people from San Antonio who entered the Alamo after the battle to tend the wounded and dying. She stated:

> "I remember seeing poor Colonel Davy Crockett as he lay dead by the side of a dying man, whose bloody and powder stained face I was washing. Colonel Crockett was about fifty years old at that

time. His coat and rough woolen shirt were soaked
with blood so that the original color was hidden,
for the eccentric hero must have died of some ball
in the chest or a bayonet thrust."[3]

These accounts suffer the same problems typical of most of
the accounts concerning the Alamo. The first by Joe appeared in
a newspaper article and obviously was edited heavily. The second may have been written as a letter by William Fairfax Grey
and appeared in the *Frankfort (Kentucky) Commonwealth* on
May 25, 1836. However, it seems as if this same account
appeared in the *Telegraph and Texas Register* two months earlier.[4] As stated earlier, when this whole letter is read it becomes
unclear whether these are Joe's or Dickinson's observations.
Whoever made the observation, it was of Crockett's dead body,
not of him dying in combat.

Dickinson's statement appeared in J.M. Morphis' *History of
Texas* published in 1875. It is impossible to tell how much editorializing Morphis himself did. It is also uncertain how much
effect the intervening thirty-nine years had on Dickinson's
memory. These accounts only describe Crockett's body. At least
they serve to disprove the accounts of his survival. The witnesses never claimed to have seen Crockett die in action. By the
same token, they never claimed that he was executed after the
battle.

Currently, the most generally accepted version of Crockett's
demise is that he was executed by a direct order of Santa Anna
after the Alamo battle had ended. It is favored by revisionist historians as well as by many traditional students of the Alamo
battle and of Crockett's life. The versions of the execution story
vary. Sometimes Crockett is executed alone. At other times he is
executed with at least one or as many as six other Alamo
defenders. One version has him executed along with the
Alamo's commander, Travis. Sometimes he is hacked to death
with swords. At other times he is stabbed by bayonets. At other
times he is shot with rifles. Sometimes Mexican officers are

Crockett's executioners. At other times Mexican enlisted men perform the grisly task.

Antonio Lopez de Santa Anna. His policy of "no quarter" brought about the executions at the Alamo and elsewhere in Texas.

From Albert C. Ramsey, *The Other Side: or notes for the History of the War between Mexico and the United States* (New York: John Wiley, 1850). Courtesy of the Institute of Texan Cultures, San Antonio, Texas.

The bases for our belief that Crockett was executed are the earliest newspaper reports which melded Crockett's name with the story of executions at the Alamo. Many of these newspaper reports refer to the defenders of the Alamo as "murder" victims rather than casualties of battle.[5]

In the one hundred twenty years following the battle, seven seemingly unrelated accounts surfaced that, for many, prove that Crockett was executed. They are all purported to be and have been used and cited as firsthand eyewitness accounts. When used as such these accounts are usually identified as those of:

1) An unidentified Mexican officer (given in the spring of 1836).
2) Colonel Juan N. Almonte or an unidentified informant (given on July 18, 1836).
3) Colonel Fernando Urriza (given in late April 1836).
4) Sergeant Francisco Becerra (given sometime around 1875).
5) General Martin Perfecto de Cos (given in 1836).
6) Colonel José Juan Sanchez-Navarro (written as a journal in 1836).
7) Lieutenant José Enrique de la Peña (written as a diary in 1836).

Six officers and a sergeant are a pretty impressive array of witnesses when taken at face value. However, when you scratch the surfaces of these accounts they reveal themselves to be other than pristine firsthand accounts. More accurate descriptions of these accounts are:

1) An article in the *Morning Courier and New York Enquirer* published on July 9, 1836, reporting the story of an unnamed reporter (probably William H. Attree), who is reporting the statement of an unidentified witness (never identified as a Mexican officer). Hereafter referred to as the *Attree* account.
2) The *Detroit Democratic Free Press* of September 7, 1836, printing a letter by George M. Dolson, describing an

alleged secret interview with Col. Juan N. Almonte (or an unidentified informant, depending on one's interpretation of the letter). Hereafter referred to as the *Dolson* account.

3) Nicholas Labadie describing from memory an interview with Col. Urriza that allegedly occurred twenty-three years earlier and was published in the *Texas Almanac* in 1859. Hereafter referred to as the *Labadie* account.

4) John S. Ford describing the memories of Francisco Becerra. Given as a speech in 1875 and published in the *Texas Mute Ranger* in 1882. Hereafter referred to as the *Becerra* account.

5) William P. Zuber describing an account allegedly given to him by Dr. George M. Patrick, that allegedly was given to him by Gen. Cos, written from memory in a letter in 1904 and published in a book in 1939. Hereafter referred to as the *Zuber* account.

In these first five there are no documents that link the eyewitnesses to their alleged stories directly. In other words, there is no independent documentation from Cos or Urriza or Becerra, etc., in which they described in their own words the ones attributed to them. Also, there is no way to know how much handling, editing, and reshaping each story had gone through before it appeared.

The last two accounts are more accurately described as:

6) Allegedly Col. José Juan Sanchez-Navarro, first appearing in 1938. Hereafter referred to as the *Navarro* account.

7) Allegedly Lt. José Enrique de la Peña, first appearing in 1955. Hereafter referred to as the *Peña* account.

I use the word *allegedly* in referring to these two documents because I have considerable doubt as to their authorship. Others do not share this opinion and have used and continue to use these accounts as absolutely authentic and factual.

The first six of these accounts were published between 1836 and 1938. They have been cited in histories of the Alamo and biographies of Crockett. They also have served as the basis of dramatic scenes in fictional tellings of the story. When cited or published, these accounts usually were done so as possibilities, just as many of the other legendary stories of the Alamo were. In 1955 the last of these accounts was published in book form in Mexico. This is the Peña account. It too was cited in books and articles but never treated as an absolute. In 1975 it was published in English in the United States. The media picked up on the one controversial paragraph concerning Crockett's execution. The account was publicized widely and caused quite a row. Newspapers seemed to revel in the belief that Crockett was executed and somehow extrapolated that into the belief that he was less than heroic, even cowardly. Crockett supporters came to the defense of his reputation, and some went overboard. It should be noted the Peña account does not state that the person described as Crockett surrendered nor that he behaved cowardly.

Carmen Perry, former archivist of the Daughters of the Republic of Texas Library at the Alamo and translator of the account into English, became the brunt of the overreaction. She began receiving threats, crank phone calls, and hate mail. Her only crime had been to translate the words of someone else from Spanish to English. In 1977 Dan Kilgore came to Perry's defense. Kilgore was president of the Texas State Historical Association. At his presidential address to the Association he described the other accounts of Crockett's execution (numbers 1 through 6). His was not an in-depth investigation into Crockett's death, but he did bring all of the execution stories together for the first time. He laid out these accounts as if to show that Perry was not putting forth this theory, but that many others had done so before. One year later his speech was expanded into book form and titled *How Did Davy Die?* It was published by Texas A&M University Press, which also had published Perry's book.

Once again the media played up the story of a cowardly, unheroic Crockett. This time the abuse shifted from Perry to Kilgore. He was labeled everything from a "commie" to a "mealy-mouthed intellectual," and was even challenged to fight.[6]

Kilgore's contribution to the story is important. By his bringing together these conflicting and disparate accounts in one volume he advanced their perception as a solid body of irrefutable evidence pointing toward one conclusion—Crockett's execution. Once this idea had taken hold, professional historians began to offer opinions on the Peña account and Crockett's death. Kilgore's presentation of these other accounts was enough for writer Richard Boyd Hauck to declare the Peña description of Crockett's death as "well authenticated." Professor Stephen L. Hardin called it "the best" account of the Alamo battle and of Crockett's death. Professor Paul Andrew Hutton, a well-respected and well-known historian, stated that of all the Mexican accounts of the Alamo battle none was "more reliable" than that of Peña.[7]

Kilgore's book is a slim volume but contains a good deal of information. It has to be read carefully. Kilgore included the Peña description of a Crockett execution scene and went on to say, "Six other Mexican soldiers [the six mentioned above] support de la Peña's testimony that Crockett was one of several Texans who was captured or who surrendered and then was killed." This statement gives the impression that the other six are all authenticating the Peña account. Later he wrote:

> Until 1955, however, available sources really afforded little reason to believe that Crockett was murdered by Santa Anna's order. The early accounts by Urissa [Urriza] and Becerra have a ring of folklore instead of history, and Zuber's letter mentioning General Cos certainly lends no credence to the story. But in 1955 came the publication in Mexico, in original Spanish, of Lieutenant Colonel de la Peña's diary.

Now it is the Peña account validating some of the others. Still later he states:

Little doubt now remains that Mexican troops captured several Texans in the final moments of the storming of the Alamo. Statements from seven of Santa Anna's men who were present as eyewitnesses say specifically that David Crockett was one of those taken alive.[8]

Now, the seven accounts are on an equal footing again. The question that was never asked was "Which accounts are the ones being authenticated and which accounts are the controls used to validate the others?" Kilgore explained that the seven accounts were "...mutually corroborative."[9] In other words, they all validate one another. Still, however, we do not have one account firmly set in stone that validates all of the others. That has been the problem with the Peña account since it appeared on the historical scene in 1955. Until recently, everyone has treated it as an absolute. Writers and historian have used it and cited it as a source without ever weighing its reality. Regarding the "mutual corroboration" of the seven accounts, Tom Lindley correctly has pointed out that seven false things can be mutually corroborative if they are all false about the same thing.

The following are the accounts upon which the theory that Crockett was executed are based:

The Attree account (also known as the unidentified Mexican officer account):

> After the Mexicans had got possession of the Alamo, the fighting had ceased, and it was clear day light, six Americans were discovered near the wall yet unconquered, and who were instantly surrounded and ordered by Gen. Castrillón to surrender, and who did so under a promise of his protection, finding resistance any longer in vain —indeed, perfect madness. Castrillón was brave and not cruel, and disposed to save them. He marched them up to that part of the fort where

stood "His Excellency," surrounded by his murderous crew, his sycophantic officers. DAVID CROCKETT was one of the six. The steady, fearless step, and undaunted tread, together with the bold demeanor of this hardy veteran—"his firmness and noble bearing," to give the words of the narrator, had a most powerful effect on himself and Castrillón. Nothing daunted, he marched up boldly in front of Santa Anna, looked him steadfastly in the face, while Castrillón addressed "His Excellency," "Sir here are six prisoners I have taken alive; how shall I dispose of them?" Santa Anna looked at Castrillón fiercely, flew into a most violent rage, and replied, "Have I not told you before how to dispose of them? Why do you bring them to me?" At the same time his brave officers drew and plunged their swords into the bosoms of their defenseless prisoners!! So anxious and intent were these blood-thirsty cowards to gratify the malignity of this inveterate tyrant, that Castrillón barely escaped being run through in the scuffle, himself. Castrillón rushed from the scene, apparently horror-struck—sought his quarters and did not leave them for some days, and hardly ever spoke to Santa Anna after. This was the fate of poor Crockett, and in which there can be no mistake. Who the five others were, I have not been able to learn. Three other wounded prisoners were discovered and brought before "His Excellency," and were ordered to be instantly shot. There are certain reasons why the name of the narrator of these events should not be made known. I will only repeat that he was an eye-witness.[10]

This account is unique for a number of reasons. The other early newspaper accounts of the Alamo battle and executions

Crockett, unarmed yet defiant, is put to death
as a Mexican officer calmly looks on.

Woodcut from *The Life of Colonel Davy Crockett*, 1869. Courtesy of the
Center for American History, University of Texas at Austin.

and Crockett's death radiated out from San Antonio north and east. This account started in New York City (at least that location is the earliest one we have been able to place it so far). From New York it traveled south and west. It appeared in the *Morning Courier and New York Enquirer* on July 9, 1836, in the *Richmond (Virginia) Enquirer* on July 15, and in the *Frankfort (Kentucky) Commonwealth* on July 27. It also is unique in that it specifies Crockett as one of those executed.

A calculated guess can be made as to the identity of the unnamed reporter. The evidence for this is a letter of introduction to David G. Burnet from Billings Hayward, the editor of the *New York Transcript*. The letter is addressed from New York City on March 4, 1836, and reads:

> Though personally unknown to you, permit me to introduce to your notice, as a public man, the bearer William H. Attree Esqr. a gentleman who for the last three or four years has been connected as a writer with the leading journals of this City, & in particular with the Courier & Enquirer, the Star, & my own paper the Transcript, which he has ably edited since its commencement, & which through his talents & exertions has attained the unparalleled daily circulation of 18,000. In his capacity as an editor he has most ably advocated and supported the cause of Texas against Mexican tyranny; he has travelled through most of the States during the last five months to induce the departure of volunteers for Texas, & believing it to be his duty to support in the present emergency that cause by his sword which he has hitherto advocated with his pen & purse, he sacrifices pro. tem. his prospects here, & leaves us to join the Texian Army. While in Texas Mr. A. will at all times have the control of the columns of the above named journals as a correspondent from your country. He is an honorable,

talented & brave young man, & as such I herewith commend him to your notice.[11]

According to Hayward, Attree would "... at all times have the control of the columns" emanating from Texas to the New York papers. Attree was known in New York City for his flamboyant writing style and his lurid stories, especially crime stories. Attree began his career as a printer in the type foundry of Conner and Cooke. He moved on to being a police and court reporter for several of the New York papers. He wrote sensational stories while building a reputation of indifference to the feelings of those he wrote about. Sometimes he was the subject of stories himself. A short time after he began working for the *Courier and Enquirer*, he was stabbed and bludgeoned in the street by a subject of one of his stories. At the inception of the Texas Revolution, Attree left his journalistic duties and spent five months traveling around the United States, helping to raise volunteers for Texas. In 1836 he left for Texas and served as a dispatch rider for the Texan army, while also sending his news reports north. In September of 1836 he returned to New York. He later went to work for James Gordon Bennett's *New York Herald*, a paper committed to Texan independence, later the annexation of Texas, and Manifest Destiny in general. Bennett admonished him to "... be as lascivious as ever you like, Attree, but damn it, don't be vulgar!"[12] By 1842 Attree had taken over the *Herald*'s Washington bureau.

The witness Attree reported on was unidentified, but writers Walter Lord and Dan Kilgore both felt he was Ramón Caro, the civilian secretary of Santa Anna. Tom Lindley has pointed out that Attree's account is the first to mention General Manuel Fernández Castrillón as the officer who brings the prisoners to Santa Anna. One year later, in 1837, Caro published his own account of the revolution. In it he named Castrillón as the officer but does not mention Crockett as one of those executed. Also, his account mentions five, not six prisoners being executed. Caro's account states:

Among the 183 killed there were five who were discovered by General Castrillón hiding after the assault. He took them immediately to the presence of His Excellency who had come up by this time. When he presented the prisoners, he was severely reprimanded for not having killed them on the spot, after which he turned his back upon Castrillón while the soldiers stepped out of their ranks and set upon the prisoners until they were all killed.

In a footnote Caro continues:

We all witnessed this outrage which humanity condemns but which was committed as described. This is a cruel truth, but I cannot omit it. More cruel falsehoods have been promulgated against my character.[13]

My opinion of this first execution account is that it cannot be relied on as an absolutely factual report. We have seen that newspaper articles are not necessarily accurate records of events. We do not have an original transcript of information Attree may have gotten from this witness or what he or the newspaper editor may have added to it. We do not know if Attree may have been influenced by news reports of the Alamo mentioning Crockett's name in close proximity to the story of the executions. These reports already were traveling north while Attree was traveling south.

I believe Attree may have interviewed Caro. Caro's description of the executions mentions five Texans. Attree added Crockett and made it six, with another group of three wounded prisoners executed separately. I do not believe he did this to denigrate Crockett but simply in the interest of the Texan cause. Attree was committed to raising volunteers for Texas. The inclusion of Crockett's name in the execution story was key to raising emotions and men for Texas.

Also, James W. Webb, Attree's editor at the *Courier and Enquirer* was involved in Texas land speculation with Samuel Swartwout, the Collector of the Port of New York. They were members of the New Washington Association and had a great deal of money invested in Texas lands. There is some evidence that Attree rode dispatch in Texas for Thomas Jefferson Green. Green himself was very interested in raising volunteers for the Texan army since a coveted rank of brigadier general went along with raising a certain number of men. Green embarked on a vigorous recruiting drive in the United States fueled by the emotional impact of the Alamo's fall. Recognizing the propaganda value of the "big names" at the Alamo, he even recruited for a company in David Crockett's district in Tennessee and also attempted to raise a company around James Bowie's brother Rezin as commander. Green was also interested in Texas land, especially the area of New Washington. One year after the revolution had ended Swartwout wrote to Colonel James Morgan, also a member of the New Washington Association, that "Genl. Green and his Brother are very anxious to possess an interest in the City of New Washington—They are crazy for it."[14] It was in their interest to prevent Santa Anna from regaining power and possibly Texas after his defeat at San Jacinto. The portrayal of the bloodthirsty Santa Anna as ordering the execution of the popular Crockett was insurance toward that end.

Tom Lindley concurs with this opinion of Attree and his account. Others disagree, most notably Prof. James E. Crisp. Crisp, referring to me as a "...master of historical character assassination," rehabilitates Attree as a witness by pointing out that contemporary criticism of Attree's reporting style was not directed at the *imprecision* of his stories but rather their *explicitness*. He also points to Attree's promotion as head of the *Herald's* Washington bureau. Crisp goes on to say:

> So! Attree was a stenographic reporter who recorded the debates of the United States Congress, and who became a Washington bureau chief for the

New York Herald! This may not be a journalist on the level of the *National Enquirer*, after all![15]

But, then again, maybe he was.

The Dolson account (also known as the Almonte account or that of an unidentified informant):

> I am employed a considerable part of my time in interpreting Spanish for Colonel James Morgan, commander of this section. He sent for me yesterday and told me there was a communication of importance from one of Santa Anna's officers, which he wished me to interpret; accordingly the officer of the day was dispatched for the Mexican officer, who came in a few minutes, and the Colonel's quarters were vacated of all, save us three. The Mexican was then requested to proceed with the statement according to promise; and he said he could give a true and correct account of the proceedings of Santa Anna towards the prisoners who remained alive at the taking of the Alamo. This shows the fate of Colonel Crockett and his five brave companions—there have been many tales told, and many suggestions made, as to the fate of these patriotic men; but the following may be relied on, being from an individual who was an eye witness to the whole proceedings. The Colonel had taken the whole in writing, with the officer's name attached to it, which he observed to him, if he had the least delicacy, he might omit, but he said he had not and was willing to be qualified to it in the presence of his God, and General Santa Anna, too, if necessary. He states that on the morning the Alamo was captured, between the hours of five and six o'clock, General Castrillón, who fell at the battle of San Jacinto, entered the back room of the Alamo,

and there found Crockett and five other Americans, who had defended it until defense was useless; they appeared very much agitated when the Mexican soldiers undertook to rush in after their General, but the humane General ordered his men to keep out, and placing his hand on one breast, said "here is a hand and a heart to protect you; come with me to the General-in-chief, and you shall be saved." Such redeeming traits, while they ennoble in our estimation this worthy officer, yet serve to show in a more heinous light the damning atrocities of the chief. The brave but unfortunate men were marched to the tent of Santa Anna. Colonel Crockett was in the rear, had his arms folded, and appeared bold as the lion as he passed my informant (Almonte.) Santa Anna's interpreter knew Colonel Crockett, and said to my informant, "the one behind is the famous Crockett." When brought to the presence of Santa Anna, Castrillón said to him, "Santa Anna, the august, I deliver up to you six brave prisoners of war." Santa Anna replied, "who has given you orders to take prisoners, I do not want to see those men living—shoot them." As the monster uttered these words each officer turned his face the other way, and the hell-hounds of the tyrant dispatched the six in his presence, and within six feet of his person. Such an act I consider murder of the blackest kind. Do you think that he can be released? No—exhaust all the mines of Mexico, but it will not release him. The one half nor two thirds, nor even the whole of the republic would not begin to ransom him. The combined powers of Europe cannot release him, for before they come to his release, Texas will have released him out of his existence; but I coincide with the secretary of war, as to the disposal to be made of him, that is, to try him as a felon. Strict justice demands it and reason sanctions it.[16]

This letter is believed to have been written by George M. Dolson, a sergeant in the Texan army, to his brother. It is dated July 19, 1836, and it is addressed from Galveston Island, Texas. It was published in the *Detroit Democratic Free Press* on September 7, 1836. It was rediscovered and published in the *Journal of Southern History* in 1960. In recent years this account has received considerable attention. Since the wheels have begun to fall off the Peña account as the "best" and "most reliable" of its kind, the Dolson account is now being embraced by historians.

The account is attributed to Colonel Juan Nepomuceno Almonte, of Santa Anna's staff because, well, that is what the letter says. Historians who have cited this in the past have referred to it as the "Almonte" account. This would have been impossible, however, since Almonte was not on Galveston Island at the time this account was given. After the Battle of San Jacinto on April 21, 1836, Santa Anna, his civilian secretary Ramón Caro, his aide Colonel Gabrial Nuñez, and Almonte were held prisoner on board the schooner *Independence* in port. By May 10 Santa Anna and his small entourage were moved to Velasco where they remained until the end of the month. By July 19 Almonte was with Santa Anna at Bell's Landing in Columbia. So, it would have been impossible for Almonte to have given this account. This fact should have negated this account as a credible source. However, historians have found a way to rehabilitate it.

Dan Kilgore stated that Dolson's words were "... garbled in transcription" from the form of Dolson's letter to the newspaper article. He correctly stated that the account "... does not make sense." Kilgore reasoned and other historians have agreed that the line "... as he passed my informant (Almonte.) Santa Anna's interpreter knew Colonel Crockett..." had been punctuated incorrectly by the newspaper. They believe that the original sentence read "... as he passed my informant. Almonte, Santa Anna's interpreter knew Colonel Crockett..."[17]

If this adjustment is made, then it is not Almonte giving the account to Dolson (which would have been impossible) but an unnamed informant. Almonte becomes the one identifying Crockett. This is important for making a case since Almonte was educated in the United States, and for that reason alone it is believed that he would have known Crockett on sight. Actually, Almonte was educated in New Orleans in 1815, a good fifteen years before Crockett ever achieved national prominence.

Jim Crisp, who shares Kilgore's belief regarding the punctuation, also has an explanation for this. He acknowledges that Crockett's and Almonte's paths may not have crossed until the morning of the Alamo battle. He also is able to place Almonte in Louisiana in 1834 and in New York City in 1835. He feels it is possible that Almonte may have seen lithographed portraits of Crockett or may have been able to get to New York in time to see an original portrait of Crockett that was on display there.[18] Perhaps that is possible, but it is a real stretch to think Almonte would have been able to make a positive identification even if he had seen a portrait of Crockett a year or two earlier.

The allegation that the punctuation of the letter had been changed is merely a supposition on the part of Kilgore and Crisp. We probably will never know if they are correct since no one has ever produced the original Dolson letter. It raises an interesting question regarding the historical process. We only have the Dolson account in one form, as it is written in the newspaper. The way it is written does not conform to the point that Kilgore and Crisp wished to make. Their conclusion is not that the account is flawed, therefore invalid, but that an innocent mistake was made. Once they correct the account to the way they know it should have been written, it coincidentally supports their case.

Another adjustment is made regarding the sentence that states, "The brave but unfortunate men were marched to the tent of Santa Anna." On the surface this would place the executions outside of the Alamo. However, Crockett's body was identified as being *inside* the Alamo by people who knew him. This discrepancy has never been an obstacle to those who have determined the Dolson account to be in perfect agreement with all of the other execution accounts. Jim Crisp is the first historian to address this discrepancy. He explains this very logically by pointing out that the Spanish word for tent, *pabellón*, can also be used to indicate a flag. His reasoning is that Dolson's informant stated that the prisoners were brought to Santa Anna's *banner* or *flag* when he entered the Alamo, and that Dolson misinterpreted it to mean "tent."[19] Once again, this is a possibility, but we will probably never know for sure. The one person supposedly translating (Dolson) did translate the word as *tent*.

My opinion is the Dolson account is unreliable due to its contrived nature and to the outside forces that prompted it. The Dolson account describes a secret meeting being convened between Colonel James Morgan and the unidentified officer. If Dolson was required as an interpreter, how did the Mexican officer initially convey his desire to bare his soul? The meeting is held specifically to determine "the proceedings of Santa Anna towards the prisoners who remained alive at the taking of the Alamo." Why? What was so important about the prisoners at the Alamo? This account only spoke of six prisoners. Approximately three hundred were executed at Goliad. Surely that incident was more important than the one at the Alamo.

The point of focusing on the Alamo executions was that Crockett's name could be linked with it. Since Crockett was a fairly well-known and fairly popular figure in America, the story of his brutal execution at the hands of Santa Anna was sure to raise sentiment in the United States. Even though the Texans had been victorious at San Jacinto and had captured Santa Anna, they were still on shaky ground. Mexico still had enough strength to regain Texas. Santa Anna was one of the few men with enough power and force of will to bring this about. A key to holding Texas was to keep Santa Anna a hostage or eliminate him. This was important to the men in the Texan army whose lives depended on this, but it was also of vital importance to the land speculators. They had the opportunity to make fortunes in Texas land, but only if Texas remained independent of Mexico.

Samuel Swartwout, the Collector of the Port of New York, was one of the leading figures involved in Texas land speculation. He was also in close contact via correspondence with Col. Morgan, the Texan officer in charge of the prisoners at Galveston Island. Swartwout had so much riding on Santa Anna's continued captivity and was so incensed about the possibility of his release that he even called for the death of Texas' first president, David G. Burnet. Dolson's sentiments concerning the fate of Santa Anna at the end of his account closely resembles many of those expressed by Swartwout. It was in everyone's financial interests if Santa Anna remained a hostage. If Crockett's famous name could be used to achieve such an end, so much the better. The account does not denigrate Crockett's memory, and the seed of the execution story already had been sown in other sources.

It would not have been difficult to squeeze any needed information from a Mexican prisoner on Galveston Island. Walter Lord wrote that Mexican soldiers had a "...tendency after San Jacinto to say absolutely anything that might please a Texan." This view is not just some generalized opinion. It is well known in psychology that obvious authority figures have a very strong influence in obtaining identification by witnesses, regardless of whether the identification is accurate. After San Jacinto, there were no more clearly defined authority figures than Texans holding Mexican soldiers as prisoners. Morgan, the ultimate authority figure on Galveston Island, was known to have been imaginative in achieving his ends. When he emigrated to Texas in 1830, he got around the Mexican law prohibiting slavery by turning his sixteen slaves into indentured servants—their indenture lasting for a period of ninety-nine years.[20]

To say that Mexican prisoners on Galveston Island were under some duress would be putting it mildly. Morgan was in the process of constructing Fort Travis on the island, and he freely used the Mexican enlisted men as slave laborers. The officers fared not much better. They were allocated a fifty-yard square outside the walls of the fort with no protection from the broiling sun. They suffered from the heat, insects, bad water, lack of food, and illness. The officers also suffered the humiliation of insults from newly arrived volunteers from the United States, who were not even in Texas for any of the fighting. In fact, the tale of Crockett's "execution" probably reached Galveston Island with these new arrivals, since the story had already reached the rumor stage in the U.S. newspapers. Lastly, Morgan, not especially known for his compassion, even brought the curious around to view the officers as if they were zoo specimens. After enduring these conditions for over two months, it is safe to say that the unidentified prisoner would have been somewhat open to suggestion.

At the time, feelings were running understandably high against Santa Anna. In the months immediately following the Battle of San Jacinto, he literally was held hostage to insure that Mexico would not press the attack against Texas. Some favored Santa Anna's release after signing a treaty with Texas; others wanted him returned to Goliad, the scene of mass executions by the Mexican army, to stand trial as a war criminal. Others wanted to hang him outright. Attempts were made on his life. Finally he was sent to the United States, where he traveled as far as Washington, D.C., and Baltimore and returned to Mexico by sea in 1837.

Morgan was later charged with mismanagement, by Sam Houston, in his role as commander of the island and for his works in fortifying it.[21]

Maybe this account is completely accurate. If so, the Texan officers involved were very lucky. Of all the Mexican officers and soldiers being held prisoners, they conducted a secret interview with only one. That one gave them the exact information they needed. This information painted Crockett as a tragic martyr and Santa Anna as a heartless murderer. I believe his account was contrived toward that end, perhaps with the story of the five executed prisoners as a basis. The *Detroit Democratic Free Press* was a perfect venue for painting the picture of Santa Anna as villain. The paper continued the pressure two months later with the following description of a portrait of Santa Anna on exhibition in the Mississippi Hotel:

> The expression of his [Santa Anna's] eye and the lower part of his face is that of a cold blooded assassin, smiling scornfully at the victims of his cruelty and bent upon the execution of his purpose with no other design than the gratification of a morbid ambition stimulated by the predominance of the animal propensities. The first impression of the portrait, uninfluenced by a knowledge of his deeds, is that of a man destituted of the finer feelings of the human heart, and evincing a contempt for every thing that serves not to gloat his unnatural appetite.[22]

If the Dolson account is completely accurate, does it make Crockett appear cowardly or any less the hero than he was? No. If the account is inaccurate, was it part of some great conspiracy to paint Crockett in a bad light? No. At best, it helped Texas retain its freedom and also helped the land speculators line their pockets. At worst it may have given a false rendition of a factual occurrence.

It should be mentioned that Almonte never left any record of this interview. His own journal has no mention of executions at the Alamo. Nor does any other Mexican officer leave an account that verifies this interview. In the voluminous collection of the James Morgan Papers in the Rosenburg Library in Galveston, there is no mention of Morgan having conducted this interview or of an interview such as this having taken place.[23]

Execution or combat death?
Crockett before what appears to be a firing squad, yet he still holds a
pistol with smoke coming out of the barrel as if it just had been fired.
From Theodore Roosevelt, *Stories of the American West*. Courtesy of Paul Andrew Hutton.

The Labadie account (also known as the Urriza account):

And as regards the slaughter of the Alamo,
Castrion [Castrillón] was opposed to putting the
men to death. One night, past midnight, when
Santa Anna and Castrion were planning an assault,
Santa Anna declared that none should survive. It
was then inevitable that the fort could hold out but
little longer, and Castrion was persuading the commander to spare the lives of the men. Santa Anna
was holding in his hand the leg of a chicken which
he was eating, and holding it up, he said: "What are
the lives of soldiers more than of so many chickens?
I tell you, the Alamo must fall, and my orders must
be obeyed at all hazards. If our soldiers are driven

back, the next line in their rear must force those before them forward, and compel them to scale the walls, cost what it may." I was then acting as Santa Anna's secretary, and ranked as Colonel. My name is Urissa [sic]. After eating, Santa Anna directed me to write out his orders, to the effect that all the companies should be brought out early, declaring that he would take his breakfast in the fort the next morning. His orders were dispatched and I retired. I soon after heard the opening fire. By day-break our soldiers had made a breach, and I understood the garrison had all been killed. At about eight o'clock I went into the fort, and saw Santa Anna walking to and fro. As I bowed, he said to me, pointing to the dead: "These are the chickens. Much blood has been shed; but the battle is over: it was but a small affair." As I was surveying the dreadful scene before us, I observed Castrion coming out of one of the quarters, leading a venerable-looking old man by the hand; he was tall, his face was red, and he stooped forward as he walked. The President stopped abruptly, when Castrion, leaving his prisoner, advanced some four or five paces towards us, and with his graceful bow, said: "My General, I have spared the life of this venerable old man, and taken him prisoner." Raising his head, Santa Anna replied. "What right have you to disobey my orders? I want no prisoners," and waving his hand to a file of soldiers, he said, "Soldiers, shoot that man," and almost instantly he fell, pierced with a volley of balls. Castrion turned aside with tears in his eyes, and my heart was too full to speak. So there was not a man left. Even a cat that was soon after seen running through the fort, was shot, as the soldiers exclaimed: "It is not a cat, but an American." [In response to the question of

> "What was that old man's name?" asked by Nicho-
> las Labadie, Urriza replied] "I believe they called
> him Coket."[24]

This account has been treated as a positive identification of
Crockett and an accurate description of his death.[25] The identification in this case is the sentence "I believe they called him
'Coket.'" "They" in this case remains unidentified. Were "they"
people who were present at the execution, or were "they"
people on Galveston Island who already may have been influenced by the American newspaper stories? There is no answer
to this.

Urriza was a colonel in the Mexican army and was wounded
on April 20, the day before the Battle of San Jacinto. Urriza's
account does not come directly from him but from Nicholas
Labadie, a colorful character and a doctor of sorts, who treated
Urriza's wounds. Labadie was born in Canada in 1801. He emigrated to the U.S. and studied for the Catholic priesthood until
he decided on a medical career. He apparently was self-taught
and one of his remedies for cholera called for, "...a teaspoon of
Cooking Soda, dissolved in a cup of cold water; add a few pep-
permint drops and sugar." For severe vomiting associated with
cholera he recommended the application of "...mustard to the
pit of the stomach and between the shoulder blades." Labadie
fought in the Battle of San Jacinto as a private. After the battle,
Sam Houston asked him to treat the Mexican wounded, but
Labadie refused, until he was promised to receive $300 owed to
him by Colonel Juan Bradburn, the former commander of the
Mexican garrison at Anahuac.[26]

His rendition of Urriza's account was part of Labadie's much
longer memoir of the Texas Revolution. It was published in the
Texas Almanac in 1859. His memoir has been called "...a controversial remembrance perhaps erroneously perceived and
personally biased." Following its publication he was sued for
libel in the District Court of Nacogdoches County by John
Forbes, Commissary General of the Texas Army at San Jacinto,

for his allegation that Forbes murdered a Mexican woman on the San Jacinto battlefield. After dragging on for years, this libel suit was eventually dismissed.[27]

I find this account questionable since Labadie is reporting from memory the details of an event that happened twenty-three years earlier. He was not a witness to the event himself and is merely reporting on an alleged interview concerning the event. In addition, Labadie suffered considerable trauma immediately after the Texas Revolution had ended. He experienced the tragedy of losing two children during the revolution. He lapsed into a coma for a week after the campaign, due to sickness and lack of food. When he regained consciousness he discovered he had lost his hearing. Any one of these traumatic events might have affected his memory of his conversation with Urriza, if there was one. If this interview did take place and Urriza did witness an execution, his story appears to reflect the execution of only one man, as described by Joe. In this case Crockett (or Coket) is that one man. In the previous execution stories he was one of a group.

As is the case with the previous accounts, there is no independent verification from Urriza that this conversation with Labadie ever took place or that Urriza was a witness to any of the executions. This is one of the accounts Dan Kilgore described as "... [having] a ring of folklore instead of history," until the Peña "diary" surfaced to give it credibility.

The Becerra account (as published in the *Texas Mute Ranger* by John S. Ford):

> In the main building, on the ground floor, I saw a man lying on a bed—he was evidently sick. I retired, without molesting him, notwithstanding the order of Gen. Santa Anna to give no quarter to the Texians. A sergeant of artillery entered before I had finally left the room—he leveled his piece at the prostrate man; the latter raised his hand and shot the sergeant through the head with a pistol. A

soldier of the Toluca regiment came in, aimed his gun at the invalid, and was killed in a similar manner. I then fired and killed the Texian. I took his two empty pistols, and found his rifle standing by his bed. It seemed he was too weak to use it.

In another room I saw a man sitting on the floor among feathers. A bugler, who was with me, raised his gun. The gentleman said to him in Spanish: —"Don't kill me—I have plenty of money." He pulled out a pocketbook, also a large roll of bank bills, and handed the latter to the bugler. We divided the money.

While this was occurring another Texian made his appearance. He had been lying on the floor, as if resting. When he arose I asked:—"How many is there of you?" He replied:—"Only two."

The gentleman, who spoke Spanish, asked for Gen. Cos, and said he would like to see him. Just then Gen. Amador came in. He asked why the orders of the President had not been executed, and the two Texians killed. In answer the bugler exhibited his roll of bank bills, and they were taken from him immediately by the general. In a few moments Gen. Cos, Gen. Almonte, and Gen. Tolza, entered the room. As soon as Gen. Cos saw the gentleman who spoke Spanish he rushed to him, and embraced him. He told the other generals it was Travis, that on a former occasion he had treated him like a brother, had loaned him money, etc. He also said the other man was Col. Crockett. He entreated the other generals to go with him to Gen. Santa Anna, and join with him in a request to save the lives of the two Texians. The generals and the Texians left together to find Santa Anna. The bugler and myself followed them. They encountered the commander-in-chief in the court yard, with Gen.

Castrillón. Gen. Cos said to him:—"Mr. President, you have here two prisoners—in the name of the Republic of Mexico I supplicate you to guarantee the lives of both." Santa Anna was very much enraged. He said:—"Gentleman generals, my order was to kill every man in the Alamo." He turned, and said:—"Soldiers, kill them." A soldier was standing near Travis, and presented his gun at him. Travis seized the bayonet, and depressed the muzzle of the piece to the floor, and it was not fired. While this was taking place the soldiers standing around opened fire. A shot struck Travis in the back. He then stood erect, folding his arms, and looked calmly, unflinchingly, upon his assailants. He was finally killed by a ball passing through his neck. Crockett stood in a similar position. They died undaunted like heroes.

The firing was brisk for a time. It came from all sides. Gen. Santa Anna, and most of the officers ran. Gen. Castrillón squatted down—so did I. In this affair eight Mexican soldiers were killed, and wounded, by their comrades.

I did not know the names of two Texians, only as given by Gen. Cos. The gentleman he called Crockett had a coat with capes to it.[28]

Francisco Becerra was born in Guanajuato, Mexico, in 1810. He is described as a first sergeant in the division of Gen. Ramirez y Sesma during the Mexican army's march to Texas in 1835. The account of Sergeant Becerra is one of the more controversial accounts of the Alamo battle. It originally appeared as part of the John S. Ford papers. The account itself was given as a talk before an audience at the Austin Public Library in 1875, but it did not appear in print until April of 1882 when it was published in an obscure journal, the *Texas Mute Ranger*.

Becerra's account has been described by Walter Lord as "...perhaps the most unreliable of the Mexican participants." Dan Kilgore sent out mixed messages regarding Becerra. He described him as an "...accomplished raconteur" but also stated that Becerra was a "...straightforward, truthful witness, except for the tale of his personal role in the deaths of the three heroes" (Crockett, Travis, and Jim Bowie). Kilgore used this account to support the theory of Crockett's execution and the Peña account. At the same time he stated that it had "...a ring of folklore instead of history," was "...hard to believe," and "...the most bizarre account of Crockett's death by a participant."[29]

I find the Becerra account to be unreliable based on the erroneous information it contains. Becerra states that the Mexican army suffered two thousand killed and more than three hundred wounded in the Alamo battle. This puts their casualties higher than the number of men they had in the battle. Also, he includes Travis as being executed (this time there are two executed), but this is in conflict with Joe's description of Travis' death. Joe described Travis as being killed early in the battle on the Alamo's north wall.[30]

The manner in which this account was given casts greater doubt on its reliability. John S. Ford related that Becerra's "Recollections...were prepared from copious notes, which had been read to Sergeant Becerra in Spanish and English—he spoke both languages—and he endorsed them as a true version of the affair." In other words Becerra's account is not a spontaneous first person recollection. Someone else, most likely Ford, prepared an account, read it to Becerra, and Becerra agreed with the details. This method of questioning or interviewing a witness is recognized by experts to be very susceptible to suggestion. This is the method used by investigators when their desire is to "squeeze" some bits of information out of a witness. It provides considerably less accurate information than a "free" report.

Becerra eliminated himself as a reliable witness to Crockett's alleged execution when he admitted to John S. Ford that "...he did not know them [Travis and Crockett] personally and might be mistaken as to their identity."[31]

The Zuber account (also known as the Cos account):

This account was supposedly given in 1836 when Doctor George M. Patrick visited the Mexican army prisoners of war in Anahuac. Patrick then conveyed the information to Zuber, who did not write it down until sixty-eight years later. The narrative is attributed to Cos in answer to a question by Patrick. Zuber's letter states that Patrick asked Cos "...if he saw Colonel David Crockett in the Alamo, and if he knew how he died." Cos supposedly replied:

Yes, sir. When we thought that all the defenders were slain, I was searching the barracks, and found, alive and unhurt, a fine looking and well-dressed man, locked up, alone, in one of the rooms, and asked him who he was. He replied: "I am David Crocket [sic], a citizen of the State of Tennessee and representative of a district of the State in the United States Congress. I have come to Texas on a visit of exploration; purposing, if permitted, to become a loyal citizen of the Republic of Mexico...I extended my visit to San Antonio, and called in the Alamo to become acquainted with the officers, and learn of them what I could of the condition of affairs. Soon after my arrival, the fort was invested by government troops, whereby I have been prevented from leaving it. And here I am yet, a noncombatant and foreigner, having taken no part in the fighting."

I proposed to introduce him to the President, state his situation to him, and request him to depart in peace, to which he thankfully assented. I then conducted him to the President, to whom I introduced him in about these words: "Mr. President, I beg permission to present to your Excellency the Honorable David Crockett, a citizen of the State of Tennessee, and a Representative of a district of that State in the United States Congress. He has come to Texas on a visit of exploration; purposing, if permitted to become a loyal citizen of the Republic of Mexico. He extended his visit to San Antonio, and called in the Alamo to become acquainted with its officers and to learn of them what he could of the conditions of affairs. Soon after his arrival, the fort was invested by Government troops, whereby he has been prevented from leaving it. And here he is yet, noncombatant and foreigner, having taken no part in the fighting. And now, Mr. President, I beseech your Excellency to permit him to depart in peace."

Santa Anna heard me through, but impatiently. Then he replied sharply, "You know your orders"; turned his back upon us and walked away. But, as he turned, Crockett drew from his bosom a dagger, with which he smote at him with a thrust, which, if not arrested, would surely have killed him; but was met by a bayonet-thrust by the hand of a soldier through the heart; he fell and soon expired.

Zuber added his own disclaimer to the end of this tale stating, "This story by Cos, though a gross falsehood, shows what Santa Anna would have done if it were true."[32]

Zuber served in the Texas army from March 1 to June 1, 1836. He later served in several Indian campaigns and then in the Confederate Cavalry during the Civil War. He was a charter member of the Texas State Historical Association and was even made an honorary life member on the basis of his service during the Texas Revolution. Zuber is famous in Texas history not so much for his military service, as for his ability to crank out legendary stories about the Alamo. His best-known tale is the story of Alamo commander Travis drawing the famous line in the sand and inviting those willing to stay with him and die to cross the line. Most historians and students of the Alamo now agree that this tale was a fabrication of Zuber's. He also penned an unlikely tale of Jim Bowie having his tongue cut out and being tossed on a funeral pyre alive after the battle. Since he had covered Travis and Bowie, it is fitting that Zuber supplied a story covering Crockett.

The added touch of Crockett attempting to assassinate Santa Anna comes from the bogus Crockett autobiography published by Richard Penn Smith in the summer of 1836. Cos and Patrick never left any documentation to corroborate Zuber's tale. They both had died years before Zuber had written his letter.

This account appears to be nothing more than a creation of Zuber. Its origins are in the single defender scene described by Joe.

The alleged Sanchez-Navarro account:

During the early years of the twentieth century the last survivors of the Alamo battle passed on into history. Enrique Esparza, who had been eight years old at the time of the battle, died in 1917. He had left several accounts of his childhood memories. Alejo Perez Jr., who had been an infant in the Alamo with his mother, Juana Navarro Perez Alsbury, passed away in 1918. Of course he had been too young to relate anything about the battle, but he was the last known physical link to it.

The passing of the last survivors of the Alamo did not mean an end of "firsthand eyewitness accounts" of the battle. Several accounts emerged during the twentieth century in the form of newly discovered personal "diaries" and "journals." One of the first of these is the purported journal of Col. José Juan Sanchez-Navarro. The account reads:

> Long live the country, the Alamo is ours!
> Today at five in the morning the assault was
> made by four columns commanded by general Cos

and colonels Duque, Romero and Morales. His excellency the President commanded the reserve. The fire lasted for half an hour. Our chiefs, officers and troops as if by magic topped the walls at one and the same time and they threw themselves inside continuing the conflict by the sword. By six thirty in the morning none of the enemy existed. I saw actions that I envied, of heroic valor. Some cruelties horrified me, among others the death of an old man they called "Cocran" and of a boy approximately fourteen years. The women and children were spared. Travis, the Commander of the Alamo, died as a brave man. Buy [Bowie], the braggart son-in-law of Beramendi, as a coward. The troop was granted plunder.[33]

This account does not mention "Crockett," but everyone who has ever used it as a source agrees that "Cocran" is meant to be "Crockett." It has the distinction of being used as part of the evidence proving Crockett's execution without mentioning Crockett's name and without actually describing any executions. Sanchez-Navarro was born in Saltillo, Mexico, and was a career military man. At the time of the Texan campaign he held the rank of captain and had served as the adjutant inspector of Nuevo León y Tamaulipas. He was present in San Antonio de Bexar when Texan forces defeated Cos in December of 1835, and he returned with Cos' force in the spring of 1836.

Sanchez-Navarro's account appeared in the form of a handwritten narrative of the Texan campaign tucked away on the blank pages of two large ledger books, which contained indexes of official records from his days as adjutant inspector of Nuevo León y Tamaulipas. Texan author and newspaperman Lon Tinkle wrote that this account was discovered in 1936, which coincidentally was the centennial of the Texas Revolution. The account was first published in 1938 by Carlos Sanchez-Navarro y Peón as *La Guerra de Tejas: Memorias de un Soldado.*

My opinion is this account cannot be used as evidence of Crockett's execution for reasons other than the fact that it does not mention Crockett or executions. The ledger books in which this account is contained are part of the Nettie Lee Benson Latin American Collection at the University of Texas at Austin. The two books are not dedicated solely to the journal. They contain official government records from 1831 to 1839 that are unrelated to the Mexican army's campaign in Texas. Sanchez-Navarro's alleged journal is written on what otherwise would have been blank pages between the different subdivisions of records.

Sanchez-Navarro was a scion of one of the richest land owning families in Mexico. He was also a government official. It is unlikely he would have had to rely on partly filled ledgers on which to record his personal journal. It is just as unlikely if he did use these ledgers that he or someone else would have continued to use them for official records up to and including 1839.[34]

I believe someone in the twentieth century found these two ledger books containing mundane information and forged a "journal" of Sanchez-Navarro on the blank pages. On April 5, 1836, one month after the Alamo battle, an account of the battle by an anonymous Mexican soldier was published in a Mexican newspaper, *El Mosquito Mexicano*. Portions of this letter are so similar to the alleged Sanchez-Navarro account that they had to have been written by the same hand. This has caused many to believe that the anonymous letter writer was Sanchez-Navarro. I believe just the opposite is true. It is my opinion that whoever wrote the account in the ledgers appropriated portions of this letter, adding his or her own details. (The letter makes no mention of the death of an old man named "Cocran.") This addition, with the misspelling or mispronunciation of the name, gives readers a chance to realize or "discover" the identity of the person the writer meant.

There is no record of this document earlier than its appearance in 1936-38. This lack of provenance is a red flag regarding

Crockett at bay but still defiant. The question is "what happened next?"

Illustration by Henry Pitz, from Albert Britt, *The Boy's Own Book of Frontiersmen*.
(New York: Macmillan, 1935). Courtesy of Paul Andrew Hutton.

historical fakes. The original publisher of the account, Carlos Sanchez-Navarro y Peón, gave no indication where the ledger books came from or how he obtained them. Also, there is little information on how or from whom the University of Texas obtained the ledger books. In 1991 the head of Public Services at the Barker Texas History Center (now the Center for American History) at the University of Texas at Austin stated that "...information on its acquisition is sketchy," and that the little documentation the university has on this purchase, "...fails to indicate from whom the university bought the material or what was paid." There is some evidence that the university was prepared to offer a Mrs. Suarez del Real $1,500 to $2,000 for it in 1950.[35]

To my knowledge, no forensic tests have ever been performed on these ledger books to determine their authenticity.

The alleged Peña account:

The description of the Texans' execution is contained in one paragraph that is part of a much longer narrative of the Texan campaign. This paragraph picks up after the battle had ended and just before a speech by Santa Anna to his men. The account states that his speech was met coldly by his assembled battalions due to the executions. The paragraph reads:

> As the speech of Santa Anna very nearly proceeded an unpleasant event which, happening when the heat of the strife had already passed, was seen as contemptible murder and greatly contributed to the coldness noted. Some seven men had survived the general massacre and guided by general Castrillón, who sponsored them, were presented to Santa Anna. Among them was one of great stature, well formed and of regular features, in whose countenance there was imprinted the sentiment of adversity, but in which was noted certain resignation and nobility that commended him. He was the naturalist David Crocket [sic], very well

known in North America for his strange adventures, who had come to travel over the country and had been in Bejar in the moments of surprise had locked himself up in the Alamo, fearful that his quality as a foreigner would not be respected. Santa Anna answered the intervention of Castrillón with a gesture of indignation and immediately directing the sappers, who were the troops most near to him, ordered them to shoot them. The chiefs and officers were irritated by this behavior and did not second the voice, hoping that the first moment of fury had passed, these men would be saved; but various officers who were around the President who perhaps had not been there in the moment of danger, were made notable by an infamous act; exceeding the soldiers in cruelty, they placed themselves before them, in order to flatter their chief, and sword in hand they threw themselves upon these unfortunate defenseless ones, in the same way that a tiger throws itself upon its prey. They tormented them before they were made to die, and those unfortunate ones died moaning, but without humiliating themselves to their executioners. It is said that general Ramírez y Sesma had been one of them: I do not testify to this, because although I was present, I set apart this sight horrified in order not to see such a barbarous scene. Remember, companions that fierce moment, that horrified us all equally, and which shook our souls, which a short while ago had thirsted for vengeance. Do not our hearts beat quickly, filled with indignation against those who so vilely bloodied their swords. As for me, I must confess I shake only at the memory and the sound is always in my ears the pitiful and penetrating accent of the victims.[36]

As far as Crockett execution accounts go, this is the biggie. This is the one that corroborated all of the others and, at the same time, was corroborated by them. This is the one that set in stone the tale of Crockett's execution for historians. This is the one that is written, argued, and debated about. This is the one that is cited in books and is considered "the best" and "most reliable." It is a favorite of revisionist historians who revel in putting a new slant on Crockett's life and death. I do not believe this is an accurate or even an authentic rendition of Crockett's death. As stated earlier, I believe the Peña narrative is a modern-day forgery. My reasons for this belief are detailed in a later chapter.

There is one more description of the executions within the Alamo's walls that does not identify Crockett or anyone else. This account is found in the papers of the artist Theodore Gentilz (1819-1906), who did a number of paintings on the subject of the Alamo. It comes to us thirdhand in the convoluted manner most Alamo accounts do. This particular statement comes from his research for the painting *The Death of Dickinson* (1896). Maria Jesusa Peña was the wife of Antonio Cruz y Arocha, from whom Gentilz obtained this account. Cruz y Arocha and his wife lived in a jacal close to the Alamo. On the night Juan Seguin left the Alamo in order to rally aid, Cruz y Arocha waited for him with a horse by the acequia. He apparently accompanied Seguin on his mission. His wife's account via Gentilz states:

> [She] saw from a little window of a jacal on the west side facing the church all or part of what was happening. After the cease-fire, Santa Anna entered by the south west door. Some Texans still hiding came to kneel before him, each one with a little white flag. The foot-soldiers surrounding them hesitated to kill them; but Santa Anna in passing signaled with his head and his sword and suddenly they were pierced with blows of the bayonets.[37]

Her account does not mention Crockett, but there is nothing to be made from that. Even if he were one of those executed and even if she did witness the executions from her jacal, she probably would have been too far away to make any specific identifications anyway. It is interesting that she mentioned the prisoners as kneeling down and carrying a white flag. If her account is true (like all the other accounts of the executions, it has never been proven true or false) and the men did carry a white flag and knelt down, then why did none of the other execution accounts mention this touch?

CHAPTER THREE

Died Fighting

· · · ◆ · · ·

The evidence is fairly clear. There are no eyewitnesses to Crockett dying in combat, but there are several separate eyewitness accounts of him being executed.
—James E. Crisp

There is not a single, reliable eyewitness account of Crockett's death in battle.
—Paul A. Hutton

Not one report of an eyewitness has been found by Alamo scholars to support the popular notion that Crockett went down while desperately clubbing Mexican soldiers with the barrel of his shattered rifle.
—Dan Kilgore

THERE ARE A NUMBER of alleged eyewitness accounts that state or at least hint at the fact that Crockett died in combat at the Alamo. These accounts are no more convincing than the execution accounts. Most of them come from second- and third-hand sources and some are of questionable authenticity. There are two major differences concerning the "execution" accounts and the "died fighting" accounts. The "died fighting" accounts have never been used as a cohesive, mutually corroborative body of evidence as the "execution" accounts have. This is understandable since they are neither cohesive nor mutually corroborative. Neither are the "execution" accounts, but they are used as cohesive and mutually corroborative sources. The second difference is that the "died fighting" accounts are usually ignored by proponents of the execution theory as if they do not exist at all. They are not studied, explained, and dismissed—just ignored. They are no more or less authentic or accurate than the "execution" accounts, but they deserve to be treated on an equal footing.

The "died fighting" accounts, like the execution accounts, have an outward appearance and a separate reality to them. Those accounts that describe Crockett as dying in combat, or at least not being executed, are those of:

1) Andrea Castañon de Villanueva (Madam Candelaria) (1890)
2) Andrea Castañon de Villanueva (Madam Candelaria) (1899)
3) Sergeant Felix Nuñez (given prior to 1889)
4) Captain Rafael Soldana (given at the end of the Mexican War)
5) An unidentified Mexican army captain (given at the beginning of the U.S. Civil War)

They are more accurately described as:

1) Andrea Castañon de Villanueva (Madam Candelaria) in an interview given to William Corner in 1888 and included in his book *San Antonio de Bexar: A Guide and History* in 1890. Hereafter referred to as the *Candelaria 1890* account.
2) Andrea Castañon de Villanueva (Madam Candelaria) as published in the *St. Louis Republic* and repeated in the *San Antonio Light* after her death in 1899. Hereafter referred to as the *Candelaria 1899* account.
3) A professor George W. Noel from an account allegedly given to him by a Sergeant Felix Nuñez and then passed on to an unidentified staff writer for the *San Antonio*

Express and published in 1889. Hereafter referred to as the *Nuñez* account.

4) James T. DeShields reporting an account allegedly given to him by Creed Taylor who allegedly obtained the information from a Capt. Rafael Soldana at Corpus Christi at the end of the Mexican War. Hereafter referred to as the *Soldana* account.

5) James T. DeShields reporting an account allegedly given to him by Creed Taylor, who allegedly obtained the information from an unidentified former Mexican army captain just prior to the U.S. Civil War. Hereafter referred to as the *unidentified captain's* account.

The Candelaria 1890 account:

> Returning to the subject of David Crockett, the old Señora said he was one of the first to fall; that he advanced from the Church building "towards the wall or rampart running from the end of the stockade, slowly and with great deliberation, without arms, when suddenly a volley was fired by the Mexicans causing him to fall forward on his face, dead.[1]

Candelaria's account does not say Crockett was executed, nor does it say that he died fighting. In this case it is more like he died "traveling" from the church building towards the Alamo's wall. It is a safe compromise. Crockett does not die flailing away at Mexican soldiers with his rifle. He is even unarmed at the time. However, he is advancing in the direction the Mexicans would have been coming from. This account held some attraction for writers and historians for the same reasons the execution stories do. It presents a novel, nontraditional Crockett death.[2]

I do not find Candelaria's account particularly convincing. One reason for this is the considerable doubt cast upon her participation in the battle. Another is the substantial difference between this tale and one she supposedly told ten years later. Possibly the truest part of this account is the unremarkableness of Crockett's death. However, there is no evidence of this either way.

The Candelaria 1899 account:

He was one of the strangest-looking men I ever saw. He had the face of a woman and his manner was that of a young girl. I could not regard him as a hero until I saw him die. He looked grand and terrible standing in the door and fighting a whole column of Mexican infantry. He had fired his last shot, and had nothing to reload. The cannon balls had knocked away the sand bags, and the infantry was pouring through the breach. Crockett stood there swinging something bright over his head. The place was full of smoke and I could not tell whether he was using a gun or a sword. A heap of dead was piled at his feet and the Mexicans were lunging at him with bayonets, but he would not retreat an inch. Poor Bowie could see it all, but he could not raise up from his cot, Crockett fell and the Mexicans poured into the Alamo.... Every man at the door fell but Crockett, I could see him struggling with the head of the column, and Bowie raised up and fired his rifle. I saw Crockett fall backwards.[3]

This account attributed to Candelaria offers a considerably "jazzed up" version of Crockett's death. This one is no more convincing than her earlier one. If Candelaria actually did relate this tale, she did so at an advanced age. There is no way to know how much editorializing was provided by the various newspapers. This account has plenty of inaccuracies. It describes Travis as being killed toward the southeast section of the Alamo rather than at the north wall as described by Joe. It describes Crockett as arriving at the Alamo only days before the Mexican army's

The poised bayonet leaves little doubt as to what will happen next.
This traditional image is symbolic of the Texans' stand at the Alamo.

From Cyrus Townsend Brady, *Border Fights and Fighters* (New York: McClure, 1902).
Courtesy of Paul Andrew Hutton.

invasion, when he had been in San Antonio several weeks before. Lastly, the account centers all of the action around the Alamo church rather than the whole sprawling mission complex. At the time this account was published, the small church was the only original building left standing.

The Nuñez account:

> To recount the individual deeds of valor, of the brave men who were slain in the Alamo, would fill a volume as large as the History of Texas; nevertheless there was one who perished in that memorable conflict who is entitled to a passing notice. The one to whom I refer was killed just inside of the front door. The peculiarity of his dress, and his undaunted courage attracted the attention of several of us, both officers and men. He was a tall American of rather dark complexion and had on a long cuera (buck skin coat) and a round cap without any bill, and made of fox skin, with the long tail hanging down his back. This man apparently had a charmed life. Of the many soldiers who took deliberate aim at him and fired, not one ever hit him. On the contrary he never missed a shot. He killed at least eight of our men, besides wounding several others. This fact being observed by a lieutenant who had come in over the wall he sprung at him and dealt him a deadly blow with his sword, just above the right eye, which felled him to the ground and in an instant he was pierced by not less than twenty bayonets. This lieutenant said that if all Americans had killed as many of our men as this one had, our army would have been annihilated before the Alamo could have been taken. He was about the last man that was killed.[4]

Other than this account there is no record of Felix Nuñez. George W. Noel is also a bit mysterious. Like the account attributed to Candelaria, this one centers most of the action around the Alamo church. This tends to cast some doubt on the account, but one does not know if Nuñez was supplying this description or if Noel or the unidentified newspaper editor applied Nuñez's description of a larger Alamo mission to the only building that was left, which was the church, at the time the account was given.

This account does not mention Crockett by name, but it is generally assumed that the person described is meant to be Crockett. It certainly is the account most used in histories and fiction when writers portray Crockett as having died fighting. It offers a description of clothing that is close to the traditional Crockett garb of coonskin cap and buckskin coat. In recent years some writers have taken great pleasure in pronouncing that Crockett "... never wore a coonskin cap."[5] Next to the combat death this is the Crockett association that detractors love the most. It has little to do with any historical aspect of Crockett. Some writers just seem to enjoy upsetting a certain established image of Crockett. The modern view of Crockett as a coonskin-capped frontiersman has its roots in the Walt Disney television show. Those who make the absolute pronouncement that Crockett never wore a coonskin are not that familiar with or are ignorant of a number of contemporary references to Crockett all identifying him as wearing a coonskin cap. These were all given long before the Disney merchandizing bonanza in children's coonskin (rabbit skin) caps. The point of this is that Crockett was associated with the coonskin cap long before the 1955 television series. In 1842, when Texas was again being threatened by Mexico, a volunteer group raised in east Tennessee sported coonskin caps and called themselves "the Order of Captain Davy Crockett."[6]

This question of Crockett's headwear does not prove a case either way. If an account was being concocted or at least embellished in 1889, the person doing so may have known enough about Crockett to have added that little embellishment. If the Nuñez account is accurate, it may provide a clue to Crockett's fate. Of all the defenders of the Alamo he is the only one who is ever identified as wearing a coonskin cap.

The many problems and inaccuracies of the Nuñez account were brought to light in 1990 in a critical article by Stephen L. Hardin. His article marked the first time the account had been published in its entirety since 1889. Much of the criticism of this account stems from its inconsistency with other descriptions of the battle from the Mexican side, most notably that supposedly written by Peña. In this case the unproven, unauthenticated Peña account is used as a control to debunk another account.

The Soldana account:

We have seen earlier that the DeShields/Taylor/Soldana account gave us a description of an Alamo defender, "Kwockey." The account continues to describe "Kwockey's" death:

> When the final assault was made upon the walls these men fought like devils. [When asked by Creed Taylor if any begged for quarter he replied by saying that] he had never heard that any of them offered to surrender or that a single man had begged for his life. "Kwockey" was killed in a room of the mission. He stood on the inside to the left of the door and plunged his long knife into the bosom of every soldier that tried to enter. They were powerless to fire upon him because of the fact that he was backed up against the wall and, the doorway being narrow, they could not bring their guns to bear upon him. And, moreover, the pressure from the rear was so great that many near the doorway were forced into the room only to receive a deadly thrust from that long knife. Finally a well-directed shot broke this man's right arm and his hand fell useless at his side. He then seized his long gun with his left hand and leaped toward the center of the

room where he could wield the weapon without obstruction, felling every man that came through the doorway. A corporal ordered the passage cleared of those who were being pressed forward, a volley was fired almost point blank and the last defender of the Alamo fell forward—dead.[7]

The unidentified captain's account:

He [the unidentified captain] said Crockett was the last man slain and that he fought like an infuriated lion. He stated that his last stand was in a small room and with gun in hand he brained every Mexican that tried to enter the door. He used his gun as a club until a shot from without the door broke his right arm, and his gun barrel (the stock had been broken off) fell to the floor. Seeing this the Mexican soldiers made a rush into the room with fixed bayonets, but drawing a large knife with his left hand he rushed upon his assailants and, parrying their thrusts, killed several before he was finally slain. He said he did not hear of a sick man being bayoneted while helpless on his bed but there was a sick man who got out of his bed when the Mexicans entered the fortress and died fighting with the rest. He also stated that Santa Anna could not have done otherwise than to put the defenders of the Alamo to the sword, since they were in open rebellion, held a government fortress, and had refused all overtures looking to a surrender.[8]

The DeShields/Taylor accounts and the newspaper editor/Noel/Nuñez account fall short of being firsthand accounts, just as the execution accounts do. They are too tenuous to build a rock solid case for Crockett having died fighting. I do not believe these accounts prove that Crockett died fighting. They are simply more evidence in the case and more fuel for argument on a par with the execution accounts. As stated earlier, it has been more convenient to many to ignore these accounts. To consider them requires some type of evaluation to be applied to them. In fairness the same standards would have to be applied to the execution accounts.

There is one other account that may have some bearing. In his 1907 interview Enrique Esparza is quoted as saying:

> ... [Crockett] was everywhere during the siege and personally slew many of the enemy with his rifle, his pistol and his knife. He fought hand to hand. He clubbed his rifle when they closed in on him and knocked them down with its stock until he was overwhelmed by numbers and slain. He fought to his last breath. He fell immediately in front of the large double doors which he defended with the force that was by his side. Crockett was one of the few who were wide awake when the final crisis and crash came. When he died there was a heap of slain in front and on each side of him. These he had all killed before he finally fell on top of the heap.[9]

Opposite: The Alamo church and surrounding area are those most associated with Crockett:

A) Susanna Dickinson's account in Morphis' *History of Texas* stated that she recognized Crockett's body between the church and the two-story barracks building. Most Alamo scholars interpret her statement to mean this area.

B) A strict interpretation of her words would also take in this area in the Alamo's horse corral.

C) In 1890 Madam Candelaria stated that Crockett was one of the first to fall while advancing, unarmed, from the church to the wall rampart running from the end of the stockade.

D) An 1899 account attributed to Candelaria stated that Crockett died defending the sandbagged doors of the church, inside the building. Enrique Esparza's 1907 interview states that Crockett fell immediately in front of the large double doors. This is generally interpreted to mean on the outside of the church doors.

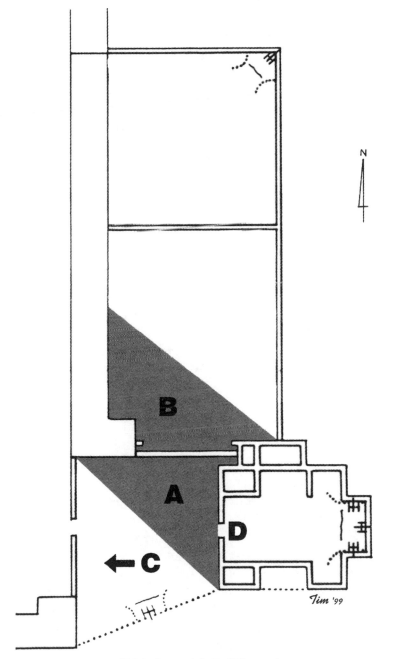

(Original artwork by Rod Timanus.)

Esparza never claimed that he actually witnessed Crockett's death. We do not know if the passing of many years had affected his memory of events. He does place Crockett's body in the same general area in front of the Alamo church that Susanna Dickinson described in Morphis' *History of Texas*.

The statement of Francisco Ruiz, the Alcalde of San Antonio de Bexar, may support the placing of Crockett's body in this area. Following the battle, Ruiz was pressed into service by Santa Anna to accompany him into the Alamo and identify the bodies of Travis, Bowie, and Crockett. Ruiz's account was translated into English by a J.A. Quintero and appeared in the pages of the *Texas Almanac* in 1860. It is unknown if Quintero's translation remained true to what Ruiz described since there is no original document from Ruiz. The account states "Toward the west in a small fort opposite the city, we found the body of colonel Crockett."[10]

This statement continues to confuse historians since "Toward the west" is interpreted to mean "near the west wall of the Alamo plaza," since this wall faced the town of San Antonio. However, there was no structure in the vicinity of the west wall that could have been considered a "small fort." Some historians are now interpreting this to mean one of the artillery emplacements along the west wall. My (and others') interpretation of Ruiz's statement is that he was speaking of the area directly in front of the Alamo church. This small walled-in area fits the description of a "small fort" very well.

Ruiz's statement was probably given and translated not much earlier than its publication. By that time the outer walls of the Alamo proper had long since disappeared. Anyone speaking about the Alamo at that time would have used the church, that was (and still is) standing as a logical reference point. I believe "Toward the west" means "to the west of the church." The facade of the church faces west, onto the walled-in area. This is the same area that Esparza claims Crockett was defending and where Dickinson said she saw his body. The words "opposite the city" did not necessarily mean opposite San Antonio proper.

Across the San Antonio River from the town was a collection of huts and dwellings, a neighborhood if you will, called La Villita, or "little village." This section was on the same side of the river as the Alamo, south of the Alamo, and opposite the area in front of the Alamo church. The word "city" is likely a misinterpretation of "La Villita."

This is a relatively simple explanation to Ruiz's description of the location of Crockett's body. As stated earlier, some agree with this, while others do not. Still others have their own interpretation of Ruiz's words.

Historian William C. Davis was admittedly mystified by my opinion. He concocted his own scenario to explain Crockett's location. Immediately before the description of Crockett's body, Ruiz's account states that Travis' body was found on the "north battery." This would have been one of the artillery positions on the Alamo compound's north wall. Since the Crockett description comes after this, Davis interpreted it to mean "toward the west" of the "north battery." He then goes on to explain that "Either Mrs. Dickinson was mistaken [in identifying Crockett's body] or Ruiz identified the wrong man in 1836, or he had a false recollection in 1860, or Crockett's body was *unaccountably moved across the compound* [?] between the time Susanna saw it and Ruiz' arrival."[11]

Davis' research for his book on the Alamo triumvirate of Travis, Bowie, and Crockett uncovered a long forgotten account in the Mexican archives. This account is by General Joaquin Ramirez y Sesma, who commanded the Mexican cavalry at the Alamo. The account adds credence to several others that said groups of Texans sallied out of the Alamo when the Mexican soldiers took possession of the Alamo's walls.[12]

In an article Davis speculated:

Perhaps Crockett made it into the open, only to be ridden down by enemy lances, in which case, if Susanna did see his body, then she must not have left the church until *after the Texan dead were brought back into the compound by Sesma's men.*[13]

Crockett may have tried to escape with the scores of other Alamo defenders who opted for the open prairie. However, Dickinson's and others' identification of his body inside the Alamo argues against his having made it outside the walls. Davis' statement about the Texan dead being "...brought back into the compound by Sesma's men" is made with such offhandedness that it comes off as a foregone conclusion. Brought back in? The bodies of the Alamo defenders were burned in three pyres outside the Alamo's walls. What would have been the point of bringing their bodies into the Alamo only to drag them out again to be burned?

I think there is enough evidence to place Crockett's body in the area in front of the Alamo church, to the exclusion of any other place. Whether he died fighting, was executed, was shot down unarmed, or was retreating with his comrades when he was killed in that area remains a mystery.

Opposite: The 1860 account by Francisco Antonio Ruiz in which he claims to have identified Crockett's body "Towards the west and in a small fort opposite the city," can be interpreted in a number of ways. The "small fort" may have been:

1) The enclosed area to the west of the Alamo church, opposite La Villita;

2) An artillery position on the west wall, opposite the town of San Antonio de Bexar;

3) The northwest artillery position, to the west of where Ruiz identified Travis' body (4) and opposite San Antonio;

5) The outer works protecting the Alamo's main gate, opposite La Villita;

6) A fortified area outside the west wall, opposite San Antonio that is shown on two maps purported to have been done by Mexican officers during the siege.

N

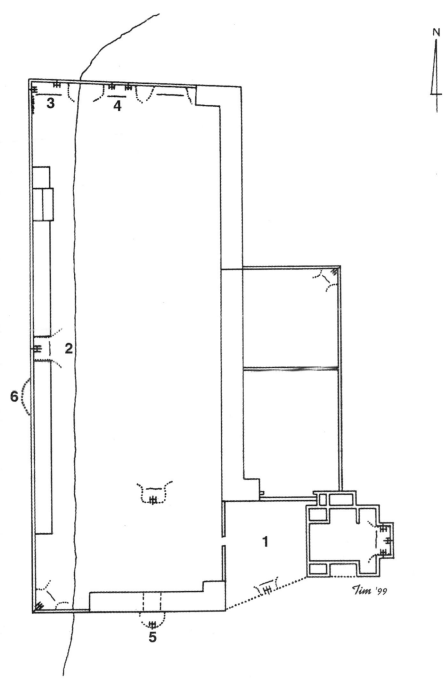

3

4

2

6

1

5

Tim '99

(Original artwork by Rod Timanus.)

CHAPTER FOUR

Other Deaths—Other Mysteries

· · · ◆ · · ·

Like most passionate nations Texas has its own private history based on, but not limited by, facts.
—John Steinbeck, *Travels With Charley*

The report of my death was an exaggeration.
—Mark Twain

THE QUESTIONS SURROUNDING THE DEATH of Crockett and the variety of descriptions of his death are not surprising. A legendary man, a legendary event, a traumatic battle, confusion, false memories, the passage of time all contribute to the problem. Crockett was not the only Alamo defender whose death was interpreted in a number of ways. Travis and Bowie, the Alamo's leading figures, are perfect examples. The following are some of the ways their deaths were reported in the days, weeks, months, and years after the Alamo's fall.

Travis

> Travis killed himself...
> E.N. Gray, March 11, 1836.[1]

Travis, 'tis said, rather than fall into the hands of the enemy, stabbed himself...
    Sam Houston, March 13, 1836.[2]

Col. Travis, the commander of the fortress, sooner than fall into the hands of the enemy, stabbed himself to the heart and instantly died.
    B.B. Goodrich, March 15, 1836.[3]

Travis and all his men [were] captured and murdered.
    John T. Mason, March 20, 1836.[4]

The chief they called Travis died like a brave man with his gun in his hand, in back of a cannon...
    Unidentified Mexican soldier, April 5, 1836.[5]

Col. Travis sprang from his blanket with his sword and gun, mounted the rampart and seeing the enemy under the mouths of the cannon with scaling ladders, discharged his double barreled gun down upon them; he was immediately shot; his gun falling upon the enemy and himself within the fort. The Mexican General leading the charge mounted the wall by means of a ladder, and seeing the bleeding Travis, attempted to behead him; the dying Colonel raised his sword and killed him!
    Joe, April 12, 1836.[6]

Travis sprung up, and seizing his rifle and sword, called to Joe to take his gun and follow. He mounted the wall, and called out to his men—"Come on Boys, the Mexicans are upon us, and we'll give them Hell." He immediately fired his rifle—Joe followed his example. The fire was returned by several shots, and Travis fell, wounded, within the wall, on the sloping ground that had recently been thrown up to strengthen the wall....As Travis sat wounded, but cheering his men, where he first fell, General Mora, in passing, aimed a blow with his sword to despatch him—Travis rallied his failing strength, struck up the descending weapon, and ran his assailant through the body. This was poor Travis' last effort. Both fell and expired on the spot.

Joe, May 25, 1836.[7]

On the north battery of the fortress lay the lifeless body of Col. Travis on the gun-carriage, shot only in the forehead.

Francisco Ruiz, 1860.[8]

Cols. Travis and Bonham were killed while working the cannon, the body of the former lay on top of the church.

Susanna Dickinson, 1875.[9]

A soldier was standing near Travis, and presented his gun at him. Travis seized the bayonet, and depressed the muzzle of the piece to the floor, and it was not fired. While this was taking place the soldiers standing around opened fire. A shot struck Travis in the back. He then stood erect, folding his arms, and looked calmly, unflinchingly, upon his assailants. He was finally killed by a ball passing through his neck.

Francisco Becerra, 1875.[10]

After that we all entered the Alamo, and the first thing we saw on entering a room at the right was the corpses of Bowie and Travis.

Manuel Loranca, 1878.[11]

At this time our cannon had battered down nearly all the walls that enclosed the church, consequently all the Americans had taken refuge inside the church, and the front door of the main entrance fronting to the west was open. Just out side of this door Col. Travis was working his cannon...Our troops rallied and returned a terrible fire of cannon and small arms. After this the cannonading from the Alamo was heard no more. It is evident that this discharge killed Travis...

Felix Nuñez, 1889.[12]

Colonel Travis was the first man killed. He fell on the southeast side near where the Menger hotel stands.

Madam Candelaria, 1899.[13]

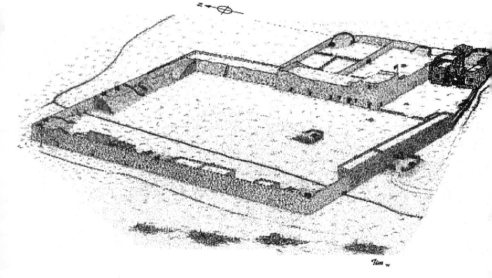

The Alamo 1836.

(Original artwork by Rod Timanus.)

Travis, the commander of the Alamo, died as a brave man.

Published version of the alleged Sanchez-Navarro journal, 1938.[14]

Travis was seen to hesitate, but not in the death which he chose. He took some steps and stopped turning his face to us with an air to discharge his shots, well he fought like a soldier. Finally he died, but he died after having sold his life very dearly.

Published version of alleged Peña diary, 1955.[15]

Bowie

Bowie was killed lying sick in bed.

E.N. Gray, March 11, 1836.[16]

Col. Bowie was sick in his bed, and was also murdered.

Sam Houston, March 11, 1836.[17]

... our friend Bowie, as is now understood, unable to get out of bed, shot himself as the soldiers approached it.

Sam Houston, March 13, 1836.[18]

Col. Bowie was murdered, sick in bed.

B. B. Goodrich, March 15, 1836.[19]

Colonels James Bowie and Crockett were among the slain; the first murdered in his bed in which he had been confined by sickness.

A. Briscoe, March 16, 1836.[20]

The pervert and braggart Santiago Bowie, died like a woman, almost hidden under a mattress.

Unidentified Mexican soldier, April 5, 1836.[21]

Col. Bowie was found dead in his bed, in one of the rooms of the south side.

Francisco Ruiz, 1860.[22]

Col. Bowie was sick in bed and not expected to live, but as the victorious Mexicans entered his room, he killed two of them with his pistols before they pierced him through with their sabres.

Susanna Hannig (Dickinson), 1875.[23]

After that we all entered the Alamo, and the first thing we saw on entering a room at the right was the corpses of Bowie and Travis.

Manuel Loranca, 1878.[24]

... four soldiers brought a cot, on which lay a sick man, and set it down by the captain and one of them remarked, "Here, captain, is a man that is not dead." "Why is he not dead?" asked the captain. "We found him in a room by himself," said the soldier. "He seems to be very sick, and I suppose he was not able to fight, and was placed there by his companions, to be in a safe place and out of the way." The captain gave the sick man a searching look and said, "I think I have seen this man before." The lieutenant replied, "I think I have too," and, stooping down, he examined his features closely. Then raising himself, he addressed the captain, "He is no other that the infamous Colonel Bowie."

The captain then also stopped, gazed intently upon the sick man's face, assumed an erect position, and confirmed the conviction of the young lieutenant.

The captain looked fiercely upon the sick man and said: "How is it, Bowie, you have been found hidden in a room by yourself and have not died fighting, like your companions?" To which Bowie replied in good Castilian: "I should certainly have done so, but you see I am sick and cannot get off this cot." "Ah, Bowie," said the Captain, "you have come to a fearful end—and well do you deserve it. As an immigrant to Mexico you have taken an oath before God to support the Mexican Government; but you are now violating that oath by fighting against that government which you have been sworn to defend. But this perjury, common to all your rebellious countrymen, is not your only offense. You have married a respectable Mexican lady and are fighting against her countrymen. Thus you have not only perjured yourself, but you have also betrayed your own family."

"I did," said Bowie, "take an oath to support the Constitution of Mexico, and in defense of that Constitution I am now fighting. You took the same oath when you accepted your commission in the army and you are now violating that oath and betraying the trust of your countrymen, by fighting under a faithless tyrant for the destruction of that Constitution and for the ruin of your people's liberties. The perjury and treachery are not mine, but yours."

The captain indignantly ordered Bowie to shut his mouth. "I shall never shut my mouth for your like," said Bowie, "while I have a tongue to speak." "I will soon relieve you of that," said the captain.

Then he caused four of his minions to hold the sick man, while a fifth, with a sharp knife, split his mouth, cut off his tongue, and threw it upon the pile of dead men. Then, in obedience to motion of the captain's sword, the four soldiers who held him, lifted the writhing body of the mutilated, bleeding, tortured invalid from his cot, and pitched him alive upon the funeral pile.

William P. Zuber (relating the alleged tale of Apolinario Saldigna), 1882.[25]

Colonel Bowie...was in bed very ill of typhoid fever, and that as she was in the act of giving him a drink of water the Mexican soldiery rushed in, wounding her in the chin—showing an old scar —and killing Bowie in her arms. She demonstrated this scene in quite an active fashion and showed us exactly how she was holding Bowie, her left arm around his shoulders and a drinking cup in her right hand.

Madam Candelaria, 1890.[26]

Colonel Bowie died in my arms only a few minutes before the entrance to the Alamo by the soldiers. I was holding his head in my lap when Santa Anna's men swarmed into the room where I was sitting. One of them thrust a bayonet into the lifeless head of Colonel Bowie and lifted his body from my lap.

Madam Candelaria, 1892.[27]

She saw the Mexican soldiers enter, bayonet Bowie, then while he still lived, carry him upon their bayonets into the Plaza below, and there toss him up and catch him upon the bayonets 'til the blood ran down upon their arms and clothes. Then a Mexican cavalry officer dashed in amongst the butchers, with drawn sword. Lashing them right and left and forced them to desist.

Juana Alsbury, 1898.[28]

A dozen or more of the Mexicans sprang into the rooms occupied by Colonel Bowie. He emptied his pistols in their faces and killed two of them. As they lunged towards him with their muskets I threw myself in front of them and received two of their bayonets in my body. One passed through my arm and the other through the flesh of my chin. Here, señor, are the scars; you can see them yet. I implored them not to murder a sick man, but they thrust me out of the way and butchered my friend before my eyes.

Madam Candelaria (published after her death), 1899.[29]

Bowie, although ill and suffering from a fever, fought until he was so severely wounded that he had to be carried to his cot, which was place in one of the smaller rooms on the north side of the church. Even after he was confined to his cot he fought, firing his pistol and, occasionally, his rifle at the enemy after the soldiers of Santa Anna had entered the church and some of them got into his room. He loaded and fired his weapons until his foes closed in on him. When they made their final rush upon him, he rose up in his bed and received them. He buried his sharp knife into the breast of one of them as another fired the shot that killed him. He was literally riddled with bullets. I saw his corpse before we were taken out of the building.

Enrique Esparza, 1907.[30]

Buy [Bowie], the braggart son-in-law of Beramendi [Veramendi], [died] as a coward.

Published version of the alleged Sanchez-Navarro journal, 1938.[31]

The circumstances surrounding the deaths of less well known Alamo defenders are subject to similar confusion.

Almeron Dickinson was one of the Alamo's officers. His wife and young daughter were with him inside the Alamo during the siege but survived the battle. His final moments were recorded by alleged witnesses or those who interviewed witnesses. Susanna Dickinson did not witness his death but remembered a variety of parting scenes:

Almeron Dickinson

> Lieutenant Dickinson, who had a wife and child in the fort, after having fought with desperate courage, tied his child to his back, leaped from the top of a two story building, and both were killed by the fall.
>
> Sam Houston, March 11, 1836.[32]

> During the closing struggle Lieut. Dickenson [sic], with his child in his arms, or tied to his back, as some accounts say, leaped from an upper window [a notation to a map indicates that Potter was referring to the north side of the apse of the church], and both were killed in the act.... Lieut. Dickinson commanded a gun in the east upper window of the church. His family was probably in one of the two small upper rooms of the front. This will account for his being able to take one of his children to the rear platform while the building was being stormed. A small irrigating canal runs below the window referred to; and his aim in the desperate attempt at flight, probably was to break his fall by leaping into the water; but the shower of bullets which greeted him rendered the precaution as needless as it was hopeless.
>
> Reuben M. Potter, 1860.[33]

> "...my husband rushed into the church where I was with my child and exclaimed: "Great God, Sue, the

Mexicans are inside our walls! All is lost! If they spare you, save my child."

Then, with a parting kiss, he drew his sword and plunged into the strife, then raging in different portions of the fortifications.

Susanna Hannig (Dickinson), 1875.[34]

Toward the close of the struggle Lieutenant Dickenson [sic], with his child in his arms, or, as some accounts say, tied to his back, leaped from the east embrasure of the chapel, and both were shot in the act. . . . Lieutenant Dickenson [sic] commanded the gun at the east embrasure of the chapel. His family was probably in one of the small vaulted rooms of the north projection, which will account for his being able to take his child to the rear of the building when it was being stormed. An irrigating canal ran below the embrasure, and his aim may have been to break the shock of the leap by landing in the mud of that waterless ditch, and then try to escape, or he may have thought that so striking an act would plead for his life; but the shower of bullets which greeted him told how vain was the hope. The authenticity of this highly dramatic incident has been questioned, but it was asserted from the first, and was related to me by an eye-witness engaged in the assault. . . .

In a footnote the author added:

I had for several years in Texas as a servant one of the Mexican soldiers captured at San Jacinto, Sergeant Becero [Becerra], of the Battalion of Matamoras. He was in the assault and witnessed Dickenson's [sic] leap.

He went on to say that Becero [Becerra] did not know Dickinson by name.

Reuben M. Potter, 1878.[35]

She was then a young woman and had a child one or two years old, which some writers have stated was killed in his father's arms. This statement, she says, is incorrect.... The last she ever saw of her husband he rushed into the room and said, "My dear wife, they are coming over the wall, we are all lost!" He embraced her and the babe, saying "May God spare you both!" then drew his sword and went out. His body when found was riddled with bullets, and later burned by the inhuman victors with the rest of the slain.

Charles W. Evers, reporting an interview with Susanna Hannig (Dickinson), 1878.[36]

What became of her husband Al Marion [Almeron] Dickinson, she cannot tell, but saw him last when he went from her presence with gun in hand to die for his country.

An unidentified reporter of the *San Antonio Express* reporting on an interview with Susanna Hannig (Dickinson) during her visit to the Alamo in 1881.[37]

... another American appeared on top of the roof with a little boy in his arms, apparently about three years old, and attempted to jump off, but they were immediately riddled with bullets and both fell lifeless to the ground.

The Nuñez account, 1889.[38]

... she said that the husband of Mrs. Dickinson was fighting as one of the defenders of the Alamo and that when he saw the cause was lost he hastened down from the walls and took his son, a little child and tied him around his waist in front of him, got to the top of the wall at the front of the Church and jumped down among the fighting Mexicans below and both were killed. This is very dramatic but it is not I believe elsewhere recorded.

William Corner, reporting his interview with Madam Candelaria, 1888.[39]

Artist Theodore Gentilz combined the story of a defender leaping from the Alamo's wall with a child in his arms, with Cruz y Arocha's story of kneeling defenders with white flags.

The Death of Dickinson by Theodore Gentilz.
Courtesy of the Daughters of the Republic of Texas Library at the Alamo.

On the day of the fall, Sunday, her husband kissed her goodbye in the morning, and she never saw him again. [Speaking of the Dickinsons.]

Mary A. Maverick's memoirs published by her granddaughter, 1921.[40]

Along the south side was a dirt wall or embankment up which the Texans would run and fire. Some of them were killed when they did this – Lieutenant Dickerson [sic] was among these.

Howard R. Driggs and Sarah S. King recording a talk before school children by Enrique Esparza supposedly given sometime between 1908 and 1917.[41]

An unfortunate father was seen with a little son in his arms throw himself from a considerable height and both perished at the same blow.

The alleged Peña account, 1955.[42]

Walker, Wolff, and Evans—what Susanna saw

The description or the memory of what someone actually witnessed can change with the passage of time. We know that Susanna Dickinson was at the Alamo. She was sheltered away in one of the rooms, probably of the church, and could not see the progress of the battle. However, there is evidence that she did witness some of the violence. It is often described that Dickinson witnessed an execution, or executions. Due to the reporting, editorializing, and probably dramatization of her statements by others, we cannot be sure if what she saw was part of a formal execution (after the battle and by Santa Anna's direct order), or simply the withholding of mercy to Alamo defenders who had ceased resisting. These second- and thirdhand statements attributed to her can be interpreted in any number of ways:

...of the five [Alamo defenders] who, for a moment survived their companions, and threw themselves on the victor's clemency, two were pursued into her room, and subjected in her presence to the most torturing death. They were even raised on the points of the enemy's lances, let down and raised again and again, whilst invoking as a favor, instantaneous death to terminate their anguish, till they were at last too weak to speak, and then expired in convulsion.

William Parker who obtained the information from William Hadden who allegedly obtained it from Dickinson, 1836.[43]

...three unarmed gunners who abandoned their then useless guns came into the church where I was, and were shot down by my side. One of them was from Nacogdoches and named Walker. He spoke to me several times during the siege about his wife and four children with anxious tenderness. I saw four Mexicans toss him up in the air (as you would a bundle of fodder) with their bayonets, and then shoot him.

Susanna Hannig (Dickinson) in Morphis' *History of Texas*, 1875.[44]

The only man witness saw killed was a man named Walker from Nacidoches [sic], who was bayonetted [sic] & shot.

Description of testimony by Susanna Dickinson, September 23, 1876.[45]

She says that only one man, named Wolff, asked for quarter, but was instantly killed. The wretched man had two little boys, aged 11 and 12 years. The little fellows came to Mrs. Dickinson's room, where the

Mexicans killed them, and a man named Walker, and carried the boys bodies out on their bayonets.

Susanna Hannig (Dickinson) from an interview with Charles W. Evers. Ca., 1878.[46]

It was in this room that she saw the last man fall, and he was a man named Walker, who had often fired the cannon at the enemy. Wounded, he rushed into the room and took refuge in a corner opposite her own. By the time the Alamo had fallen and the hordes of Santa Anna were pouring over its ramparts, through its trenches and its vaults. The barbarous hordes followed the fated Walker, and, as Mrs. Hannig describes the scene, "they shot him first, and then they stuck their bayonets into his body and raised him up like a farmer does a bundle of fodder with his pitchfork when he loads his wagon." Then she says they dropped the body.

Susanna Hannig (Dickinson) interview with unidentified reporter from the *San Antonio Express*, 1881.[47]

Probably she and the Mexican women, who were her companions, saw the bayoneting of the last American; when the shooting was over, a soldier crawled into the room where they were, not to seek refuge, but to carry out an order previously given, and generally understood, which was that if the garrison fell someone was to try to fire the powder supply; and this man named Evans, wounded and spent with weariness, was killed while making his painful way to the powder room.

Mary A. Maverick's version of Dickinson's story, published by Maverick's granddaughter, 1921.[48]

Dickinson may have witnessed one man killed, or two men, or three, or two men and two boys. If her story as reported by Parker via Hadden is true, then she was aware at the time that one group of five men were executed (two in her presence). At least the story of five men being taken alive was circulating earlier than April 29, 1836, when Parker's letter was published in the newspaper the *Free Trader*. One year later Ramón Caro added credence to this number in his pamphlet. Before that, however, Crockett's name was added to the group to bring the number up to the six reported in the Dolson and probably Attree reports, adding a known name and a little extra drama to the story.

Going to the mattresses

Another area of confusion regarding the executions at the Alamo is the question of how the prisoners were taken or where they were found. A description often used in renditions of the story is that the prisoners were found "hiding under mattresses," or "hiding under a pile of mattresses." This may or may not be so. The only problem is you cannot find this description in any of the accounts by eyewitnesses or alleged eyewitnesses. The earliest reference to the executed prisoners being discovered under mattresses is found in Reuben M. Potter's 1860 *The Fall of the Alamo: A Reminiscence of the Revolution of Texas*. In it Potter writes:

> Half an hour or more after the action was over a few men were found concealed in one of the rooms under some matrasses [sic]. Gen. Houston, in a letter of the 11th says as many as seven; but I have generally heard them spoken of as only three or four. The officer to whom they were first reported entreated Santa Anna to spare their lives; but he was sternly rebuked and the men ordered to be shot, which was done.[49]

Actually, Houston's letter mentions seven men executed but makes no mention of men hiding under mattresses. It is uncertain what Potter used as a source for this. Potter was an agent of a commercial house in the town of Matamoras, Mexico, and was there during the Texas Revolution. He kept track of the goings-on of the Revolution and interviewed Mexican soldiers returning after the debacle at San Jacinto. He did not set his information down in writing until some twenty years later while he was assigned to duty in San Antonio with the U.S. Army's Quartermaster department.

In 1878 Potter published a revised edition of "Fall of the Alamo" as an article in the *Magazine of American History*. After the lengthy paragraph detailing the discovery of the prisoners, Potter cited in a footnote the previously mentioned Sergeant Becero (Becerra).

Since Potter was in Mexico during and after the Alamo's fall, he may have been influenced by the newspaper article account of the unidentified Mexican soldier that stated, "...the braggart Santiago Bowie, died like a woman, almost hidden under a mattress."[50] In some translations of this passage mattress is replaced by "bedding." It is also possible that he obtained this information from Becerra.

John S. (Rip) Ford also used Becerra as a source for his work on the Alamo. Either Becerra did not tell him the same information he told Potter, or if he did, Ford may have felt some delicacy about describing Alamo defenders as hiding under mattresses. Perhaps Potter misinterpreted Becerra's information. Becerra's account as published by Ford stated:

> There was a long room on the ground floor [of the church building]—it was darkened. Here the fight was bloody. It proved to be the hospital. The sick and the wounded fired from their beds and pallets.[51]

In the setup for his execution story Becerra also stated that in another room he saw a man "...sitting on the floor among feathers," who turned out to be Travis. Crockett rises from the floor in the same room. Travis and Crockett are then taken outside and executed. If Becerra had related to Potter the same information as he did Ford, his description of the sick and wounded in their beds and the Texans on the floor among feathers (a possible stuffing for bedding) may have been misinterpreted or not remembered correctly by Potter. If he did tell the two historians the same information, Potter remembered a few (three or four) prisoners, but Ford only mentioned two. Perhaps Becerra did not tell Potter anything about this. If that is the case we do not know where Potter got his information.

This has not stopped later writers and historians from incorporating this tale into the Alamo story, thus establishing it as an accepted fact of the battle. John Myers Myers wrote in his 1948 *The Alamo*:

> They were picking their way among the corpses in the plaza when a Mexican officer reported to [Santa Anna] with a critically wounded Texian, who had been found hidden in a pile of mattresses in an upper room of the long barracks.

Ten years later Lon Tinkle stated in his *13 Days to Glory*:

> Caro, after admitting many previous falsehoods in order to be now believed, claimed that after all the fighting was over, five Texans were discovered hidden away under mattresses in one of the far barrack rooms against the west wall. [Actually Caro never mentioned mattresses or rooms along the west wall.]

In 1961 Walter Lord in *A Time to Stand* wrote:

> Santa Anna devoted himself to poking around the rubble and idly inspecting a few of his victims. He was still at it when a commotion erupted toward the main gateway. The troops had just found six

Texans still alive hidden under some mattresses in one of the barracks rooms.[52]

Paul Hutton added a novel twist on this story by working Crockett's name into it in his article "Davy Crockett—Still King of the Wild Frontier" in *Texas Monthly Magazine*. He wrote:

> A few men, discovered hidden under mattresses in the long barracks, were taken prisoner. General Manuel Fernandez Castrillón, a brave and humane officer who had led the assault against the northeast wall, then halted the advance of his soldiers on another tiny band of exhausted, bloodied defenders. He offered them clemency and persuaded them to surrender. He gathered all the prisoners, numbering only seven, and marched them into the courtyard between the church and the long barracks. Crockett was among those men, although it is impossible to tell which group he belonged to. It is difficult to envision him hiding beneath mattresses, and so to soothe our psyches we can assume that he was with the band taken prisoner by Castrillón.[53]

Perhaps the best example of how stories related to the Alamo evolve can be found in the latest interpretation of the mattress story, although in this case the mattress becomes a full bed. Alex Shoumatoff in his *Legends of the American Desert: Sojourns in the Greater Southwest* writes that "Davy Crockett ...according to recent research, hid under a bed throughout the fighting [at the Alamo] and tried to surrender rather than fight to the death."[54] Shoumatoff failed to mention whose "recent research" uncovered this information.

Such are the stories born in the blood, smoke, and dust of the former mission San Antonio de Valero, also known as the Alamo, on the morning of March 6, 1836.

CHAPTER FIVE

José Enrique de la Peña and His Diary

· · · ◆ · · ·

But in 1955 came the publication in Mexico, in original Spanish, of Lieutenant Colonel de la Peña's diary.
—Dan Kilgore, 1978

. . . none was more reliable than the diary of José Enrique de la Peña.
—Paul A. Hutton, 1989

Carmen Perry translated and edited the diary of Mexican officer José Enrique de la Peña.
—Stephen L. Hardin, 1990

. . . the narrative diary of Lt. Col. José Enrique de la Peña.
—James E. Crisp, 1994

. . . based on an original diary but with extensive additions and revisions made by de la Peña in the months and perhaps years following the Texas campaign.
—James E. Crisp, 1995

I believe it is [an authentic memoir], *yes.*
—Stephen L. Hardin, 1998

... *De La Peña's* journal, *or diary as it is often mistak-
enly labeled.*
—Paul A. Hutton, 1999

Oy!
—Bill Groneman, 1999

As A PIECE OF THE EVIDENCE in the question of Crockett's death the Peña account stands out, not necessarily for its quality but because a status has been bestowed on it above and beyond the rest. It is the account by which the case is proven and gives credence to all the other bits of evidence. Since this is the case, a discussion of Peña and his alleged "diary" are in order.

We know that Davy Crockett was a legendary figure in his own time. As we have seen, reports of his death are consistent with those of other legendary or famous historical figures. There are many conflicting versions, even some that kept Crockett alive after he was gone. The story of Crockett's death is unique in one way, however. Conventional historical wisdom now dictates the exact manner of his death. That is, death by execution as described by the account attributed to José Enrique de la Peña. Almost every other aspect of the Alamo battle is clouded by myth, legend, conflicting reports, and in many cases just a general lack of information. With Peña, however, historians are now able to cite his account as the definitive answer as to how Crockett died.

As the Peña account caught on in popularity in the late 1970s, Crockett's reputation began to suffer. This was due to the newly accepted information that he died by execution rather than in combat. Even though the account did not say "Crocket" did anything dishonorable, he began to be portrayed as some type of coward or shirker who denied his role in the fighting in order to save his life. As Crockett's stock fell, the reputation of the little-known Peña began to rise. Peña's growing reputation and the reliability of his alleged "diary" developed a synergistic relationship. As historians and writers used the account, Peña began to be portrayed as noble, brave, and absolutely reliable, because, after all, an account so wonderful and so rich in detail could only have been produced by someone who was noble, brave, and reliable. The more this image of Peña caught on, the more credible his account became. After all, a brave, noble, and reliable person could only produce an account that was completely authentic.

American Heritage Magazine described Peña as "Brimming with patriotism, machismo, and a professional soldier's love of battle...." Jeff Long, in his bitter diatribe *Duel of Eagles* wrote that Peña was "...one of Santa Anna's best and brightest officers ..." and that "Where ever he found Mexico's enemies, de la Peña fought them."[1] Peña was accepted by historians as a very competent, aggressive, and professional soldier. Actually his troubled fifteen-year career was something less than brilliant.

The following biographical information on Peña comes from the introductory material in Jesús Sanchez Garza's *La Rebelion de Texas*, and from Miguel A. Sanchez Lamego's *Apuntes Para La Historia del Arma de Ingenierós en Mexico: Historia del Batallón de Zapadores*, published in 1943.

Peña is believed to have been born in Jalisco in 1807. His military service began in 1825 when he entered the Mexican navy as an eighteen-year-old cadet aboard the corvette *Libertad*. He may have served, not so much as a sailor but as a marine in the navy. In two years he had risen to the rank of second lieutenant. At this time he ran into trouble because of his outspoken opposition to the appointment of an American, David Porter, as commander of the Mexican navy. He may have resigned his commission at this point, or he may have been reassigned. Sources indicate he was serving the Army Corps of Engineers that same year, but later records still referred to him as a second lieutenant of the naval service. Peña obviously was dissatisfied with this assignment. In 1827 he submitted the first of several requests to be attached to one of the Mexican legations in Europe. He also worried over the fact that his request would not be granted.

From July to November of 1828 he wrote a series of articles for the newspaper *El Sol*, condemning the management of the navy. He wrote under the pseudonym of "Lover of the Navy" and signed off the final article as "Always lover of the Navy." That same year Peña was assigned to Vera Cruz for duty aboard ship. While on his way there he met the commander of the state of Vera Cruz, Antonio Lopez de Santa Anna. Santa Anna had not yet come to power in Mexico, but he was on his way. Peña managed to get Santa Anna's permission to remain with him in Jalapa rather than continue on to his assignment.

In 1829 Spain, ousted from Mexico in 1821, reinvaded Mexico in an attempt to regain its lost colony. A Spanish force under Brigadier General Isidro Barradas invaded Tampico. Santa Anna met this force in late August of 1829 and quickly forced Barradas into an unconditional surrender. This probably was Peña's first taste of action, and it is said that he distinguished himself with brilliance in this campaign.

In September of 1829 Peña completed his criticism of the navy with two final articles. His association with Santa Anna must have emboldened him since he did not use his pseudonym "Lover of the Navy," but signed with his initials "JEP." In November, after seeking the permission of President Bustamente, he obtained permission to serve as adjutant and secretary to General Melchor Musquiz. He served with Musquiz until February of 1830. He then requested to be assigned to the physician corps of the artillery, but it is unknown if this request was granted.

In the spring of 1830 Peña became ill with "abominable smallpox" and remained housebound for about three months. He was back on his feet by August but felt that he had not regained his full strength. In 1831 Peña was commissioned by the navy department to study mathematics at the Mexican

Military College. He did well in his studies of arithmetic, algebra, speculative geometry, and plane trigonometry.

In October he was ordered to take a company of students to Acapulco for shipboard duty and the study of navigation. For reasons unexplained Peña failed to carry out this assignment. He later claimed that it was due to illness and that he would have been able to prove it through a doctor, had he only been given the chance. However, there is no evidence that he ever did.

Finally, he was compelled to proceed to Acapulco for duty aboard the corvette *Morales* after begging to be allowed to do so. His other request, at the time, for assignment in California as an alternative to shipboard duty, was met with a silence from his superiors that Peña found insulting. This incident seems to have resulted in an end to Peña's academic career. He later blamed this on "political convulsions."

In January of 1833 Santa Anna came to power in Mexico. Within one month of Santa Anna's arrival in Mexico City, Peña petitioned for promotion to lieutenant colonel based on his service against the Spanish. Santa Anna tended to agree, but when he met with the junta in the Federal District to discuss Peña's promotion, they decided that such a promotion was prohibited by law. Instead they promoted Peña to captain of cavalry on March 9, 1833. This rank never really pleased Peña.

Two months later Peña's six-year-old request to be assigned to a European legation was finally granted. Peña, however, had changed his mind. In September he made a flowery plea to Santa Anna, denouncing the enemies of the Supreme Government and pledging his love for the system. He requested to be freed from his current orders and instead be assigned to Santa Anna's own Federal Division of the President General. In December his request was granted. Peña seems to have been comfortable in Santa Anna's Federal Division. At least there is no record of request for reassignment.

During this time certain parts of Mexico became dissatisfied with Santa Anna's move toward dictatorial powers. On May 11,

1835, Santa Anna brutally put down a revolt in the town of Zacatecas. He returned to Mexico City ten days later. On May 22, the day after Santa Anna returned, Peña requested permission to be assigned to the Mexican legation in the United States. Four days later he was assigned to a legation, but to the one in London. Peña withdrew his original request in light of this new development.

While he waited to depart for London, Peña stepped up his campaign for a higher rank. In June he made an urgent request for promotion. In the following month he made another petulant request in which he complained about the slowness of advancement in his career and supplied papers testifying to his services in the Guanajuato campaign, for which he received a rank that "...he was not interested in." He summed up by begging for a promotion that he felt he was worthy of. The Director of Engineers was also contacted to testify to Peña's record. But although he could commend his good civil conduct, he was not able to comment on his military conduct and admitted that Peña had only been attached to the Engineers to receive his pay and to engage in studies.

Peña had no reason to believe he was not on his way to Europe. As long as he was going, it made sense to try for an assignment that was a little more glamorous than London. In September he requested permission to be assigned to France. He also complained that his request for legation duty dated back to 1827, yet he had never even made the waiting list of those to be assigned.

By this time the citizens of Texas also had enough of Santa Anna's policies. The sparks of revolution had ignited. Texan forces already had been involved in skirmishes with Mexican troops at Gonzales and Goliad, and now Gen. Cos was ordered to San Antonio de Bexar with a force to restore order. By the end of the month the Texans would have this force besieged in Bexar.

In October of 1835 Peña made an urgent request to be assigned to France, instead of London, and even offered reasons for such a request. It seems he felt that the climate and language of England would not agree with him, and the cost of living was just too expensive. However, Peña need not have worried about this. In November he found himself a lieutenant in the Zapadores Battalion, preparing to march to Texas. Although he was assigned to the Zapadores, his designation was that of a staff officer.

On December 7, while Cos and his men were fighting the Texans at San Antonio in the Battle of Bexar, Peña presented another urgent request, which actually dated back to June. This time he complained about the slow advancement of his career compared to those of men who had entered the service after he did. Ten days later an order was issued for Peña to report to the Battalion of Public Safety, or in his default, another officer was to be named. Since Peña had already been assigned to the Zapadores, he asked that someone else be assigned to the Battalion of Public Safety.

This point in Peña's career has been misinterpreted by historians and accounts for much of our misconceptions concerning him. Carmen Perry stated that he was "...granted permission" to march to Texas. Implicit in this statement is that Peña *requested* permission to go. Jeff Long took the misinterpretation one step further. He stated that Peña "...threw his safety to the wind...and secured permission to head north to Texas."[2]

Actually, aside from his requests for promotions and assignment to France during the war in Texas, the only request Peña made was to have someone else assigned to the Battalion of Public Safety since he was already attached to the Zapadores. There is no evidence that he requested permission to march to Texas.

There is also some evidence that the military executive board that handled these requests and assignments came to the opinion that Peña, through the Director of Engineers, should offer his services to the Inspector of Active Militia. It is likely that Peña was already committed to service in the Texan campaign when this suggestion was made.

Although he was technically assigned to the Zapadores Battalion, Lieutenant Peña managed to land a job as an assistant or aide to Colonel Francisco Duque, commander of the Toluca Battalion. The vanguard of the Mexican army arrived at San Antonio de Bexar on February 23, 1836, and the siege of the Alamo began. Col. Duque, his aide, Peña, and the Toluca Battalion arrived on March 4. Santa Anna had been awaiting these reinforcements. After Duque's arrival, Santa Anna held a council of war and decided that the Alamo would be taken by assault. He chose Col. Duque to lead one of the four assault columns. Duque had been so impressed by Peña during the march from Mexico and had developed such confidence in him that, while the attack assignments were being given out, he requested that Peña be right by his side during the assault. Santa Anna immediately acceded to Duque's request.

The Battle of the Alamo began in the predawn hours of March 6, 1836. As per the wishes of Duque, Peña was right with him when his column assaulted the fort's north wall. Peña pressed on with Duque to the vicinity of the wall until Duque fell wounded. With his commanding officer down, Peña promptly headed toward the rear where he encountered General Castrillón. Castrillón was second in command of Duque's column and was at that time leading the rear guard of the reserve of the column. Peña informed him that Duque was out of the action. He then returned to the front and back to the rear at least twice, delivering important messages.

The Mexican army was victorious at the Alamo at a cost of several hundred dead and wounded. The wounded were particularly unlucky, since Santa Anna had failed to provide any type of efficient medical unit to march north with the troops. Peña was lucky enough to survive the battle with only a serious bruise. He saw no further action during the Texan campaign but was very helpful during the Mexican retreat following Santa Anna's defeat by Sam Houston at San Jacinto.

On June 16, 1836, Peña struggled back into the Mexican town of Matamoras with the Zapadores. It was at this time that

This single sheet of the Peña papers mentions David Croket [sic].
The reverse side contains the story of his execution.

Courtesy of the Center for American History, University of Texas, Austin.

Peña was promoted to captain, since the officer's corps of the Zapadores called for the assignment of two captains. There was a vacancy, and Peña happened to be available. Once he was in Matamoras, Peña began collecting letters of commendation from a few officers, attesting to his actions at the Alamo and during the retreat of the Mexican forces. He received one from Lieutenant Colonel Ampudia on June 22, one from Duque on July 1, from Lieutenant Colonel Amat on August 17, and finally from Urrea on September 10. Urrea cited Peña's actions at the Alamo, even though he was not there to witness them himself. He based his praise on information he had obtained from Duque and other officers, possibly even Peña himself.

On December 15, 1836, Peña testified at an inquiry into the actions of General Vincente Filisola, a native of Italy and Santa Anna's second in command during the Texan campaign. Filisola ended up with the weight of responsibility for the retreat from Texas on his shoulders. Filisola was later exonerated of blame, but not necessarily by Peña. On February 3, 1837, a letter of his was published in the newspaper *El Mosquito Mexicano* vehemently condemning Filisola. Although Peña used the pseudonym "An Admirer of Texas," Filisola knew who was doing the writing. One week later he fired back an article in which he referred to Peña as "Peñita."

Between February 21 and 28 Peña published a lengthy and rambling article in which he defended himself and again lashed out at Filisola. He had probably been waiting for just such an opportunity, since he also published the letters of commendation from Duque and the others, which were actually quite good. In this article, Peña also made first mention of having kept a "Diario" but made no mention of any executions at the Alamo.

On April 11 Peña was ordered to Sonora by Urrea, who had become Peña's mentor and best hope for advancement since Santa Anna was captured in Texas. He was also breveted to the rank of lieutenant colonel. On January 7, 1838, he delivered a fiery proclamation to the garrison he commanded in the District of Baroyeca in praise of liberty, the United Mexican States, and

Urrea. One week later he delivered a similar pronouncement to the garrison of another town, ironically enough, Los Alamos, which was published in *El Cosmopolita* on February 21.

By June Peña's loyalty to Urrea had led him into armed conflict. On June 6 he found himself under the command of Colonel José Maria de la Cueva and bottled up in the port of Mazatlán, with government troops under General Mariano Paredes closing in fast. Peña surrendered, along with his commander, as soon as favorable terms were offered. Had he thought of Tampico and the Alamo, he would have remembered that the Mexican army did not offer surrender terms. He was immediately apprehended and tossed into the military prison at Guadalajara.[3]

There are at least two documents thought to have been written by Peña while he was in prison. One is a condemnation of Santa Anna, written under the pseudonym "Scipion." This statement includes a description of the executions at the Alamo. It states:

> If those in the cultured countries name us savages and assassins, none more than general Santa Anna has given an occasion to this. In the Alamo he ordered the murder of a few unfortunates who had survived the catastrophe, and whom general Castrillón presented imploring his mercy. Among those had been a man who pertained to the natural sciences, whose love of it had conducted him to Texas, and who locked himself up in the Alamo not believing it safe by his quality of foreigner, when general Santa Anna surprised Bejar.[4]

There has never been found an original of this document. So far, this account is known only to exist as an appendix in Garza's *La Rebelion de Texas*. Interestingly enough, the description makes no mention of David Crockett. It also does not state that Peña actually witnessed the executions himself. The other is a pamphlet entitled "Una Victima del Despotismo," which will be mentioned later in this chapter.[5]

It is believed that sometime between 1839 and '40 Peña was dishonorably discharged from the Mexican army, possibly as a result of a new law covering the desertion of military officers and applied retroactively to him, thus ending the career of one of Santa Anna's "best and brightest officers." It is likewise believed that sometime between 1841 and '42 Peña died. Much like David Crockett, the actual details of his life could never match the myths and legends concocted about him in later years.

Jesús Sanchez Garza

The Peña account first appeared in book form as *La Rebelion de Texas: Manuscrito inedito de 1836 por un oficial de Santa Anna [The Rebellion of Texas: Unpublished 1836 Manuscript by an Officer of Santa Anna]*, in March of 1955. The book's editor was Jesús Sanchez Garza. One month after publication the United States Copyright Office received an application by Garza for "Registration of a claim to copyright in book form or periodical in a foreign language published outside the United States of America." On May 9, 1955, the Copyright office received one copy of the book. A second edition of the book was published on June 20, 1955. The only difference between this and the original was the illustration on the title page.

Garza was born on October 14, 1891, in Piedras Negras, Coahuila, Mexico. His father, Jesús Sanchez Herrera, was a representative to Coahuila's state congress. Garza began his education in Mexico but later attended Draughon's Business College, located on Alamo Plaza in San Antonio, Texas. Garza made his living as an antiquarian who dealt in used books, old documents, coins, paper money, and assorted bric-a-brac. He lived at 624 San Francisco in Mexico City. His garage was piled high with his collectibles and used goods. He sold his merchandise at a store on or near Calle Medellin and also at the outdoor Lagunilla Sunday Market.

Garza was also a coin collector and was especially interested in coins of the Mexican Revolution of 1913. In 1932 he is credited with publishing a book, *Historical Notes on Coins of the Mexican Revolution, 1913-1917.* The book was published in Mexico, but in English, translated by Garza's American wife, Adelia Frank. The book is actually supplementary notes to American numismatist Howland Wood's *Coinage of the Mexican Revolutionists*, published in New York in 1928. One year later Garza published his notes and Wood's book in Mexico under the title *La Moneda Revolucionaria de Mexico 1913-1917.* This time it was published in Spanish, translated and annotated by Manuel Romero de Terreros.

In 1955 Garza self-published *La Rebelion de Texas* in Mexico. The book's exclusive distributor is listed as "A. Frank de Sanchez" with an address of 624 San Francisco, but this actually was Garza's wife and their home address. Besides the alleged "diary" of Peña, Garza provided approximately forty pages of introductory material on Peña and his military and literary careers. It also contained ninety pages of supporting documents.

When first published, Garza's book had little impact historically. It had been published in Spanish in Mexico, and American writers and historians had only limited access to it. It was used by James Presley in his article "Santa Anna in Texas: A Mexican Viewpoint" in the *Southwestern Historical Quarterly* in 1959, and by Walter Lord in his 1961 *A Time to Stand*. No great theories or irrefutable proof of anything related to the Alamo was attributed to Peña's alleged narrative in those early days. Both writers used it for colorful quotes by Peña to enhance their works. Its greatest strength was in the belief that it was a pristine, firsthand eyewitness account of the Texas Revolution. Writers and historians today still use it for dramatic "sound bites" in their works on the Alamo and the Texas Revolution. Texan writer Lon Tinkle mentioned the account in his 1958 book *13 Days to Glory* and described it as a "private diary of Col. Gonzales Pena (who fought at the Alamo)." He described it as one of two of the "most interesting contributions to Alamo investigation in recent years," but he really did not use it as a source in his book due to the amount of inaccuracies contained therein.[6]

Garza, the original publisher of the "diary," is somewhat of an enigmatic figure. The Special Collections section of the John Peace Memorial Library at the University of Texas at San Antonio became the repository of the document for almost twenty years. The library's records did not even have his name listed correctly. When the head of the Special Collections was asked about his background, she could only offer that he "...was a Mexico City businessman and an avid collector. Outside of that I know nothing more about him."[7]

Much of the current information on him comes from a friend and fellow numismatist of Garza's, Clyde Hubbard. Hubbard describes Garza as a memorable personality who had an enthusiastic, almost explosive way of talking. He is described as short, somewhat plump, bald, and round-faced. He was a wonderful conversationalist whose eyes flashed as he spoke on topics of interest. Hubbard found his anecdotes about people and Mexican history colorful. Later he was able to confirm his stories as true and not just inventions to impress people. Hubbard states that he never had any unsatisfactory dealings with Garza. To this day he owns an inscribed copy of the second edition of *La Rebelion*.

Hubbard recalls a number of conversations with Garza. On one occasion Garza said that someone offered him sixteen or seventeen boxes of official documents, which Garza believed were pilfered from the Mexican National Archives. Garza reassured him that he did not buy them, though. Garza also told Hubbard the story of a prolific author of books on Mexico, Nicholas de Leon of Oaxaca, who had forged coins and archeological items to sell to Americans. Hubbard later verified this information through a prominent historian from Paxaca whom he does not name.[8]

Some additional information on Garza comes from a short biographical blurb in the book *Tesoro de la Música Polifónica en México*. This was a collection of musical manuscripts that Garza's wife donated to the Mexican National Institute of Fine Arts three years after his death. His biographical blurb is somewhat misleading. For instance, it makes no mention of his life as an antiquarian. It cites his numismatic books but does not mention Howland Wood's connection to them. It also states that Garza was the founder and first president of the Numismatic Society of Mexico. However, the first newsletter of the society indicates otherwise. Although it lists Garza as one of thirty-two founding members, it does not list him as president. Furthermore, Hubbard (another founding member) states that Garza simply " .. declared his intention of becoming a founding member but never became a member, much less president of the club." He also stated that since Garza was not listed among the

Jesús Sanchez Garza at the Lagunilla Sunday Market in Mexico.
Courtesy of Clyde Hubbard.

first twenty-five members, he apparently never paid any dues into the organization. Hubbard does not recall ever seeing him at a meeting nor was he able to find any photos of him in the society's publications.[9]

One person does not share Hubbard's fond memories of Garza. José Tamborrel Jr. *was* the first president of the Numismatic Society of Mexico. Hubbard asked Tamborrel for information on Garza since Tamborrel was more closely acquainted with him. Tamborrel claims he had once bought some coins from Garza that were counterfeit and they had originated with Garza. Hubbard knew of my investigation into the Peña account as a possible forgery. He asked Tamborrel if Garza might have forged the manuscript. Hubbard reports that Tamborrel answered with a "...very positive yes," and added, "You may quote me." When I asked Hubbard to clarify this, he stated that Tamborrel meant Garza had the *capability* of forging Peña's "diary."[10]

Regardless of his connections, or lack of them, with the numismatic community of Mexico, Garza is best remembered today for bringing the Peña narrative to the world. Since Garza's book was self-published, he was able to bring it to the world without it ever having undergone any scrutiny by an editor or publisher willing to risk money and reputation on the final product.

Acquisition and Acceptance

Carmen Perry has had a distinguished career as a Spanish teacher, the director of the Daughters of the Republic of Texas Library at the Alamo, head archivist at the University of Texas at San Antonio and at the San José Mission Research Center, and as an author. She entered the fray surrounding Crockett's death in 1975 when she translated and published the Peña narrative with Texas A&M University Press. Perry had been aware of Garza's book *La Rebelion*. Local history teachers sometimes would ask her to translate parts of it for them. Since there was interest in the narrative on the Texas side of the border she approached Garza's widow for permission to do an English translation of it. Señora Garza was unwilling to give her permission, though.

According to the currently accepted story, Perry then went to John Peace Jr. and interested him in the project. Peace was the chairman of the board of regents of the University of Texas and a well-known and respected political leader. He was also a collector of Texana and Mexican documents. The story goes that Perry accompanied Peace and his wife to Mexico in 1974 where Peace bought the document. The most recent information, now being investigated, indicates there may have been others who accompanied them to Mexico and other owners of the document. Whomever he bought the papers from, he brought them to Texas and gave Perry permission to do her translation. It was published in 1975 under the title *With Santa Anna in Texas—A Personal Narrative of the Revolution by José Enrique De La Peña*. Peace passed away in August of 1974, and Perry dedicated her book "To the memory of John Peace who brought the de la Peña diary to Texas and made possible its publication." The handwritten document and a variety of supporting documents eventually became part of the Special Collections at the University of Texas at San Antonio.

The publication of *With Santa Anna* ignited the present-day debate over Crockett's death. Perry was put on the defensive when headlines such as those in *People Weekly* magazine declared "Did Crockett die at the Alamo? Historian Carmen Perry says no." She took great pains to explain "In the first place, I'm not a historian—I'm an archivist. And I didn't write it—I just translated it." She also explained that neither she nor the document itself ever mentioned the words "surrender" or "capture," a fact that was lost on a number of reporters and historians for years to come.[11]

In the course of the Peña document being purchased, brought to Texas, translated, published, and installed at the University of Texas at San Antonio, there is no record of anyone ever trying to establish the document's authenticity. From the first, it has been accepted as absolutely authentic without anyone questioning it in the least. Perry never expressed any doubt in it. If there was any questionable information contained in it, she might not have been familiar enough with other sources to pick it out. By her own admission she was not a historian. There is no evidence that Peace made any attempt to test the papers or establish their authenticity. He solely went by Perry's opinion and his own knowledge of historical documents. There is no evidence that anyone at the University of Texas at San Antonio ever questioned it, nor is it likely that anyone would have. The document and its accompanying papers were loaned by John Peace Jr. and were kept in the John Peace Jr. Memorial Library at the University of Texas, which is located on John Peace Jr. Boulevard. It is unlikely that Texas A&M University Press ever questioned its authenticity since they did publish it and have kept it in print for the last twenty-four years.

With its acquisition and publication the Peña tale's roots were set firmly into Alamo history. Three years later Kilgore's *How Did Davy Die?* was published, giving further credence to it. At the time, Kilgore never cast any doubts upon the Peña account. He certainly never felt the need to authenticate it since no one at the time voiced any doubts about its authenticity. During the 1980s the account began to be embraced lovingly by the academic community. There is no evidence that those who proclaimed it to be the best and most reliable of its kind ever looked beyond Perry's version of it. There is no record of any of the historians, who had used it as a major source in the earlier days, ever evaluating the handwritten pages of the manuscript or their contents for authenticity. Today, of the true believers in the account, only Jim Crisp has spent any considerable time with the manuscript itself.

To sum up: The account was self-published in Mexico; a handwritten version of the account was purchased and brought to Texas (but there are gaps in this part of the story that still need to be filled); the account was published in the United

States by a university press; the handwritten document was placed in the special collections of a university library; a book was written to support the account; and prominent historians have used the account as a major source for their works while lavishing unrestrained praise on it. The account also has achieved the distinction of solving a historical mystery by giving us the exact, unquestionable answer as to how Crockett died. All of these things occurred without anyone along this evolutionary path saying, "How do we know it's real?"

CHAPTER SIX

The Peña Account as a Fake

$\cdots \blacklozenge \cdots$

When I turned the pages of those volumes, my doubts gradually dissolved. I am now satisfied they are authentic.
    —Cambridge Historian Hugh Trevor-Roper (on the Hitler diaries)

I have no doubt that they are authentic. They have passed every test.
    —James E. Crisp (on the Peña papers)

We are absolutely confident in the authenticity [of the Peña papers].
    —Gregory Shaw

So prevalent are historic forgeries today, and so gullible are the press and the general public, that outrageous fakes, which wouldn't fool a ten-year-old, are successfully marketed.
    —Charles Hamilton

I DO NOT BELIEVE the Peña account is authentic. I believe it is a twentieth-century forgery. This was the basic premise of *Defense of a Legend*. I cannot prove it is a fake, although I do feel it can be proven a fake with certain kinds of tests. It was never my intention to prove it was a fake, nor do I feel obliged to do so. No one has ever proven it is authentic either. In writing *Defense* I wanted to point out to historians, writers, and readers of Alamo history that the Peña account has always been treated as if it were chiseled in stone, but that is not the case. There is plenty we do not know about it, and there are a number of factors that were unknown to those using the account as the best firsthand eyewitness account of its kind.

People often ask, "What would be the motive in faking something like the Peña account?" Regarding the motives of forgers of historical documents, document dealer Kenneth W. Rendell states:

> The forging of manuscript material has most commonly been done to change history rather than for financial gain... The most famous modern forgery cases, most notably the Hitler diaries, have contained elements of both; efforts to change history and swindle money.

Handwriting and document expert Charles Hamilton wrote:

> For many forgers the ultimate goal is not to get rich by swindling easy marks but to see their fabrications touted as authentic by historians.... Every year new discoveries (actually forgeries) of rare letters and manuscripts are announced with a ruffle of drums in the newspapers, and there is always some historian or "expert" naïve or inexperienced enough to authenticate and launch these imposters into the eternal jigsaw puzzle of literature or history.[1]

The following does not prove the Peña account is a fake. If people were to tell me they wanted to use the Peña account as a major source for a work on the Texas Revolution, the Battle of the Alamo, or Crockett's death, I would tell them to go right ahead and do so if it was really important to them. I would also advise them to familiarize themselves with the account and its history first. Had John Peace Jr. been aware of any of this information, maybe he would have investigated further before he bought the document. Maybe Texas A&M University Press

CHARLES HAMILTON
HANDWRITING EXPERT
166 E. 63RD STREET
NEW YORK, NEW YORK 10021
(212) 888-0338

October 18, 1993

C E R T I F I C A T I O N

I certify that I have carefully examined the document allegedly written by JOSE ENRIQUE DE LA PENA, entitled PERSONAL NARRATIVE WITH SANTA ANNA IN TEXAS, and find that it is a forgery by John Laflin, alias John Laffite. I have compared the handwriting in the PERSONAL NARRATIVE with other exemplars forged by Laffite that are illustrated in my book GREAT FORGERS AND FAMOUS FAKES (pp. 122-29) and noted that the NARRATIVE bears the same characteristic script, slightly modified, that appears in his other fabrications in English, French and Spanish.

Charles Hamilton
Handwriting Expert

Gregory Shaw of Butterfield & Butterfield speculated on whether or not Joseph Musso forged Hamilton's signature on this certification. Musso disproved this by producing cancelled checks to Hamilton's firm.

Courtesy of Joseph Musso.

would have investigated further before they published it. If the historians who have passed judgment on the account had known this information earlier, maybe they would not have declared it the best of its kind.

If someone were to ask my opinion as to why I believe the document a fake and thus the account unreliable, I would tell them the following:

1) There is no record of this document before 1955 (the year that marked the height of Crockett popularity due to the Disney television series). This lack of provenance is a red flag when dealing with historical documents. There is no record of where the document came from or how Garza obtained it. His only reference to it is the vague statement:

> ... his [Peña's] manuscripts revolved from hand to hand and from generation to generation; maybe to some relative or to some friend (since he had no children), poorly kept, exposed to humidity, the moth and the rats as its traces indicate, until reaching us wrapped in a thin paper and already partly ruined.[2]

In all the pages of introductory material in *La Rebelion* Garza failed to mention where the document came from. This omission is suspicious enough. This coupled with the total lack of provenance is a recognized symptom (not proof) of historical forgeries.[3]

2) There are many factual errors in the account. For example, the account describes the death of a defender identified as the Alamo commander, William Barret Travis:

> Travis was seen to hesitate, but not about the death that he would choose. He would take a few steps and stop, turning his proud face toward us to discharge his shots; he fought like a true soldier. Finally he died, but he died after having traded his life very dearly.[4]

This stirring account is very compelling. The only problem is that Travis' slave, Joe, who was right by his side during the assault on the Alamo, reported that Travis was struck in the head by gunfire and killed after discharging his gun over the wall only once, minutes after the battle began. The Peña account is wrong when it mentions that a defender named Evans was commander of the Alamo artillery. Captain William R. Carey of Virginia was commander of the Alamo garrison's artillery company, which he called his "Invincibles." Major Robert Evans, originally from Ireland, was the head of the Alamo garrison's ordnance department. A trivial discrepancy? Maybe, but if one had to label the account right or wrong on this point, it would clearly be wrong.

Also of interest is the fact that this is the only alleged "first-hand account" that mentions Evan's name at all. He is listed on some pre-Alamo siege letters and muster rolls, but never as commander of artillery. He is mentioned, years later, in an account by Susanna Dickinson. He is also mentioned in books years *after* the battle, and in some he is listed as being of the artillery.

The number of survivors of the Alamo battle is incorrectly given in the Peña account. Peña states that "...only an elderly lady and a negro slave..." survived. Actually, the noncombatant survivors of the Alamo battle were closer to twenty.[5]

Some of these errors can be attributed to the fact that "anyone can make a mistake," but some of them are things the writer of the account would have seen or known if he had been on the scene. The Peña account mentions the burning of the Texan bodies after the Alamo battle and states, "...within a few hours a funeral pyre rendered into ashes those men...." This mentions a (one) funeral pyre and the reduction of the bodies (200-250) in a matter of hours. Other accounts by San Antonio civilians that appeared in newspapers years later stated there were at least two and possibly three funeral pyres, and these pyres were burning for at least two days. The stench and the grisly remains were a horrible and shocking experience to these people. One would think it would have been mentioned in the Peña account.[6]

There are other examples of factual errors within the account. Charles Hamilton called attention to these types of errors in a list of ways to spot forgeries. He called them "Little errors of place or date which fail to dovetail with our other knowledge...." Once again this does not prove the Peña account is a fake, but it is another symptom of historical forgeries that is contained therein.[7]

3) Much of the account (including the section on Crockett) appears to have been pieced together from many other published accounts. Some of these other accounts were published during Peña's lifetime, others were not. Peña is believed to have died sometime around 1841 or '42. Some are from sources Peña would never have been able to access. Some of the passages in the Peña account are similar in wording with these others. In some cases it is not word for word, but the gist of a particular passage compares closely with others. Regarding this aspect of the Peña account, no one has done more research than Tom Lindley. When his findings are published they will change substantially the view of the Peña papers. A few examples are:

Peña account
"Numerous feats of valor were seen in which many fought hand to hand; there were also some cruelties observed.

The alleged Sanchez-Navarro account (published in 1938)
I saw actions of heroic valor I envied. I was horrified by some cruelties.... [8]

Peña account
...within a few hours a funeral pyre rendered into ashes those men who moments before had been so brave that in a blind fury they had unselfishly

offered their lives and had met their ends in combat.

Becerra account (published in 1882)

The bodies of those brave men, who fell fighting that morning, as men have seldom fought, were reduced to ashes before the sun had set.[9]

Peña account

He was the naturalist David Crocket [sic], very well known in North America for his strange adventures, who had come to travel over the country and had been in Bejar in the moments of surprise had locked himself up in the Alamo, fearful that his quality as a foreigner would not be respected.

Zuber account (published in 1939)

I am David Crocket [sic] .... I have come to Texas on a visit of exploration; purposing, if permitted, to become a loyal citizen of the Republic of Mexico. I extended my visit to San Antonio, and called in the Alamo to become acquainted with the officers, and learn of them what I could of the conditions of affairs. Soon after my arrival, the fort was invested by government troops, whereby I have been prevented from leaving it. And here I am yet, a noncombatant and foreigner, having taken no part in the fighting.[10]

The account's description of the hardships faced on the march north from Mexico follows very closely that made by General Vincente Filisola in his *Memoirs of the History of the War in Texas* Vol. II, first published in 1849. Both make similar remarks on the chaos of regiments being lost in a freak snowstorm; the depth of the snow; the death of Ramón Muzquiz's nephew at the hands of the Comanches; the Mexican soldiers goading oxen along with the points of bayonets; and the description of the civilian camp followers as locusts. Filisola could not have obtained this information from Peña since Peña's account was not published until 1955. These men were bitter enemies after the Texan campaign. They were not about to compare notes or share their personal observations about anything.[11]

4) It seems to have been influenced by later sources, some of which did not appear until the twentieth century. The Peña account contains an often-repeated description of an Alamo defender jumping from the walls with a small child in his arms as the fort is being overrun. Perry's translation does not indicate that Peña himself actually witnessed the defender jump from the walls. It merely states that a man "was seen to" do this without specifying by whom. This can be written off as just a detail of the battle that Peña obtained from other sources while preparing his account later on. The source for this story was a New Orleans newspaper article of April 1836, which reproduced a letter from Sam Houston to James Fannin. In it the defender is identified as Lt. Dickinson. In fact, all of the early descriptions of this tale are consistent in that they identify the defender as Dickinson. It was not until 1878 that this story was refuted by Dickinson's wife and his name was eventually deleted from the tale. If Peña did obtain this information from contemporary sources, why does he not name Dickinson? The account's author certainly was not shy about naming Alamo defenders. The account mentions Travis, Bowie, Crockett, and Evans by name. The Peña version of the scene reflects the later nineteenth and early twentieth centuries telling of the tale.

The Peña account mentions that the Alamo was armed with fifteen pieces of artillery, and then in a footnote it states there were "19 of different calibers." Tom Lindley has done extensive research on the subject of the Alamo artillery. He reports that the only source he has been able to find which numbers the artillery as fifteen is a map by Andrew Jackson Houston done early in the twentieth century. The closest source to mentioning nineteen pieces is Amelia Williams' "A Critical Study of the Siege of the Alamo and of the Personnel of its Defenders" of the 1930s which numbers the artillery as "18 or more."[12]

5) It contains language that may be questionable. In at least two places the writer of the account uses the term "crimes against humanity." Once it is written in Spanish as "... crimen de lesa humanidad," and the second time as "... crimen contra la humanidad." This is not strictly an anachronistic term. It is not as if the writer used something like "the sound barrier," or "blitzkrieg." Anyone could have put those three words together in that particular order at any time. In a diligent search of nineteenth-century documents someone probably would find these three words used together, eventually. However, the term was not really used to describe war atrocities until World War I. It did not come into general use as a catch phrase description of war crimes against civilians until it was defined at the London Conference of 1945 and finally used as a charge at the Nuremberg Trials. Here it appears twice, in a document that is first introduced to a post-World War II society.[13]

6) There are several passages in Peña that are somewhat similar in tone and subject matter to those of a suspected fake. The Peña account and the alleged journal of Gulf Coast pirate Jean Laffite both contain passages that portray their subjects as writers deeply concerned about the accuracy of their stories; as noble defenders of the truth; as selfless patriots; as anti-elitist heroes of the lower classes; as faithful, determined, and honest; and as sensitive soldiers.

Peña account

I had to take some time to verify those acts which I was not an eyewitness and to obtain more accurate information about, important objectives which I achieved by collecting the daybooks from the various sections that constituted the Army.

Alleged Laffite journal (published in 1958)
The manner in which I shall begin this story of my life will no doubt involve me in some years of research before I can collect the necessary proofs of authenticity.

Peña account
... the accumulation of lies told to falsify the events published in National as well as international newspapers... the honor and self esteem of every military man who participated, so deeply hurt by the great inaccuracies in the official records as to dates, deed and places and above all the honor of the country, deeply compromised by its leaders and not less by the truth and atrocity of its crimes—these are the principal causes which compelled me to publish the diary I kept during the time I served in this unfortunate campaign.

Alleged Laffite journal (published in 1958)
... only in this way shall I be free of the fear of contradiction and only in this way can I hope that my words will expose the deceit and cunning of degenerate writers—both present and future—and their slanderous conjectures and erroneous fairy tales about me. At the same time, I may hope to prevent others from multiplying such conjectures and perpetuating a false legend.

Peña account
... who expects no compensation...

Alleged Laffite journal (published in 1958)
... without receiving any compensation for myself ...

Peña account
> If in bringing forth my notes I accomplish the noble objectives I have pursued in vindicating the honor of this unfortunate nation and its army...

Alleged Laffite journal (published in 1958)
> ...at one time I did all I could to save that same nation from complete annihilation in order to preserve the liberty founded on that most sacred document, the Declaration of Independence...

Peña account
> The bodies, with their blackened and bloody faces disfigured by a desperate death, their hair and uniforms burning at once, presented a dreadful and truly hellish sight.

Alleged Laffite journal (published in 1958)
> The spectacle of three thousand wounded and dead English soldiers on that marshy battle field [New Orleans] was a dreadful and horrible sight.[14]

7) There are handwriting similarities between the Peña document and another suspected forgery. The Isaac Millsaps letter was believed to have been written during the Alamo siege by the defender of the same name. Recent scrutiny of this letter has shown considerable evidence that it is a forgery. The writer of the Millsaps letter made reference to Texan army officer James W. Fannin but for effect misspelled the name as *Fanning*. One page of the Peña manuscript mentions Fannin three times, and the name is spelled *Fanning* all three times. According to Joseph Musso of California, the Millsaps' "Fanning" and the Peña "Fannings" appear to have been done by the same hand. Musso is an expert on the life of Jim Bowie, on period weaponry, and also on Mexican army uniforms of the time. He is also a graphic artist. He does not claim to be a handwriting expert, but he does

look at this aspect of the evidence with an artist's eye. His observation does not prove there is anything wrong with the Peña document, but maybe some professional scrutiny should be directed at this comparison.[15]

8) Charles Hamilton has certified that samples of handwriting he saw in photocopies of pages of the Peña document were that of a known forger. During his lifetime Hamilton earned a reputation as one of the foremost handwriting experts in the world. He testified in court many times as an expert witness and helped prosecutors in a number of cases of criminal forgery. He has also been subject to the ire of a number of detractors. Hamilton did not give an opinion on the paper of the document, the ink, or the historical content of the documents. He only gave his opinion in the area of his expertise—the handwriting. His opinion, in a certification obtained by Joe Musso, was that the samples of handwriting he saw were that of John Laflin, also known as John Laffite. Laflin claimed to be a descendant of the pirate Laffite. He was known during the 1940s, '50s, and '60s to have forged a number of documents and signatures relating to Texas history, including those of Crockett and Bowie.

The most famous document associated with Laflin is the alleged journal of Jean Laffite. Laflin was said to have inherited this journal from his grandfather along with a number of other related papers and family Bibles, etc. Coincidentally Laflin is also the leading suspect in the authorship of the Millsaps letter. Despite claiming losses of much of his material in two fires, Laflin never had a shortage of the stuff. He continued to hawk his documents after both fires.

Laflin had a reputation among book dealers in Kansas City, Missouri, for his intense interest in acquiring old paper. Apparently, he was successful. He obtained enough of the paper to be able to use it as personal stationery. Hamilton was thoroughly familiar with Laflin's work. He devoted a chapter to him in his book *Great Forgers and Famous Fakes*.[16]

There are other factors that cast some doubt on this document. The Peña of the account is almost like a character in a

at Galvez reception Club room

It was the opinion of Charles Hamilton that some of the handwriting in the Peña document was that of John Laflin, also known as John Laffite.

Courtesy of the Jean Laffite collection, Sam Houston Regional Library and Research Center, Liberty, Texas.

historical novel. He travels all through the story, reporting on dramatic scenes and developments. He never seems to be tied down to any particular unit or mundane responsibilities. He is also all-knowing. He knows how many men were in the Alamo on the night of February 22, 1836, even though Peña did not enter Bexar until March 4. He describes the manner of James W. Fannin's execution at Goliad although Peña was not present. He describes things that went on in Sam Houston's camp before the Battle of San Jacinto. He cites contents of a dispatch written by

Houston. He can describe what was in the minds and hearts of the Texans as they charged across the field at San Jacinto.[17]

As stated earlier, these are some of the reasons that have caused me to doubt the authenticity and reliability of the Peña account. These opinions about the account were not brought out until after it had been elevated to the level of the best and most reliable of its kind.

The Argument

The publication of *Defense of a Legend* started an argument that continues to this day. The argument, which at times is more like an academic version of a pier-six brawl, is not about the manner of Crockett's death per se. It centers on the Peña account, its authenticity, its reliability, what is or is not historical evidence, etc. This most recent battle of the Alamo was joined when Jim Crisp published his scathing rebuttal to *Defense of a Legend* as an article in the *Southwestern Historical Quarterly* in October 1994. *Defense* was published in February of that year. I met Crisp in San Antonio in March 1994 and made him aware of the book. I thought he would be interested in it since it was along the same lines as an article he had written exposing a speech falsely attributed to Sam Houston. Crisp's rebuttal was savage and at the same time condescending—the quintessential professor straightening out the errant student. The next step came in March of 1995 when I gave an abridged version of *Defense* as a talk at the meeting of the Texas State Historical Association. (The *Southwestern Historical Quarterly* is the journal of the Association.) The talk had come about when I queried the Association (of which I am a member) about doing a biographical entry on Peña for their revision of the *Handbook of Texas*. Despite the fact that the six-volume *New Handbook* contains more than 23,000 entries related to Texas, the Association was not interested in a biography of Peña, whose alleged "diary" was considered the best account of the Texas Revolution. Instead, it was suggested that I put together a panel for their annual meeting and give a talk on the Peña document as a forgery.

The 1995 meeting was held in San Antonio. Our panel was entitled "The Alamo: Questionable Historical Sources." The panel included Tom Lindley, who spoke about the Amelia Williams doctoral dissertation on the Alamo; William R. Chemerka, editor of the *Alamo Journal*, who acted as commentator; myself; and Chuck Parsons, who presided. Our session attracted an audience of approximately three hundred fifty people. We were told it was the largest audience for such a panel in the Association's one hundred-year history. Crisp was in attendance and asked some pertinent questions. Within hours of this session he gave a rebuttal to my talk before an amateur history organization. As with his rapid response to my book, it seemed important to refute my beliefs immediately, before they could catch on. At the time I considered his efforts to steal the show on the same day as our Association meeting session to be tasteless grandstanding. However, I later saw a tape of his session and realized that although he was part of it, he was not the organizer of it. His presence seemed to have been an expediency to the organizers of this meeting to air their own personal arguments.

The next exchange came in the fall and winter of 1995/96 when Crisp and I salvoed a series of articles back and forth in the pages of *Military History of the West*. By now, others had been drawn into the fray. Tom Lindley and Crisp began a battle of theories in the pages of the *Alamo Journal*. This time the discussion shifted from the Peña account to those of Attree and Dolson. The argument continued to spread in ever-widening circles.

Michael Lind, poet, author, and staff writer at the *New Yorker, New York Times*, and *Washington Post*, published an epic poem, *The Alamo*, in 1997. In the verses of his poem he describes Crockett as parrying Mexican soldiers with his gun until he is cut by a saber on the temple and shoulder. As he raises his arm to protect himself, he is stabbed to death by three bayonets. In an appendix to his poem Lind explained his disbelief in the Peña narrative and the whole body of evidence that goes with it.[18]

The poem was the subject of a hissy fit review by columnist and author Garry Wills, in the *New York Times Book Review*. Wills describes the Peña account as having been called a forgery "...by Texans clinging to myths." He also describes Lind as accepting the "desperate claim of forgery." Newsman Dan Rather, a native Texan, came to Lind's defense in a letter to the editor of the *Times Book Review* a few weeks later. Wills fired back with a press release stating that "Texans are rarely sane on the subject of the Alamo, as Newscaster Dan Rather recently proved..." He also stated that "Mr. Rather's credentials as a broadcaster are safer than his claims to be an historian."[19]

Lind went on to pen an article, "The Death of David Crockett," in an issue of the *Wilson Quarterly*. This, in turn, prompted letters to the editor in the following issue by myself and Crisp, and a reply by Lind. And so it continues. It is difficult to wade into these waters without finding one's self up to one's neck. Everyone has an opinion on the subject, and very few are shy about sharing it. The *Alamo Journal* has featured a number of articles concerning Crockett's death and the ongoing debate. (See "Davy Deathiana" later in this book.)

In the course of this never ending argument, some truths have been revealed and new information has been brought to light. This information does not solve the question of Crockett's death but only gives us a new wrinkle on some of the evidence. Crisp has graciously acknowledged that the historical profession is in my debt, "not because he is right about the...Peña diary, but because he has substantially advanced our understanding of this document in the course of being wrong about it."[20]

One of the results of our simultaneous, if not agreeable, investigations is that we now know there was never an edition of the Peña account published in Mexico in the 1830s. This had been a common error since the account began to be cited in other works. The belief in an 1830s edition added an air of authenticity to the account and helped many of its early proponents toward acceptance of it. Today, writers and historians still cite Perry's *With Santa Anna in Texas* with Peña's name as if he actually wrote and published a book by that title in 1836.

Another aspect of the Peña document has been revealed by Crisp and Lindley in their scrutiny of the handwritten pages. This is the fact that the Garza and Perry transcriptions of the account are not exact transcriptions or translations of what is in the handwritten papers. Crisp describes the handwritten papers as having been written in two drafts. One is a narrative in diary entry form, and the other is a more lengthy second draft. Lindley calls them the "rewritten diary" and the "final draft." Both agree there is no original holograph "diary" that Peña would have written while on campaign.

In early newspaper interviews Perry hinted that Garza's transcription was not exact, but that she "followed de la Peña word for word" in her translation. That seems not to be the case, and Crisp has indicated that she followed Garza's book, rather than the handwritten document when preparing her own book.[21]

For instance, the handwritten papers contain Travis' famous letter of February 24, 1836, addressed to the "People of Texas & all Americans <u>in the world</u>," without any explanation as to how the account's author would have gotten access to the contents of this letter. The original letter reads:

> Commandancy of the Alamo
> Bejar, Fby. 24th 1836 —
>
> To the People of Texas & all Americans <u>in
> the</u> world —
> Fellow citizens & compatriots —
>
> I am besieged, by a thousand or more of the
> Mexicans under Santa Anna— I have sustained a
> continual Bombardment & cannonade for 24 hours
> & have not lost a man— The enemy has demanded
> a surrender at discretion, otherwise, the garrison

are to be put to the sword, if the fort is taken— I have answered the demand with a cannon shot, & our flag still waves proudly from the walls— <u>I shall never surrender or retreat.</u> Then, I call on you in the name of Liberty, of patriotism & & [sic] every thing dear to the American character, to come to our aid, with all dispatch— The enemy is receiving reinforcements daily & will no doubt increase to three or four thousand in four or five days. If this call is neglected, I am determined to sustain myself as long as possible & die like a soldier who never forgets what is due to his own honor & that of his country—

<u>Victory or Death</u>

William Barret Travis
Lt. Col. Comdt
[rubric]

P.S. The Lord is on our side— when the enemy appeared in sight we had not three bushels of corn — We have since found in deserted houses 80 or 90 bushels & got into the walls 20 or 30 head of Beeves—

The handwritten Peña document contains the letter twice (in two different handwritings). Neither is a full translation. They are the same but leave out some sentences from the original. When Garza included the letter in his book he added sentences that do not appear in the handwritten document but bring it closer to the original. Perry seems to have used the original letter and left out corresponding sentences. Yet, that was not done with complete accuracy.[22]

The appearance of the letter in the handwritten document twice indicates that one version probably falls within the "rewritten diary." This indicates that Peña would have had access to the letter for his original "diary." However, the handwritten version does not reflect the only version of the letter that was circulating in Texas, in broadside form, in 1836. The version in the handwritten document is closer to shortened versions of the letter that appeared in books by Chester Newell in 1838 and by Frederick C. Chabot in 1936.[23]

Another example is the inclusion in the Garza and Perry books of a footnote that describes the Texan casualties at the Alamo. This note begins "See the accompanying documents, the second of which states exactly the number of losses sustained by us." It then goes on to include word for word a passage that appeared in a book published by Gen. Filisola in 1849. Garza's and Perry's books give the impression that this passage was a note by Peña himself. By going back to the handwritten account, Crisp rehabilitated this anachronism by pointing out that this passage is not contained in the original. Instead there is a line that translates to "The following report shows exactly that [Crisp interprets this to mean "the loss"] which we had. (Here the report)." This line is scratched through, and a line is inserted in the margin that translates to "Let the documents be seen n . . . the second of which shows exactly that which we had." Crisp goes on to explain that Peña had intended to include the Mexican losses (but did not) and Garza, in an act of good faith but poor editorial policy, inserted this passage. What is not apparent in this explanation but is in the illustration of the page Crisp provided is that the marginal note is in what appears to be a different handwriting than the rest of the page. The note does appear to resemble the handwriting on the page concerning Crockett. That page's handwriting also changes just before the part about Crockett.[24]

There are other examples of the handwritten pages not transcribing or translating into the written books. One is a "lost week" of entries discovered by Crisp that is now included in an expanded edition of *With Santa Anna in Texas*.[25] Another is that both Garza and Perry showed some delicacy in leaving out of their books a vulgar reference to Mexican Minister of War Tornel and Santa Anna, and a snide ethnic reference to Santa Anna's second in command, Filisola. The manuscript refers to them respectively as "carajo," "carajote," and "an Italian."[26]

These examples only go to prove that what you see in the handwritten version of the account is not exactly what you get in the published ones. Most everyone agrees that a word-for-word, page-for-page translation of the account, without any editorializing, is what is needed.

In *Defense of a Legend* I raised the fact that the Peña account, purported to be a "dairy" written in 1836, cites another document that was not published until 1838. This was not proof the document was a forgery, but it did heighten my suspicion that there was something wrong with it as a firsthand eyewitness account. This bit of evidence was negated quickly by Crisp when he pointed out that the handwritten version makes no claim that it is written solely in 1836. In addition, he supplied evidence of references by Peña that his account was still a work in progress after 1836. So, the mention of an 1838 document would not be a fatal anachronism.[27] It also should be noted that his observation does not prove the Peña document is authentic. If Peña did refer to an account as a work in progress, we do not know that the much publicized handwritten "diary" is that work.

This aspect of the argument raises other questions about Peña's account. For years it has been treated and cited by writers and historians as a firsthand eyewitness report, written in 1836. Why was I the first to notice that it made mention of an 1838 work, and why was Crisp the first to attempt to explain it? This hints at the fact that those who have used it and have passed judgment on it have done so without really studying it too closely. The main point of interest in the account was and now is the one passage concerning Crockett. It is likely that those who declared the account the "best" and "most reliable" of its kind never looked beyond that one passage.

Another contribution to the Peña history and argument by Crisp was his discovery of a long-forgotten pamphlet attributed to Peña. He discovered this in the Manuscripts and Archives Department of Sterling Memorial Library at Yale University. It is a printed pamphlet entitled "Una Víctima del Despotismo" apparently written by Peña and published in 1839. The pamphlet is addressed to Anastasio Bustamente and is a sixteen-page, rambling complaint about the imprisonment and harsh conditions Peña had suffered since the previous year. There is some information contained in this pamphlet that Crisp uses to support the authenticity of the Peña account. He uses the line "In good time I will explore the causes which have prevented me from publishing my diary and the observations which I have almost completed...." to show that Peña was still working on his "diary" as late as 1839 and that later material could have been incorporated into it.[28] The pamphlet contains a line that is probably the best argument for the authenticity of the Peña "diary." This line translates to:

> ...in writing about the Texas campaign, my principle object was to vindicate the honor, tarnished in it, of the nation and the army,...the noble goal which I have set for myself will give me the courage necessary to face all difficulties.

The Peña "diary" contains the line:

> If in bringing forth my notes I accomplish the noble goals which I have set for myself in vindicating the honor of this unfortunate nation and its army, which has recently been tarnished...[29]

To Crisp and others this is irrefutable proof that the Peña "diary" is authentic, since two documents bearing Peña's name contain such similar passages. To others this presents a situation similar to that presented by Kilgore's *How Did Davy Die?* of an unverified document or account being used to verify another unverified document or account. There is no concrete provenance to the pamphlet at Yale, and no one seems to know when the pamphlet became part of the collection. Crisp discovered this pamphlet listed in the *National Union Catalog Pre-1956 Imprints,* so its arrival at Yale would have been before that date.

He describes his discovery as an act of serendipity. This is important because it conveys the idea that no one else could have ever seen the pamphlet before he did. If the pamphlet is authentic, it originated in Mexico and it is doubtful the copy at Yale was the only one printed. Right now it is the only known copy in any collection in the U.S. or Mexico. The possibility that Garza or someone else in Mexico or the U.S. would have had access to a copy cannot be dismissed. We cannot eliminate the possibility that the copy in Yale actually passed through Garza's hands. To myself and others the similarity of passages indicates more evidence of the "diary" as a researched or "cut and paste" account.[30]

The discovery of this pamphlet has been mentioned a number of times in Crisp's writings with a certain dramatic flair. There is the possibility that some may construe this discovery as a verification of things written in the Peña account. It should be noted that the pamphlet contains no mention of Crockett, no mention of executions at the Alamo, nor any mention of the Alamo battle itself.

Since I regard the Peña account as a fake, I do not consider it any more a reliable piece of evidence of Crockett's death than all the others. Those of us who argue against the Peña account as a reliable source are always in a position of trying to topple it from its lofty perch as the "best" and "most reliable." The account achieved this status not by any inherent qualities it possesses but simply because historians have bestowed those titles on it. They did this without considering or even being aware of the many questionable aspects of it.

A number of people from both sides of the argument have called for testing of the papers. Both sides are sure that such testing will vindicate their theories. There are a number of ways to test for forgeries. Those involved in the argument agree that a test to determine when the ink was put on the paper would be the conclusive one in this case. There is a test that can determine when the ink was put on the paper plus or minus fifteen years. However, these tests are prohibitively expensive and are not readily available.

If the Peña papers were to be tested using this method, there is the question of what is to be tested. The handwritten pages in the papers comprise two hundred separate sheets. Most are folded in half so they present a sheet with four writing surfaces. Obviously, all of these cannot be tested. If a page or pages are tested selectively, there is the possibility it may reveal that the writing does date back to Peña's time. It is possible that some of the Peña papers are authentic and that someone, later on, enhanced them by adding all of the interesting parts.

There are a number of different handwritings in the papers, and they change right before dramatic scenes such as the executions and Travis' death. Charles Hamilton has written, "In my fifty years of examining manuscripts and thirty-five years as a dealer and manuscript historian...I have never seen a manuscript of any length that was part genuine and part fake." However, much of his belief is based on the assumption that a forger would not ruin an already valuable document (such as one done by Hitler) by adding false things to it.[31] This could be a possibility, and the Peña document may be an exception to the rule. Shorter documents such as letters are often enhanced by the later addition of a famous signature or notable reference. An examination of the papers certainly does not rule this out since they are written in a number of different handwritings.

If the Peña papers are only partially authentic, a test of certain writing that happened to be Peña's could give a false authenticity to the whole document. Since most of the argument of the Peña papers revolves around the question of Crockett's death, most advocates of testing agree that the page containing the reference, and more specifically Crockett's name, should be tested.

I have never advocated the testing of the papers since I feel the question can be resolved intellectually through the examination of historical evidence. I also feel that it is not my place to demand expensive tests of papers that I do not own. The past and present owners of the papers obviously believe they are authentic. Why would they spend a great deal of money on tests to prove something they already believe. It is interesting to note that a number of professional historians, whose business it is to resolve historical questions by research and evidence, are calling upon another discipline, science, to answer this question.

Even if the papers were tested and found to be authentic for their purported time period, it does not guarantee the accuracy of the contents. Historians would still have to consider whether Peña actually wrote the thing and if he did, whether he was writing about things he actually witnessed himself and whether his information was factual. This has never happened with the Peña account. Its acceptance has always been a case of "It's here, in writing, therefore it is real and absolutely factual."

The argument for and against the Peña papers and account is a complex one. The Peña document is at the same time a physical artifact, a piece of evidence, a historical source, an absolute, and the final word to a historical mystery. In the end, the staunch defense of the account by its proponents, brought on by the close scrutiny it has been subjected to lately, may cause the account to self-destruct. The main strength of the Peña account has always been the belief that it originated as a *diary*. It was an exact telling of events by an eyewitness and was written down by the witness himself as events unfolded. For these reasons alone it was considered unquestionable. Proponents will argue that the papers themselves contain no such claim, and this is only an error by those who have used the document as a source. Maybe that is true, but most of the citations of, uses of, and publicity of the account since 1955 have been as if it were a personal diary. When it was spoken about, written about, or referred to, it was as a diary. Historians felt secure enough to throw their support behind it because the general perception of it was that of a firsthand, eyewitness report written as a diary.

Recently, however, there has been a change. In the past year a good deal of attention has been directed to the Peña account and papers due to the public auction of the Peña collection.

There were many newspaper and television interviews in which both sides of the argument had an opportunity to air their views once again. In the course of these interviews proponents of the account began to refer to the papers as Peña's *memoir* as opposed to his *diary*. Actually, this idea began to be put forth by Crisp in his articles of the past few years. As the evidence against the papers began to mount, the position of defending it as a "diary" became untenable. So, the diary simply became a memoir. In other words, instead of Peña writing down his personal, daily observations, he researched and compiled information from other sources and added these to his own observations. This was stated in a letter allegedly written by Peña to Mariano Mando and dated September 15, 1836, and used as an introduction to the Peña narrative in both Garza's and Perry's books.[32]

Perhaps this is true, but if the Peña account is a memoir rather than a diary, it loses all of the firsthand immediacy for which it had been noted. It is no more authoritative than any of the other accounts that describe Crockett's death and is no less subject to question and examination. It does not become "mutually corroborative" with the rest of the execution tales but instead "similarly questionable."

At worst, the Peña document is a twentieth-century fake. Maybe it is partially authentic with twentieth-century additions. If that is the case, it is no more a reliable source than a complete fake. At best it is now a memoir padded with researched material. If that is so, we do not know if the references to Crockett and the executions were researched from the newspaper articles circulating at the time. What it is not is a firsthand eyewitness diary—the quality for which it received all of the attention in the first place. As Crisp wrote in his doctoral dissertation: "I have avoided a reliance on memoirs in order to reduce the distortions which arise from the almost inevitable projection of later attitudes into these reminiscences."[33] As the final word on Crockett's death, the Peña diary or memoir or account just fails to stand up.

CHAPTER SEVEN

History for Sale

$\cdots \blacklozenge \cdots$

Half the truth is often a great lie.
—Benjamin Franklin, *Poor Richard*

Packaging in America is an art with liabilities. The people are prone to be charmed with the package and disregard the contents.
—Hans Bendix

God help us if we ever take the theater out of the auction business or anything else. It would be an awfully boring world.
—*Wall Street Journal*, September 18, 1985

THE PERCEPTION OF THE PEÑA ACCOUNT as a memoir casts doubt on it as a reliable historical source and as the final word on Crockett's death. One aspect of it not affected by this perception is that of the Peña papers as a collectable artifact. This was proven beyond all doubt in the fall of 1998 when the papers were sold at auction for $350,000. Of this amount $37,500 went to auctioneer's fees.

At the time I wrote *Defense of a Legend* I was not aware that the late John Peace Jr.'s family still owned the papers. I was under the impression that they had been donated to, and were the property of, the University of Texas at San Antonio. The truth is the papers were *loaned* to the Special Collections department of the university by the Peace family. This information was not volunteered by anyone at the Special Collections during my visits or correspondence with the John Peace Memorial Library.

In the spring of 1998 a rumor began to circulate that the Peña papers were about to be taken out of the University of Texas at San Antonio and placed in the Institute of Texan Cultures in downtown San Antonio. Later, in May, the story broke in the *San Antonio Express-News* that the Peace family intended to sell the papers. Initially the newspapers reported that John Peace III decided to remove the papers from the university because he had heard the rumor that his father's collection was to be broken up. He explained that the Peña material was not included in the collection donated by his father. His mother only loaned the Peña papers to the university after the death of his father.[1]

In later months Peace admitted that his family was "... selling it for the money, first of all." He also stated, "We'd have been more receptive to keeping it here, but for all the people calling, coming by. I've been interviewed about ten times, been on the BBC. It's fine for a while, but it's not my avocation to be a Davy Crockett buff." Still later he agreed that the Peña papers were among his father's prized purchases, and it had been his wish that the papers remain at the university library forever. He speculated that if his father were alive today, he would not want them to be there anymore. "The times have changed, the people involved with the university have changed, and the politics of colleges are much more transparent these days. If people were aware of how libraries treat their donations, they'd think twice," he said. He also complained that the university was not utilizing it properly. "It's been there for twenty-five years, and it has been neglected."

Peace's comments finally elicited a response from Michael Kelly, director of the John Peace Memorial Library:

You can take all those explanations that he gives you with whatever you think they are worth.... The document has received very intensive scrutiny here. I don't know what he thinks should have been done with it, and I don't know if he really thinks those are the reasons for doing what he did. He complained about it being kept in a box. Well, that's what you do with documents. You keep them in document boxes.... You can draw your own conclusions as to why somebody would want to sell a document for $200,000.

Peace fired back with "The money's a factor, but my motivation certainly isn't the money.... I just think that it deserves a better shot than it has had."[2] No one asked, "A better shot at what?" I found Peace's complaints as perplexing as Kelly. If one wanted to examine the papers, one would make an appointment, visit the library, and the staff would bring out the boxes containing the papers. One could study them until the library closed. The library's staff was always more than helpful.

An owner of the papers may have had grounds to complain since the papers were accessible to any researchers, including those who believed they were bogus, but this does not seem to have been the case. It also should be pointed out that there is no indication the Peace family simply wanted to unload the papers at this particular time due to all of the attention and doubts cast upon them. Whatever the reasons, the Peña papers were removed from the John Peace Memorial Library at the University of Texas at San Antonio and placed in a bank vault.

The solution to Peace III's perceived mistreatment of the papers and to his concerns about becoming a "Crockett buff" was simple. He decided to sell the capstone of his father's collection to anyone for a great deal of money. Once the decision to get rid of the papers was made, approximately two hundred dealers from around the country were notified. Peace also placed an ad in *AB Bookman's Weekly*. The prize of auctioning the papers fell to the firm of Butterfield & Butterfield in California. The date was set for November 18, 1998.

In the two months between the announcement and the auction, the sale of the papers received a good deal of attention in headline stories in newspapers across the country as well as in television news broadcasts. This only served to show that the question of Crockett's death was still of great interest to people, and that the sole importance of the Peña papers was that they contained one passage concerning his death. The stories that appeared during this time raised the perception of the impending sale to one of regional concern and pride. Calls went out resembling Travis' appeals for help from the Alamo. Headlines appeared stating, "Texas may lose Alamo diary," and "Texans may lose their historic Alamo diary." On the day before the auction the *San Antonio Express-News* ran a story entitled "Alamo diary rescuer sought—Local buyer sought to save Alamo diary." It went on to say that "... a call went out for someone in a 'white Stetson' to ensure the document stays in San Antonio." Steve Hardin, who heavily relied on the Peña account from Perry's *With Santa Anna in Texas* in his book *Texian Illiad*, was inaccurately quoted as stating, "I'm just afraid it will end up in the Bancroft Library in California or, worse yet, in Yale...I don't want the Yankees to have it." He also stated "I really hope the document stays in Texas. I think it's vitally important. It's part of our history." By "our history" he obviously was referring to that of Texas, not the United States.[3]

This new attitude regarding the Peña papers constitutes what is commonly known in Texas as "a hoot." If the Peña papers (or diary or memoir or account) are authentic, are they not a Mexican diary, memoir, or account rather than an Alamo diary, memoir, or account? If Texans were worried about losing the papers, one can imagine how Mexicans may have felt about it. As far as Mexico is concerned Texans are counted among the Yankees. As it turned out there was a greater danger to the Peña papers than the dreaded Yankees. Jim Crisp was quoted in an article in the *New York Times* as saying, "My greatest fear is that some right-wing nut case will put down a bunch of money and then throw it in the fireplace."[4] In a CNN interview I was asked what I thought of Crisp's statement. I told the interviewer that I could not believe Crisp would have made such a statement, but if he did, he did so facetiously. I later confirmed this in a phone call to Crisp. He did toss off a facetious remark, but it was translated into a legitimate concern in the article.

In many of the articles preceding the auction there was a general confusion of facts and misquotes. In an interview for the same *New York Times* article I was asked what the motivation of a forger might be. I responded that financial gain is the usual motive for forgers, but in the case of historical forgeries, forgers often want to see history written the way they believe it to be. The *Times* used my remarks but changed them to appear as if I was speaking about *historians* who believe in the authenticity of the Peña account, rather than forgers.

Misquotes in the newspapers notwithstanding, the idea was planted that Texas was in grave danger of losing something very important to its history. It could end up in a university or archives outside of the Lone Star State. Texan historians who wished to refer to or examine the handwritten document itself then would have to travel outside of the state in order to do so. Worse still, there was the danger of it falling into the clutches of some wealthy, right-wing, psycho, document-burning Yankee.

A good part of the media coverage of the auction seemed to be made up of a public relations campaign by Butterfield & Butterfield to assure potential buyers of the authenticity of the papers. This made sense considering the auction house stood to earn a good deal of money from selling the papers. In early October Gregory Shaw, vice president of Butterfield & Butterfield, and Steve Hardin appeared on NBC's *Today Show* to speak about the Peña papers. In a segment that only lasted about five minutes Hardin reiterated his confidence in the account and the papers, but he also stated that he believed the papers should be tested. When Shaw was asked if they would be tested he responded, "We're not going to test it in terms of destructive testing, no, because we are absolutely confident of what time this manuscript was created." He failed to say whether they were confident that the manuscript was created in the 1830s-40s, or in the 1940s-50s; in either case they would not have wanted testing. He did go on to say that the main reason the manuscript would not be tested was because of the paper:

> And the paper is a high rag-content laid paper typical of the period, but there are watermarks throughout the paper and one of them actually has the name of the manufacturer of the paper on it. A watermark is like a trademark and the name is Benedetto Picardo, and with the help of the Huntington Library we were able to establish that he was a paper maker in Lisbon, Portugal. And more that it's a registered watermark and that it was manufactured between 1824 and 1832. We know that for a fact.[5]

What a revelation. The paper was never a bone of contention. Everyone who has ever seen it knows the paper is old paper. His dramatic announcement was the equivalent of saying "We believe the Peña papers are real because we have found that all of the writing is in Spanish." What he did not say was that there are anywhere from fifteen to twenty different types of watermarks from as many as ten to fifteen different paper manufacturers within the Peña papers. The question is not whether one of these pages is authentic for the time period. It is whether even one of them may *not* be of the proper time period. This has never been determined.

The Peña papers consist of three stacks of loose papers. There are also twenty-two file folders of various documents. These include handwritten papers of Garza, typescript pages, photocopies from newspaper articles, and other letters and papers allegedly written by Peña as well as some letters allegedly written to him.

Stack one consists of eighty-two pages measuring approximately 12¼" x 8½". These pages are folded in half, so that they present a sheet 6⅛" x 8½", with four sides of writing surface. There are also three single pages of approximately 6⅛" x 8½". Stack two consists of eighty-eight pages of approximately 12¼" x 8½", folded and used as in stack one; seven single pages as in stack one; and one large page 17½" x 12½", folded and used as four writing surfaces. Stack three consists of twenty-six large pages. Some are 16¾" x 12", some 17" x 12½", and others are pages taken from a ledger, 15½" x 12¼". There is also one single page approximately the size of the others in this stack. All of the smaller sheets, 12½" x 8½", and 6⅛" x 8½", show evidence of having been cut from larger sheets of 17½" x 12½".

The confusion in the amount of different watermarks and paper manufacturers is due to the fact that many of the smaller sheets of paper bear a manufacturer's name and/or watermark, while other sheets simply bear an emblem such as a star or the words "e Figli," meaning "and Son." Since these sheets were cut from larger sheets, the marks give the impression of being from two different paper makers, when, in fact, they are simply two halves of one large sheet. Along with the watermarks, chain lines are visible in the majority of pages. These lines, which run parallel through the page, indicate the manufacturing process of "laid" paper, as opposed to "woven" paper.

A different type of paper appears throughout the holograph in various places, usually as single sheets or smaller pieces, 1" or 2" wide. These sheets and pieces are glued to the normal pages of the "diary," apparently to add some later information. These single sheets and pieces do not bear watermarks or chain lines. The paper appears to be a lighter weight than the paper of the rest of the holograph, and it has a bluish-green tint. Many of the pages are stained. In some places the same stain permeates a number of pages, but never enough to eradicate the handwriting. The majority of writing is done in light brown ink. Corrections and cross-outs appear throughout the holograph, and often they are done in black ink. Some of the pages in stack two bear what appears to be "worm holes." These holes penetrate approximately twenty pages. Many of the pages in stack two also bear three small uniform holes along the fold on the left side of the sheet. This indicates that these pages were at one time bound. This is not to say the papers were ever in book form. These pages were also cut down from larger sheets, which apparently was done after they were removed from a bound volume and before they were written on.

The page containing Crockett's death is a single page, approximately 8½" x 6¼", and it appears as the eleventh page of stack one. The description of his death appears on side two of this page. The handwriting of the paragraph describing the execution appears to be different from that of the previous paragraph.

Later Shaw scoffed at the idea that the papers possibly could be forgeries:

> To be a forgery, it would require the forger to have found 700 pages of period paper, find the right kind of ink and imprint the writing on the paper in a way that doesn't feather [blur], which would happen with paper this age. The idea of forgery is ludicrous.[6]

That statement is not precisely accurate. When Shaw spoke of 700 pages he had to have been speaking of pages as writing surfaces. If you fold a sheet of paper in half, you get four writing surfaces. The separate *sheets* of paper in the three stacks of Peña papers only amount to 200 sheets. The pages in the first two stacks all show evidence of having been cut down from larger sheets of 17½" x 12¼". Eighty-eight pages of that size could have accounted for all the sheets of paper in the first two stacks. With the twenty-six sheets in stack three it still only amounts to 114 sheets of paper, and not all of those definitely have been identified as paper of that period. This is still a considerable amount of period paper, but it is considerably less than the 700 spoken about by Shaw. It may come as a surprise to some, but historical forgers collect period paper in order to produce their forgeries. Charles Hamilton tells us that a person such as Laflin was known among rare book dealers in Kansas City, Missouri, for his intense interest in acquiring old papers. Kenneth Rendell states:

> The skillful forger... can obtain the correct paper of the period without too much difficulty. Contemporary journals and account books with blank pages and the unused leaves of contemporary letters provide the sophisticated forger with his basic materials.[7]

Forgers do not have to *find* the right kind of ink. They can *make* ink that is consistent with ink of the time period they are forging documents about. Regarding the feathering of new ink on old paper, this occurs when ink is put on paper that has aged and has dried out. Joe Musso has pointed out that if old paper has been stacked tightly or if it is bound between the covers of a book, it is not exposed to air as it would be if it were loose. The drying and aging of the paper may not necessarily apply.

Catherine Williamson, manuscript cataloger at Butterfield & Butterfield, backed up the company line, stating her firm's satisfaction about the papers' authenticity. "You look at three things: the ink, the paper, and the content itself. And we're satisfied on all three points. This document has proven to be what people have said it is." She did not specify if these "people" were the papers' proponents or opponents. She also stated that the papers were written in an "elegant nineteenth-century script," with the implication that this fact makes the papers authentic.[8] This explanation should have satisfied everyone who believes that a modern-day forger, forging a nineteenth-century piece, would use copy machine paper, a ball point pen, and a twentieth-century script style.

Another bit of implied but not actual verification of the papers came from an article in the *San Antonio Express-News* on the day of the auction. Carmina Danini wrote, "Sanchez

[Garza], perhaps aware of the criticism [the account] might raise, noted that the handwriting on the manuscript matched that on letters written by de la Peña and found in military files in Mexico."[9] Danini apparently was speaking of the letter of September 15, 1836, ostensibly written by Peña and used as an introduction to both Perry's and Garza's books. This letter is signed "José Enrique de la Peña." Perry and Garza included an image of this letter in their books since it includes what appears to be a verification of Peña's signature from the Mexican Military Archives. The image of this verification in Perry's and Garza's book is reproduced in such a way as to make it seem as if the verification was written on the same page as the signature. Actually, the verification is written on a three-inch-wide piece of blue tinted paper. This piece is glued to the letter bearing Peña's alleged signature. If this verification is authentic, it could have been obtained for any document bearing Peña's name and simply attached to that letter. If the verification is authentic to the letter, it only verifies the authenticity of the signature on the letter, and not the authenticity of the whole account.

The inclusion of this verification raises an interesting question. Why did Garza (or someone else) feel the need to provide a verification of Peña's signature? It is not as if Peña was a famous historical figure or a celebrity whose signature alone would have some collectable value. If Garza (or someone else) had the Peña papers, why did he not just accept them as such? What was the point of verification unless someone suspected the papers might be a forgery or wanted to guard against the possibility of someone believing they are a forgery. It seems as if the explanation already was in place before the question was even asked. For the purposes of the auction this was just another bit of information that gave the papers the image of authenticity. What we do know is that the auction firm, whose job it was to sell the papers for as much money as possible (not buy it or use it as a historical source), had great confidence in its authenticity.

When the sale of the Peña collection was announced, a couple of institutions expressed their interest in obtaining the papers. The Daughters of the Republic of Texas Library at the Alamo definitely were interested, but the asking price was out of the Library's range. Its best hope was for a white Stetson with a rich sympathetic Texan under it. The Center for American History at the University of Texas at Austin was also interested. Don E. Carleton, director of the Center, thought it was unfortunate that a public auction should be held for what he considered a document of priceless historical value, especially one that everyone believed would have been in the possession of the University of Texas system forever.[10]

The asking price of the document was a factor. Peace III previously had put a $250,000 price tag on the papers. In his *Today Show* interview Shaw stated that the estimate on them was two to three hundred thousand dollars. He expressed his feeling that those prices were conservative. A few days before the auction Shaw may have gotten carried away. "I don't want to scare anybody off," he confided to the *Austin American-Statesman*, "but it could go for a million dollars." Don Carleton reacted to Shaw's giddy prediction:

> In his dreams. There could be some person with more money than sense who would spend a million dollars for that, but I think that's absurd, and I just don't believe it's going to happen. It has value in the realm of historical scholarship, but there's not really any monetary value attached to that. Babe Ruth didn't sign it, much less Mark McGwire.[11]

For that matter, many doubt that Peña ever signed them.

As the auction approached, Butterfield & Butterfield had to contend with the media's growing curiosity about Charles Hamilton and his opinion of the papers. Shaw also handled this particular assignment. He stated, "We know Charles Hamilton never mentioned it to anybody and didn't even refer to it in the new edition of his book about Laffite." Hamilton did not have a new book about Laffite. In fact, he did not even have an old book about Laffite. What Shaw must have been referring to was

Hamilton's 1980 book *Great Forgers and Famous Fakes*, in which he included a chapter on John Laflin/Laffite, and which did come out in a new edition in 1996. Shaw may have been a little cavalier. If he had missed the reference in the text, he need only to have looked in the book's index under "De La Pena, José, forgery of..." In the new edition of his book Hamilton stated:

> A glance at the Millsaps letter told me it was the work of John Laffite, alias John Laflin. Comparing the writing in the Millsaps letter with an early narrative on Santa Anna's Texan expedition by José Enrique de la Pena, also forged by Laflin, revealed numerous similarities in penmanship, even though one document was in Spanish and the other in English.

Hamilton also included the image of three words or portions of words from the Millsaps letter and the same words or portions from the Peña manuscript. Of these he wrote, "...the writing in the compared words is the same size and has the same slant and stroke intensity. Both reveal the writer's training in the Palmer method of penmanship."[12]

The day of the auction arrived amid much hoopla and media coverage. Joe Musso was on hand at Butterfield & Butterfield and explained to reporters about the anomalies in the Peña account and about the handwriting comparisons with the Millsaps letter. This forced Shaw to fend off some last-minute questions about Hamilton's certification that the Peña papers were fake. He played down Hamilton's expertise and even suggested that Musso may have faked Hamilton's signature on the certification. What is interesting about this tactic is that Butterfield & Butterfield was auctioning a number of documents that day. Two of them were documents of James Bowie and William Travis. The auction house's catalog of that day assures the potential bidder that the authenticity of these documents was certified by none other than *Charles Hamilton*.[13] Welcome to Oz!

The reporters got it, but they would not be the ones bidding on it. Brian Huberman, a media professor from Rice University, was there to film the proceedings for his documentary on the death of Crockett. Don Carleton was there in a last-ditch effort to keep the document within the University of Texas system. Whether or not any psycho Yankee document burners were lurking in the audience is unknown. If they were there, they did not bid. Carleton was the only person who bid from the floor. When the smoke cleared the Peña papers had gone to two unidentified bidders via a phone bid for $350,000. It later was revealed that two Texans, not necessarily in white Stetsons, had ridden (more precisely flown) to the rescue. Carleton, despite his belief that there was no monetary value attached to the papers, bid to $300,000. He was finally edged out by Thomas O. Hicks and Charles Tate. Hicks is the owner of the Texas Rangers baseball team and the Dallas Stars hockey team. He is also the chairman and chief executive officer of Hicks Muse Tate & Furst investment firm, and the chairman of Capstar. Tate is president of Hicks Muse Tate & Furst. The two were in an airplane on a business trip to Boston on the morning of the auction when Tate read about it in a newspaper. "It was inconceivable to me that it might end up outside Texas," he stated. "This would have been a tragedy for all Texans." The men placed a call to Wendy Evans Hoff, a New York antiques dealer and agent, who placed the winning bid for them.[14]

The newspaper headlines had paid off. Having never seen the papers and probably believing that they were indeed an "Alamo diary," Tate and Hicks spent $350,000 in order to keep them in Texas. The bidding started at $150,000 and jumped in increments of $25,000. Carleton, on the auction floor, bid to $300,000 but gave up when the bid went to $350,000. He stated:

> Of course, I'm disappointed. I'd love to have it at UT. I actually went higher [in bidding] than I had wanted to, but we wanted the diary and that's the main reason we made an extraordinary effort to

> come.... I consider this a rescue mission that was
> unsuccessful.... The last thing I want to see is for it
> to wind up in someone's back room and have them
> show it off to friends after dinner.[15]

He need not have worried. One month after the auction there was another surprising development. Hicks and Tate had remained anonymous up until this time. In December they identified themselves to the press along with the announcement that they intended to donate the Peña papers to the Center for American History at the University of Texas at Austin. Carleton had bid up to $300,000 on behalf of the Center. Hicks' and Tate's agent unknowingly had bid against Carleton to $50,000 more. After having walked away with the prize, Hicks and Tate then handed the papers to Carleton's institution. Go figure.

Everybody wins

The auction of the Peña papers and their donation to the University of Texas at Austin proved to be a happy ending for almost everybody. The Peace family rid themselves of the pesky papers for a fabulous windfall before (if ever) anyone proved them to be fakes, and Peace III shed the heavy mantle of Crockett buffdom. The University of Texas system won by holding on to the coveted papers. In the end they only moved a scant seventy miles north, a mere "hoot 'n holler" up the road by Texas standards. Steve Hardin is satisfied since the papers did not fall into the clutches of the Yankees. All those interested in the papers, both proponents and opponents alike, are happy that they did not end up in the fireplace of some maniacal right-winger. Don Carleton is certainly happy. His institution has the papers and still has its 300 "large." Hicks and Tate are happy. For $350,000, a mere bag of shells compared to the $1,000,000 predicted by Shaw, they became heroes by preventing an alleged Mexican diary, memoir, or account from leaving Texas soil. Greg Shaw and Butterfield & Butterfield must be delirious.

The rescuers and proud new owners of the Peña papers.
Tom Hicks (left) and Charles Tate.

Photo by John Davenport. Courtesy of the *San Antonio Express-News*.

Thank God for Texan patriotism. Someone bought the papers for more than their client was asking for them, sight unseen.

The proponents and opponents of the account are relieved because the papers are still in an accessible institution, and they do not have to sit through someone's boring dinner in order to see them. The possibility of a word-for-word, page-for-page translation of the papers is still alive, thus giving us a look at what is really written in the papers for the first time in the many years they has been known to exist. Proponents of the Peña account are happy because the purchase of the papers helps support the view of them as authentic. Nobody would spend that much money on something that was not real. Right? The doubters of the Peña account are happy since the papers (the physical papers and not just photocopies of them) should remain available for examination at the Center for American History. I say *should* because at the time of this writing there is a rumor that the papers will be copied and only the copies would be available to researchers. This would be unfortunate since one of the main questions about the papers is their authenticity. The Center for American History has always been cooperative in allowing researchers "hands-on" examination of documents in their collection, even questionable ones like the Sanchez-Navarro journals. Hopefully the Peña papers will remain as accessible as they were in the Special Collections at the University of Texas at San Antonio. The latest information indicates that the papers will be scanned and made available on the Center's World Wide Web page.[16]

Regarding the question of Crockett's death, the auction of the papers does not do anything to resolve the mystery either way. It is still an open field for researchers interested in the matter. The only people who perhaps did not win are the people of Mexico. If the Peña document is authentic, is it not a document of Mexican history? How did it ever get out of the country? Also there are the people at the John Peace Memorial Library, because it was made to look as if they had done something wrong regarding the papers. I do not believe they did.

Almost everybody wins.

CHAPTER EIGHT

Conclusions

· · · ◆ · · ·

The Safety Valve of all speculation is: It might be so.
—John Steinbeck, *The Sea of Cortez*

This is why you never as a historian say anything absolutely.
—Paul Andrew Hutton

It is, then, a rash man indeed who claims he has the final answer to everything that happened in the Alamo.
—Walter Lord

DAVID CROCKETT DIED ON MARCH 6, 1836, at the Alamo in San Antonio de Bexar, Texas. He was either killed during or soon after the battle. The exact manner of his death will never be known. Perhaps it is better that way because it keeps alive a mystery. It also leaves room for further debate, and his death will be able to be portrayed in a wide variety of ways in future books and films. The importance of the exact manner of his death is relative. To some it is important, to others it is not. The subject has been, and probably will remain, of interest to people for a long time. The story of Crockett's death has been kept alive for the more than forty years by the Peña account. The two are irrevocably linked.

Since its appearance in 1955 the Peña account generally has been accepted as true without qualification. It has only recently come under any question or investigation. I believe eventually that historians and students of the Alamo battle will distance themselves from the Peña account. This will be the result of the work of researchers such as Tom Lindley of Texas and Joe Musso of California. Their research continues to reveal evidence that the Peña papers are forgeries, independent of my own conclusions. This is not to say that the papers themselves will not be around for a while. Due to their recent sale, the papers now have a monetary worth of $350,000, and that must be maintained. It is to be expected that people will equate the document's authenticity and its historical accuracy to the fact that someone spent that much money on it.

In the various newspaper articles that covered the auction of the papers, some inaccuracies crept in that served to portray the argument over the account in a certain light. Carmina Danini reported in the *San Antonio Express-News* that I was so angered by the account of Crockett's death that I "dismissed it as a forgery." That is not true. I was never angered by the fact that Crockett could have been executed. If anything, I was somewhat surprised that historians and writers could take an account, put their own interpretation and spin on it, and pass it on to readers as if it were established fact. I was also surprised that so many people would buy into this account without ever questioning it or even trying to establish its authenticity first.

Danini also wrote, "Critics contend the diary is a forgery because of de la Peña's report that Davy Crockett was captured and executed by troops acting under order of Santa Anna."[1] Once again, that is not true. Her statements make it seem as if I and others immediately declared the papers a forgery as soon as it was published in the United States in 1975 because we did not believe what was written in them. I and the others who believe it is a fake believe so because of the many characteristics of documentary forgeries apparent in the papers. The critics of the papers all believed they were an authentic "diary" originally. It is only after years of studying it that some of us have come to the conclusion that it is a fake. This point has been a tough sell to our opponents in the debate and to some of the media who have reported it.

It is interesting that the physical presence of the papers has been enough to convince people that they are completely authentic and accurate. However, the presence of the many indications of forgeries within the papers has not been enough to convince them they are fake.

My conclusions about the mystery of Crockett's death are presented in the following form of questions and answers. As I have stated before, these are my opinions and observations after a number of years of studying this matter. Others have their own opinions.

Q) How did David Crockett die at the Alamo?

A) I do not know. There is not enough evidence to give a precise description of the exact manner of his death.

Q) Is it possible that he was taken alive and then executed after the battle?

A) Yes, it is possible. I believe that we have enough evidence to indicate that there were executions after the Alamo battle. There probably was more than one single incident. Crockett was at the Alamo, so the possibility always exists that he was one of those executed.

Q) Is it possible that he was killed while fighting?

A) Yes, the Alamo was a battle, and obviously people were killed while fighting in this battle. Since the number of Alamo defenders exceeds the number of men reported executed, I think that the odds are in favor of his having died during the action of the battle.

Q) Is it possible that Crockett was killed in the process of trying to escape with all of the others who died outside the walls?

A) It is possible, but if he made that choice, he probably did so very late in the battle since there is enough evidence to place his body inside the Alamo afterwards. According to the latest evidence uncovered, many of the others who tried to get out actually did make it outside the walls.

Q) Is there a great difference in whether he died while fighting or was executed?

A) Probably not. One can draw such a fine line between a fighting death and an execution that it gets into a very gray area. If Crockett continued defending himself until he was out of ammunition and exhausted and a group of Mexican soldiers fired at him from a distance, does that constitute a combat death or an execution?

Q) Did Crockett die as depicted by Fess Parker in Walt Disney's *Davy Crockett* series?

A) There is no evidence of that, and anyway, Parker's Crockett is never shown dying.

Q) Is there a cinematic depiction of Crockett's death that is historically accurate?

A) If there is, it is strictly by coincidence and not by any researched documentation. We will never know the answer to that because first we would have to know how Crockett died.

Q) How would Mexican soldiers in Santa Anna's force have known who Crockett was?

A) They would not have. In a victory letter by Santa Anna after the battle he mentions that Crockett was among the dead, so he was aware of his presence in the Alamo. He probably would have gotten this information from San Antonio townspeople during the siege. As far as Santa Anna knowing of Crockett's reputation or that he had been a U.S. Congressman, I have never seen any evidence that Crockett's reputation was already known in

Mexico or that any of the Mexican force would have known him by name.

Q) Are the accounts stating Crockett was executed proof that he was executed?
A) No. I am not even sure they can be considered evidence in light of what we now know about them.

Q) Are the accounts stating that Crockett was killed while fighting proof that he died so?
A) See the answer to the previous question.

Q) Is it possible that some Alamo defenders surrendered?
A) Yes. As stated before, the battle was over as soon as the Mexican troops got control of the walls. Technically there was no justification to keep fighting after that unless one was fighting for his own survival. There certainly was no hope of winning the battle or even fighting to a draw at that point.

Q) If Alamo defenders did surrender, can it be considered some kind of disgrace?
A) No, there is no disgrace is surrendering in the hopeless situation they were in. Surrenders happen in warfare.

Q) Is it possible that Crockett surrendered?
A) Yes, but I have never seen any evidence that he did.

Q) Is it possible that Alamo defenders were taken alive without actually surrendering?
A) Yes, those who were overpowered, wounded, or simply exhausted could have been taken alive without formally surrendering. There were also a number of sick and wounded in the Alamo's hospital at the time of the battle. These may have been some of those executed.

Q) If Crockett was executed, does that in any way denigrate his reputation?
A) Not at all.

Q) If Crockett was executed, does it mean he did not really fight in the battle?

A) Not at all. If he was taken alive and then executed, he may have fought right up to the moment he was taken.

Q) Did Crockett do anything disgraceful or cowardly in his final moments at the Alamo?
A) I have never seen any evidence of that. Even the accounts that say he was executed do not say that. This idea is only a later concoction of some writers fueled by the newspaper headlines such a story always inspires.

Q) Is the value of Crockett's life a measure of the number of Mexican soldiers he may have killed at the Alamo?
A) No, and I hope no one else thinks so.

Q) Is there some grand conspiracy to besmirch Crockett's reputation?
A) No.

Q) Why do the versions of Crockett's alleged execution keep getting more outlandish in published works as the years go by?
A) A story about the death of a legendary figure takes on a life and momentum of its own. Every few years a writer or researcher, new to the story, rediscovers it and puts his or her own spin on it.

Q) Is it possible that some unidentified Alamo defender was taken prisoner and tried to pass himself off as Crockett thinking that his life might be spared?
A) I suppose that is possible, but since the Mexican soldiers would not have known Crockett anyhow, this would have been somewhat of a long shot. This scenario has been portrayed in a few fictional works about the Alamo.

Q) Most of the execution stories portray Santa Anna as ordering the execution of a number of Alamo defenders with Crockett among them. The account of Francisco Ruiz states that Santa Anna made him point out Crockett's body along with those of Bowie and Travis. If Santa Anna had ordered Crockett executed, would he not have known who he was?

A) The executions seemed to have happened fairly quickly without much conversation. If Crockett was one of those executed, Santa Anna would not have known who he was. The Mexican soldiers were not checking ID cards. There is the possibility that Santa Anna could have ordered Crockett executed without knowing who he was and then later asked someone to identify his body.

Q) Do you feel the need to defend Crockett's memory as a mythological American hero?

A) No.

Q) Do you feel the need to prove that Crockett died fighting at the Alamo?

A) No. The number of men executed at the Alamo was a small percentage of those who took part in the battle. The Alamo was a battle in which men fought and died. It was not like the mass execution at Goliad after the Battle of Coleto Creek. The unusual situation at the Alamo was that a number of defenders were executed. If Crockett was executed, he was part of this unusual situation. It is up to those who believe in the unusual situation to prove it.

Q) What are the Peña papers?

A) I believe they are modern-day forgeries.

Q) If the Peña papers are forgeries, what would have been the motive of the forger?

A) We usually think of the motive for forgery as financial gain. This may have been the case, but the experts tell us that in the case of historical forgeries, the desire to rewrite history is also a motive. Some forgers just enjoy the idea of their work being accepted by historians as authentic. If the Peña papers are forgeries, we may never know the motive of the forger. However, just because we do not know the motive, it does not mean someone did not *have* a motive. As Tom Lindley has pointed out, you do not need to provide a motive in order to show that a document is a fake. You may need to show a motive in order to convict someone in a court of law of forging something.

Q) Is it possible that any parts of the papers are authentic?

A) It is possible, but document expert Charles Hamilton would have disagreed. It is unlikely but possible that parts of the papers are real and that someone, later on, enhanced them.

Q) Is it possible that the passage concerning Crockett and the executions was written by Peña?

A) I think that is unlikely, but not because of the contents of the passage. The execution scene in the Peña account shows all signs of being derivative of all of the execution stories that came before it, even ones not published until the twentieth century. This is especially true of the Zuber/alleged Cos account that describes Crockett as a casual traveler to Texas. We know he was not. The Zuber account is the only one in which "Crockett" actually makes such a claim. Zuber is recognized now as having concocted tales about the Alamo. The Zuber account was not published until 1939. In addition, the page that the Crockett passage is written on is only one of three single sheets 6⅛" x 8½" in a stack in which the other eighty-two pages are all 12¼" x 8½" and folded in half. The page looks as if it had been inserted into the stack as an afterthought. This page does not have a watermark on it, so the age of the paper cannot be determined by that.

Q) If the papers, or specifically the page with the execution passage, are ever tested and found that the ink was put on the paper during the proper time period, does that prove that Crockett was executed?

A) No. We still would not know if Peña actually witnessed the executions himself, if he was relying on other sources to describe them, if he was being completely honest in his report, or if he was motivated by other factors such as seeking revenge for his imprisonment, etc. Even if it was proven to be of the correct time period, proponents are now calling his account a researched memoir. As such it loses all of the firsthand eyewitness immediacy for which it was known. As a note, the description of the executions in the Peña papers is not contained in the section considered the "rewritten diary" but only in the "final draft."

Q) If the papers, or specifically the page with the execution passage, are ever tested and found to be a fake, does that prove Crockett died fighting or, at least, was not executed?
A) No. He still may have been executed, or he still may have died fighting.

Q) Is there any way to determine beyond a shadow of a doubt how Crockett died?
A) Barring the invention of a time machine, I do not think so.

Q) In light of the acceptance of the Peña account and the recent sale of the manuscript for $350,000, do you think you should have done anything differently?
A) Yes, I should have taken up forgery.

Crockett's Many Deaths

· · · ◆ · · ·

*The sudden death of a just man after a good life does
not lessen his merits if he dies thus.*
—The Scotichronicon, XII

THE DEATH OF DAVID CROCKETT at the Alamo has been interpreted and reinterpreted by various historians and writers over the past years. What follows is a sampling of how a variety of these historians and writers have treated the subject of Crockett's death down through the years:

1838

Chester Newell states that Crockett's death was as glorious as his career had been conspicuous, and that he and his companions had been found with heaps of dead around them.

Chester Newell, *History of the Revolution in Texas* (New York: Wiley & Putnam, 1838; reprint, New York: Arno Press, 1973), 90 (page reference is to reprint edition).

1860

Reuben M. Potter states that Crockett had sallied forth from a room in the low barrack near the gate and was shot down.

Reuben M. Potter, *The Fall of the Alamo: A Reminiscence of the Revolution of Texas* (San Antonio: Herald Steam Press, 1860), 10-11.

1878

Reuben M. Potter, in another version of his *The Fall of the Alamo*, merely states that Crockett's body was found in the west battery.

Reuben M. Potter, "The Fall of the Alamo," *Magazine of American History*, January 1878; reprint in book form, *The Fall of the Alamo* (Hillsdale, New Jersey: The Otterden Press, 1977), 33 (page reference is to reprint edition).

1890

Sidney Lanier states that Crockett died fighting in the angle of the church wall.

Sidney Lanier, "San Antonio de Bexar," printed in William Corner's *San Antonio de Bexar: A Guide and History*, 1890 (reprinted as *San Antonio*, priv. pub. by Mary Ann Guerra, 1980), n.p.

1900

John S. Ford cites Francisco Becerra, whose opinion it was that Travis and Crockett were the last two men killed. He goes on to say that Becerra may have been mistaken since he did not know Travis and Crockett personally.

John S. Ford, *Origins and Fall of the Alamo* (San Antonio: Johnson Brothers Printing Co., 1900; reprint, Austin: Shelby Publishers, n.d.), 21 (page reference is to reprint edition).

Henry Ryder-Taylor states that Crockett died in the discharge of his duty and sold his life dearly.

Henry Ryder-Taylor, *History of the Alamo and of the Local Franciscan Missions* (San Antonio: Nic Tengg, 1900), 53.

1904

Leonora Bennett states that Crockett was among the last to die at the Alamo and clubbed many a foe to death with his gun before he succumbed. His body was bullet ridden before he gave up the struggle.

Leonora Bennett, *Historical Sketch and Guide to the Alamo* (San Antonio: priv. pub., 1904), 74.

1936

Frederick C. Chabot repeats Chester Newell's opinion that Crockett's death was as glorious as his career had been conspicuous. He goes on to state that Crockett was shot down in a room of the low barrack, near the gate where he had taken refuge. However, in his next sentence, Chabot describes Crockett's body as being found just inside the doorway of the baptistry, the first room to the right, just inside the entrance to the present-day Alamo.

Frederick C. Chabot, *The Alamo: Mission Fortress and Shrine* (San Antonio: priv. pub., 1936), 45.

1948

John Myers Myers describes Crockett as having died in combat along with his Tennesseans. He states that Crockett and two of his men were reportedly found in a heap of seventeen dead Mexican soldiers. Of Crockett's alleged execution he states that a Texas memorialist, whom he leaves unidentified, made up the story as a child to impress "greenhorns" from the U.S. This tale was allegedly fabricated within ten days of the Alamo's fall.

John Myers Myers, *The Alamo* (New York: E.P. Dutton & Co., Inc., 1948), 15, 223.

1956

James A. Shackford cites Susanna Dickinson's statement about recognizing Crockett's dead and mutilated body. He later states that too much had been made over the details of how Crockett died and explains that such details are unimportant. "[Crockett] died as he had lived. His life was one of intrepid courage."

James A. Shackford, *David Crockett: The Man and the Legend* (Chapel Hill, North Carolina: University of North Carolina Press, 1956; reprint, Westport, Connecticut: Greenwood Press, 1981), 234, 238-39 (page references are to reprint edition).

1958

Lon Tinkle states that Crockett died outdoors, and when the firing was over he and his men were found at their assigned post near the stockade fence.

Lon Tinkle, *13 Days to Glory: The Siege of the Alamo* (New York, Toronto, London: McGraw-Hill Book Co. Inc., 1958), 213-14.

Robert Penn Warren, in a children's history of the Alamo, states that although there is some uncertainty concerning his death, Crockett most likely died with two fellow Tennesseans near the gate in the wall between the barracks and church, with seventeen dead Mexican soldiers around them. He mentions the execution of Texan prisoners but does not mention the fact that Crockett was alleged to have been one of them.

Robert Penn Warren, *Remember the Alamo* (New York: Random House, 1958), 154-56.

1960

Virgil E. Baugh writes that stories concerning the deaths of Bowie, Crockett, and Travis, and even their alleged "survival," range from "patently ridiculous fabrication to anecdotes that can be disproved by the testimony of eyewitnesses, by circumstances, and by our knowledge of the men involved." He also raises the question of whether or not Cos fabricated the "malicious tale" of Crockett's surrender and execution in an attempt to ruin Crockett's reputation.

Virgil E. Baugh, *Rendezvous at the Alamo* (New York: Pageant Press, 1960; reprint, Lincoln, Nebraska: University of Nebraska Press, 1985), 221-22 (page references are to reprint edition).

Thomas Lawrence Connelly writes, "Recent studies of Crockett have denied that Crockett was among the number of surrendered, but their author's appraisals of the sources are so defective that one can put no confidence in their statements."

Thomas Lawrence Connelly, "Did David Crockett Surrender at the Alamo? A Contemporary Letter," *Journal of Southern History*, 26 (1960): 368-76.

William Weber Johnson, in a children's history of the Texas Revolution, states that Crockett had one arm shattered by a musket ball and fought with his rifle as a club until the rifle broke. He then fought with his knife until he was dropped by a sword thrust.

William Weber Johnson, *The Birth of Texas* (Boston: Houghton-Mifflin, North Star Books, 1960), 138.

1961

Walter Lord remains diplomatic and cites Felix Nuñez's description of the death of a defender who could have stood for any of them, including Crockett.

Walter Lord, *A Time to Stand* (New York: Harper & Row, 1961), 161-62, 206-207.

1964

Lon Tinkle, in a children's book on the Alamo, states that Crockett died outdoors and that he died fighting against great odds.

Lon Tinkle, *The Valiant Few: Crisis at the Alamo* (New York: Macmillan Company, 1964), 61.

1967

William C. Davis writes that six men surrendered after they were discovered hiding under some mattresses in the barracks, and legend has it that Crockett was one of these men. He points out that it is unlikely Crockett or any of the other Tennesseans surrendered, since they were cut off from the barracks. Davis concludes that even if Crockett did surrender, it was no reflection on his other heroic deeds on the day the Alamo fell.

William C. Davis, "The Alamo Remembered," *American History Illustrated* Vol. 2, no. 6 (Oct. 1967), 57.

1968

Richard G. Santos states that, "According to Colonels de la Peña, Sanchez Navarro, Almonte, and Urriza, 'David Crockett, a well-known naturalist from North America' was among the captured."

Richard G. Santos, *Santa Anna's Campaign Against Texas* (n.p.: Texian Press, 1968; reprint, Salisbury, North Carolina: Documentary Publication, n.d.), 76 (page reference is to reprint edition).

J. Hefter explains that the widely held belief of Crockett's combat death has been weakened by numerous reports of his capture and execution.

J. Hefter, "Some Comments on the Battle," in General Miguel A. Sanchez Lamego, *The Siege and Taking of the Alamo* (Santa Fe: Sunstone Press, 1968), 50-53.

1971

Lowell H. Harrison writes that the exact manner of Crockett's death is unknown. He mentions the version of Crockett's surrender and execution, a version of Crockett dying with a heap of foes about him, and a version in which Crockett is shot down early in the final battle while running from the church toward the wall. Harrison concluded, "The details were not important."

Lowell H. Harrison, "David Crockett," *American History Illustrated*, Vol. 6, no. 4 (July 1971), 30.

1972

Martha Anne Turner supports the theory that Crockett died fighting. She states that "...the persistent story regarding Crockett's surrender is undoubtedly based on the spurious conclusion of the book *Colonel Crockett's Exploits and Adventures in Texas*, published after the hero's death and without foundation."

Martha Anne Turner, *William Barret Travis: His Sword and His Pen* (Waco, Texas: Texian Press, 1972), 251-52.

1976

Joe B. Frantz, in his bicentennial of Texas, merely states that on the thirteenth day of the Alamo siege, Crockett was dead and mutilated.

Joe B. Frantz, *Texas: A Bicentennial History* (New York: W.W. Norton & Co., 1976), 69.

Leah Carter Johnson states that Crockett died fighting to the very end.

Leah Carter Johnson, *San Antonio: St. Anthony's Town* (San Antonio: The Naylor Co., 1976), 147.

C. Richard King cites Susanna Dickinson's account of recognizing Crockett's body after the battle. He also mentions the de la Peña account but offers no conclusion or opinion as to Crockett's death.

C. Richard King, *Susanna Dickinson: Messenger of the Alamo* (Austin: Shoal Creek Publishing Co., 1976), 43, 140.

Archie P. McDonald writes that Crockett was one of seven men who survived the Alamo battle and were brought before Santa Anna. Santa Anna ordered them executed and they were tortured before they were killed.

Archie P. McDonald, *Travis* (Austin: The Pemberton Press, 1976), 177.

1979

Mary Ann Guerra states that Crockett died with his "Tennessee boys," without any further elaboration.

Mary Ann Guerra, *An Alamo Album* (San Antonio: priv. pub., 1979), 2.

1980

Dan Kilgore states that "[Sergeant] Becerra and at least six other witnesses include Crockett's name in the list of the slain," referring to the men executed after the Alamo battle. Later, Kilgore states that "... on the whole the recollection bears [Becerra] out as a straightforward, truthful witness except for the tale of his role in the deaths of the three heroes, [Travis, Bowie, and Crockett]."

Dan Kilgore, introduction to Francisco Becerra, *A Mexican Sergeant's Recollections of the Alamo & San Jacinto* (Austin: Jenkins Publishing Co., 1980), 7-8.

1981

Robert F. Palmquist writes that no one knows for sure how Crockett died, and he cites accounts supporting both sides of the argument.

Robert F. Palmquist, "High Private—David Crockett at the Alamo," *Real West*, Vol. 24, no. 181 (Dec. 1981), 42-43.

1982

Richard B. Hauck advances the execution theory and slightly dramatizes the scene by stating that "Mexican soldiers routed Crockett and others from various vantage points of their last stand, literally wresting their useless weapons from their hands." He also states that "It is unimportant that he did not go down busting the heads of Mexican soldiers. What is important is that he died in the style by which he lived."

Richard B. Hauck, *Crockett: A Bio-Bibliography* (Westport, Connecticut and London: Greenwood Press, 1982), 50-54.

David Lyons describes various versions of Crockett's alleged execution and combat death. He also describes stories of Crockett being taken prisoner and sent to Mexico in slavery. Lyons concludes, "Whether Davy Crockett was captured and executed by Santa Anna at the end of the battle or whether he was killed swinging his rifle at Mexican soldiers is of little importance."

David Lyons, "The Death of David Crockett," *Alamo Lore and Myth Organization Newsletter* Vol. 4, no. 3 (Sept. 1982), 1-4.

1985

Kevin D. Randle mentions the execution but does not indicate that Crockett was alleged to have been one of the victims. He writes that Crockett and his men were surrounded and quickly killed after having killed many of the enemy.

Kevin D. Randle, "Santa Anna's Signal," *Military History* Vol. 1, no. 5 (April 1985), 40-41.

Susan P. Schoelwer, in her book *Alamo Images*, and Paul A. Hutton, who wrote the introduction, both suggest that Crockett was taken prisoner and executed after the Alamo battle. The two writers do not explain why the accounts which favor the execution theory are more reliable than those which indicate that Crockett died fighting, but instead emphasize the insane reaction to Perry's and Kilgore's books. They also emphasize that film portrayals of Crockett's death are not historically accurate.

Susan P. Schoelwer, *Alamo Images: Changing Perception of a Texas Experience*, with an introduction by Paul A. Hutton (Dallas: DeGolyer Library and Southern Methodist University Press, 1985), 12-17, 159-163.

1986

Gary L. Foreman writes that Crockett was one of seven stunned, exhausted Alamo defenders found by Castrillón at the end of the Alamo battle. Castrillón prevented their slaughter and brought them before Santa Anna. Foreman cites the de la Peña "diary" as to Crockett's fate. He also cites James A. Shackford in explaining that it is not as important how Crockett died as how he lived.

Gary L. Foreman, *Crockett: The Gentleman from the Cane* (Dallas: Taylor Publishing Co., 1986), 46-55.

The Daughters of the Republic of Texas quote Francisco Ruiz who said Santa Anna asked to be shown the bodies of Travis, Bowie, and Crockett and that "Toward the west and in the small fort opposite the city, we found the body of Col. Crockett."

Daughters of the Republic of Texas, *The Alamo Long Barrack Museum* (Dallas: Taylor Publishing Co., 1986), 42.

Paul A. Hutton cites the Peña "diary" in describing Crockett's death. He also states that "Although not all students of the Alamo agree, evidence suggests that Davy Crockett was ... taken captive at the battle's end—only to be cut down without mercy on General Santa Anna's direct order."

Paul A. Hutton, "The Alamo: An American Epic," *American History Illustrated* Vol. 20, no. 11 (March 1986), 24, 36.

Paul A. Hutton writes that there is "no doubt" Crockett was one of the prisoners at the Alamo battle's end. He again cites the Peña "diary" as to Crockett's fate. He states that no account is "...more reliable than that of Lieutenant Colonel José Enrique de la Peña." He does not explain how or why he perceives Peña as the most reliable.

Paul Andrew Hutton, "Davy Crockett—Still King of the Wild Frontier," *Texas Monthly*, Vol. 14, no. 11 (Nov. 1986), 245-246.

Ben H. Proctor states that Crockett may have died fighting, but he also briefly explains the version in the Peña "diary."

Ben H. Proctor, *The Battle of the Alamo* (Austin: Texas State Historical Assc., 1986), 35-36.

Eric von Schmidt cites Peña's account as to Crockett's fate.

Eric von Schmidt, "The Alamo Remembered—From a Painter's Point of View," *Smithsonian*, Vol. 16, no. 12 (March 1986), 66.

Bob Boyd states that "Davy Crockett died fighting at the Alamo. He did not surrender. He did not ask for quarter. He did not beg for his life. He died fighting back-to-back with two of his Tennessee comrades. Before they had finished, a pile of dead enemies, estimated at between 14 and 24, lay around them."

Bob Boyd, *The Texas Revolution: A Day-by-Day Account*, edited by Soren W. Nielsen (San Angelo, Texas: San Angelo Standard, Inc., 1986), 154.

1987

Leonard E. Fisher, in a children's book on the Alamo, quotes Ruiz, stating that Crockett's body was found in a small fort opposite the city.

Leonard Everett Fisher, *The Alamo* (New York: Holiday House, 1987), 41.

Paul A. Hutton writes that the account of the unidentified Mexican officer as described by Dolson "...agrees perfectly" with that of Peña's. He also states that "...the simple mass of evidence, both direct and circumstantial [that Crockett was executed], is overwhelming," and that there is "...not a single reliable eyewitness account of Crockett's death in battle."

Paul Andrew Hutton, Introduction to *A Narrative of the Life of Davy Crockett*, Written by Himself, (Philadelphia: E.L. Carey and A. Hart, 1834; reprint, Lincoln, Nebraska and London: University of Nebraska Press, 1987), liv (page reference is to reprint edition).

1988

George A. McAlister states that Crockett and his "Tennessee boys" were cornered near the palisade and fought with savage fury. He cites Nuñez's account with the inference that Nuñez was describing Crockett's death. He also states that since there are so many conflicting reports on Crockett's death, the subject will only reflect a particular author's interpretation until some irrefutable evidence comes to light.

George A. McAlister, *Alamo: The Price of Freedom* (San Antonio: Docutex, Inc., 1988), 200-212.

1989

Paul A. Hutton writes that Crockett was taken prisoner and hauled before Santa Anna, and that Crockett "...presented himself as a tourist who had taken refuge in the Alamo." The prisoners were immediately executed. He describes Peña as an eyewitness to this event.

Paul Andrew Hutton, "Davy Crockett—He was Hardly King of the Wild Frontier," *TV Guide*, Vol. 37, no. 5, Feb. 4, 1989, 25.

Dan Kilgore repeats his theory that Crockett was one of the prisoners executed at the Alamo. He adds, "...ironically, in their efforts to pay homage to Crockett and his death, the early perpetuators of the legend, as well as many other writers who followed, have denied the historical Crockett the true dignity of his final hours." He concludes by saying that "Crockett faced death with courage and dignity and this fulfilled the legend he helped create."

Dan Kilgore, "Why Davy Didn't Die," in Michael A. Lofaro and Joe Cummings, eds. *Crockett at Two Hundred* (Knoxville, Tennessee: University of Tennessee Press, 1989), 6-17.

Paul A. Hutton states that "There really is very little room for doubt that Crockett was captured and executed at the Alamo." He again states that of the Mexican sources of the Alamo battle, "...none was more reliable than the diary of José Enrique de la Peña."

Paul Andrew Hutton, "An Exposition on Hero Worship," in Lofaro and Cummings, eds., *Crockett at Two Hundred*, 29, 34.

1990

Stephen L. Hardin, in an article concerning Crockett's appearance and manner of dress, supports the theory that Crockett was among those executed, citing Peña as the best account of Crockett's death.

Stephen L. Hardin, "David Crockett," *Military Illustrated*, no. 23 (Feb./March 1990), 35.

Wallace O. Chariton states that "Davy Crockett won his last fight and died fighting like a tiger. Nothing else seems fitting or proper."

Wallace O. Chariton, *Exploring the Alamo Legends* (Plano, Texas: Wordware Publishing, Inc., 1990), 37-63.

Jeff Long writes that Crockett surrendered and was taken alive, and that "David Crockett made a choice. The Go Ahead man quit. He did more than quit. He lied. He denied his role in the fighting."

Jeff Long, *Duel of Eagles: The Mexican and U.S. Fight for the Alamo* (New York: William Morrow and Co. Inc., 1990), 258.

Bill Groneman states that Crockett died during the Alamo battle. He explains that current popular opinion favors the theory that Crockett was one of five to seven prisoners taken during the battle and then executed on Santa Anna's orders. He also points out that a national hero failing to live up to his legendary status is fertile ground, commercially, so only that side of the story has received much press. The accounts which support the capture and execution are at best circumstantial and in no way constitute proof beyond a reasonable doubt.

Bill Groneman, *Alamo Defenders: A Geneology of the People and Their Words* (Austin: Eakin Press, 1990), 28, 169.

1992

Albert A. Nofi cites the Peña "diary" as to Crockett's death, calling it " ... the best firsthand account," and "The clearest and most detailed of Mexican accounts of the death of Crockett...." He also declares that "De La Peña's account is in most other respects quite accurate, which argues in favor of his version of the fate of Crockett." He goes on to say, "According to De La Peña, the man admitted to being Crockett and spun a complex tale apparently intended to get himself off the hook...."

Albert A. Nofi, *The Alamo and the Texas War of Independence* (Conshohocken, Pennsylvania: Combined Books, 1992), 121, 123, 211.

1993

Mark Derr states that "Crockett survived the carnage, probably in the low barracks near his outpost and was taken prisoner along with five or six other men.... Crockett told his captors that he had been exploring the country around Bexar when he heard of the Mexican advance and...had sought refuge with the Anglos in the Alamo." He then describes the executions as per Peña.

Mark Derr, *The Frontiersman: The Real Life and the Many Legends of Davy Crockett* (New York: William Morrow and Co., Inc., 1993), 248.

1996

Michael A. Lofaro states that "Crockett and five or six others were captured when Mexican troops took the Alamo...," and that they "...were bayoneted and then shot." He explains that the executed men's "dignity and bravery was, in fact, further underscored by Peña's recounting that 'these unfortunates died without complaining and without humiliating themselves before their torturers.'" [The Peña account states that they were killed by swords and that they died "moaning," not "without complaining."]

Michael A. Lofaro, "Crockett, David," in *The New Handbook of Texas* Vol. 2 ed. Ron Tyler et al (Austin: Texas State Historical Association, 1996), 409.

1997

Alex Shoumatoff writes that "Davy Crockett never wore a coonskin cap and, according to recent research, hid under a bed throughout the fighting [at the Alamo] and tried to surrender rather than fight to the death."

Alex Shoumatoff, *Legends of the American Desert: Sojourns in the Great Southwest* (New York: Alfred A. Knopf, 1997), 287.

1999

Paul A. Hutton again offers a dramatized version of the execution scenario. He describes Crockett as being one of a "...handful of bloodied exhausted defenders" who were offered clemency by Castrillón. He then describes the execution scene as per Peña but with the added touch of having Santa

Anna order his staff officers to execute the prisoners after the Sappers balked.

Paul Andrew Hutton, "Frontier Hero Davy Crockett," *Wild West* (February 1999), 44.

APPENDIX B

Crocķett's Film Deaths

... ◆ ...

Davy Crockett has remained absolutely firm from the first film in 1909 to the last time he appeared, which I guess was in the television film James A. Michener's Texas just a couple of years ago. He is always heroic, always folksie and homespun, and his death is always heroically presented.

—Frank Thompson

THE BATTLE OF THE ALAMO has always been a popular subject for movies and television shows. Naturally, the character of Crockett figures prominently in most of these productions. Film versions of Crockett's death are as varied as the literary ones. Crockett's death is usually a coda to the dramatic sweep of the final battle. A few examples follow:

Martyrs of the Alamo or Birth of Texas (1916)
Alfred D. Sears plays a checkered shirted Crockett in this silent film. During the battle, Crockett is pushed against the wall of the Alamo church and disappears under an onslaught of Mexican soldiers.

Davy Crockett at the Fall of the Alamo (1926)
Cullen Landis portrays Crockett in this silent film. This time, a bare-chested Crockett fights several

Mexican soldiers one-on-one with a sort of wild "Charlie Chaplin" style of wide-armed punches. He dispatches three of them but is then overwhelmed by four or five others who pin him to the ground. As they hold him down, a handful of other soldiers stab him to death with bayonets. As the soldiers pull back, Crockett looks into the camera and expires with a wide grin on his face.

Heroes of the Alamo (1937)

Lane Chandler is Crockett in this early sound version of the battle. Crockett is found alive after Santa Anna has entered the Alamo at the conclusion of the battle. He is noticed crawling along the ground and trying to haul himself up a ladder. Santa Anna orders him killed, and a soldier clubs him to death with a musket.

Man of Conquest (1939)

Robert Barratt plays Crockett in this film about Sam Houston. In the Alamo battle segment, Crockett is killed by a shot from a pistol and slowly slumps to the ground.

"Davy Crockett at the Alamo"

(the third and final installment of the *Davy Crockett, King of the Wild Frontier* Disney television series episode) (1955)

Fess Parker, film's most famous Crockett in film's most famous Crockett death scene, is not shown dying. After all of his close friends are killed around him, Crockett is admonished to "Give 'em what-fer, Davy" by his sidekick, Georgie Russel (Buddy Ebsen). Crockett stands with one foot on the stairway to the parapet and with one knee on the parapet. In close-up he flails away at the Mexican soldiers with his rifle "Old Betsy." The scene fades to the Alamo's flag and then to the Texas flag. We do not see what happened to Crockett, but we know.

_____ He was killed while fighting.
_____ He was captured and then executed.
(Please check your preferred ending)

The Last Command (1955)

Veteran character actor Arthur Hunnicutt turns in a popular performance as the most "down home" Crockett, in this film about Jim Bowie. In the battle scene, Crockett jumps down from the Alamo's wall near the wooden palisade to meet the charge of a Mexican cavalryman in the interior of the fort. He is knocked down, and the cavalryman and horse are also knocked down. He uses his rifle to knock three other cavalrymen off of their horses, breaking his rifle on the last horse. He yells to one of his men, "Parson, the torch!" The parson passes him the flaming torch before being shot down himself. Crockett backs into a corner where several barrels of gunpowder stand. As a group of Mexican soldiers overwhelms him he shoves the torch into one of the barrels of powder, and they all go out in a blaze of glory.

The Alamo (1960)

John Wayne's epic features the Duke himself as the most recognized Crockett after Fess Parker. Crockett defends a hastily constructed final redoubt in front of the Alamo church. The Mexican army completely fills the Alamo's main plaza, and Mexican cavalrymen are jumping their horses over the wooden palisade. With his rifle in his left hand and a burning torch in his right, Crockett retreats toward the open double doors of the church. He does a quick spin and throws his rifle at two Mexican soldiers to his left. He puts his back to the door and hits another soldier, inside the church, with the torch. Too much follow-through proves to be his undoing as a Mexican lancer, on foot, nails him to the church door with a sickening crunch and thud. Crockett breaks the heavy lance with a flick of his wrist and lifts himself off of the portion of lance still in the door. He staggers into the church, staggers back into the camera angle, and staggers back into the church to the Alamo's gunpowder magazine. He tosses the torch into the room onto the top of the barrels of powder before collapsing into the room. Ka-boom! Arthur Hunnicutt's pyrotechnic exit is a mere firecracker by comparison as the ensuing explosion blows holes in the thick walls of the Alamo's church.

"The Alamo" (episode of the *Time Tunnel* television show) (1966)

The producers of this show solved the problem of Crockett's death, saved the expense of paying an actor to portray Crockett, and relieved themselves of the hassle of trying to find a coonskin cap in one fell swoop. They did this by having the show's two time travelers go back to the 1836 Alamo only to be told that Crockett "was killed yesterday." If only they had gone back in time 130 years plus one day!

Seguin (1982)

This film tells the story of Tejano defender Juan Seguin, the highest-ranking officer of the Alamo garrison to leave the Alamo as a courier. After a rather unrealistic battle scene, a group of Alamo defenders are brought out, stood against a wall, and shot. None are identified by name, but one tall, dejected defender is wearing a coonskin cap. Hey! Maybe that was. . .

The Alamo: Thirteen Days to Glory (1987)

Veteran actor Brian Keith portrays a youth-challenged Crockett in this made-for-TV film. Crockett makes his last stand in front of the Alamo church and wildly flails at the charging Mexican soldiers with a knife. [He could have reached farther with a rifle or a torch.] Finally a Mexican soldier points a rifle with a bayonet at him. Crockett seems to grab the rifle and helps pull the bayonet into himself. He sits down on the back of a fallen Mexican soldier. The scene cuts to a different camera angle, and the body of the Mexican soldier is no longer under Crockett's legs but behind his back, probably to provide a softer landing. Through all of this action Crockett's strange "Hey look, I'm Davy Crockett and I'm not wearing a coonskin cap" wide-brimmed hat seems to be nailed to his head.

Alamo... Price of Freedom (1987)

This film was made specifically for the IMAX theater, one block from the Alamo, and is shown several times a day. It features Merrill Connally as Crockett. During the final battle, Crockett is backed up against the front wall of the Alamo church by oncoming Mexican soldiers. He crouches and holds his rifle with two hands, like a pugil stick, out in front of him. As individual soldiers charge him he hits them with short barrel and gun stock combos. Finally, one soldier comes in too close, and Crockett hits him with a backhand barrel blow. While he is turned slightly, an officer rushes in and kills him with a sword blow to the head.

Texas (1994)

This film version of James Michener's novel features John Schneider as a young, blond "surfer dude" Crockett, sporting a Veronica Lake hairdo. The complexities of the Alamo battle and Crockett's death are solved by borrowing battle scenes from *The Last Command* and then simply showing Crockett's body afterwards. Neither his death nor any executions are shown.

Appendix C

Davy Deathiana

· · · ◆ · · ·

The publications on Crockett's death form the single largest subsegment of Alamo literature.
—William C. Davis

"**D**AVY DEATHIANA" was coined by Professor Paul Andrew Hutton of the University of New Mexico to describe the ever-growing body of information regarding Crockett's death. The body of information is considerable. Many articles and a number of books have been written on the subject. A few recent books on the Alamo and on Crockett's life include a section or chapter specifically devoted to it. As far as violent deaths in Texas go, Crockett's may be second only to that of President John F. Kennedy for the amount of written material and discussion it has inspired. What follows is a list of the original sources on Crockett's death. Also included is some of the later published material that either discuss, debate, or analyze Crockett's death or one or more pieces of the evidence.

1836

Morning Courier and New York Enquirer, 9 July 1836.

This newspaper contains the earliest known (at this time) printing of the article probably written by William H. Attree. The story of an unidentified witness describes Crockett as one of six prisoners executed by Mexican officers plunging swords into their bodies.

> "'Texas—Extract from a letter written by Mr. George M. Dolson, an officer in the Texian army to his brother in this city: Dated Galveston Island, Camp Trevos [sic] July 19, 1836," *Detroit Democratic Free Press*, 7 September 1836.

This newspaper article is the only known contemporary printing of the letter by George M. Dolson. It is attributed to either Col. Juan N. Almonte or to an unidentified informant. In this version Crockett again is one of six prisoners. He and the others are ordered shot by Santa Anna. His executioners are only identified as "hell hounds of the tyrant."

1837

> Ramón Martinez Caro, *Verdadera Idea de la Primera Campaña de Tejas y Sucesos Ocurridos después de la accion de San Jacinto* (Mexico: Imprenta de Santiago Perez, 1837).

In this pamphlet Caro describes five Texans being executed by soldiers but does not mention the weapons used. This account does not name Crockett as one of those executed.

1859

> Nicholas Labadie, "San Jacinto Campaign" *Texas Almanac*, 1859.

This article contains the account attributed to Col. Fernando Urriza in which a lone prisoner is shot to death by soldiers on Santa Anna's orders. Urriza believed some unidentified "they" called the prisoner "Coket."

1860

Francis Antonio Ruiz, "Fall of the Alamo and Massacre of Travis and His Brave Associates," *Texas Almanac*, 1860.

This contains the account of Francisco Ruiz in which he describes Crockett's body as being "Toward the west, and in the small fort opposite the city."

1875

James M. Morphis, *History of Texas from Its Discovery and Settlement* (New York: United States Publishing Co., 1875).

This book contains Susanna Hannig's (Dickinson's) statement that she recognized Col. Crockett lying dead and mutilated between the church and the two-story barrack building, and even remembered seeing his peculiar cap lying by his side.

1882

[John S. Ford], "The Fall of the Alamo" *Texas Mute Ranger*, April 1882.

This article contains the account of Sgt. Francisco Becerra in which Crockett and Travis are executed on Santa Anna's orders. Crockett and Travis are shot by soldiers in this version.

1889

Felix Nuñez, "Fall of the Alamo" *Fort Worth Gazette*, 23 June 1889.

This contains the account attributed to Sgt. Felix Nuñez that an Alamo defender, dressed in the traditional manner associated with Crockett, is felled by a deadly sword blow above the right eye and then is pierced by not less than twenty bayonets.

1890

William Corner, editor and compiler, *San Antonio de Bexar: A Guide and History* (San Antonio: Bainbridge & Corner, 1890).

This book contains the story by Madam Candelaria in which Crockett is shot down while unarmed and advancing from the church building.

1899

"Alamo Massacre as told by the late Madam Candaleria [sic]" *San Antonio Light*, 22 February 1899.

This article contains the story by Madam Candelaria in which Crockett dies defending the sandbagged door of the Alamo church.

1935

James T. DeShields, *Tall Men with Long Rifles* (San Antonio: Naylor Co., 1935).

This book contains the story attributed to Capt. Rafael Soldana in which an Alamo defender named "Kwockey," dressed in traditional frontier garb, dies in one of the Alamo rooms while swinging his rifle as a club. It also contains the story attributed to an unidentified Mexican captain stating that Crockett was killed in a room while defending it with his knife.

1938

Carlos Sanchez-Navarro y Peón, *La Guerra de Tejas: Memorias de un Soldado* (Mexico: Editorial Polis, 1938).

This book is a transcription of the alleged journal of Col. José Juan Sanchez-Navarro in which Sanchez-Navarro was horrified by "...the death of an old man they called 'Cocran.'"

1939

J. Frank Dobie, Mody C. Boatright, and Harry H. Ransom, eds., *In the Shadow of History* (Austin: Texas Folklore Society, 1939).

This book contains the story by William P. Zuber and attributed to Gen. Cos in which Crockett, alone, is executed by the bayonet thrust of a soldier.

1951

Helen Hunnicutt, "A Mexican View of the Texan War—Memoirs of a Veteran of the Two Battles of the Alamo" *Library Chronicle*, Summer 1951.

This article is an edited English version of the Sanchez-Navarro account.

1955

J. Sanchez Garza, *La Rebelion de Texas: Manuscrito Inedito de 1836 por un Oficial de Santa Anna* (Mexico: A. Frank de Sanchez, 1955).

This is the transcription of the alleged diary of Lt. José Enrique de la Peña in which David Crocket [sic] and six others are executed by Mexican officers wielding swords on Santa Anna's orders.

"1836 Paper Tells Story of Davy's Death" *Knoxville News-Sentinel*, 5 May 1955.

1956

James A. Shackford, *David Crockett: The Man and the Legend* (Chapel Hill, North Carolina: University of North Carolina Press, 1956).

Shackford included nine pages on Crockett's death before the question of his death was an issue. He settled on Madam Candelaria's undramatic version of Crockett's death.

1960

Virgil E. Baugh, *Rendezvous at the Alamo* (New York: Pageant Press, 1960).

Baugh provides five emotionally charged pages on Crockett's death, concentrating on the Zuber and Becerra accounts.

Thomas Lawrence Connelly, "Did David Crockett Surrender at the Alamo? A Contemporary Letter" *Journal of Southern History* 26, 1960.

The subject of this article is the Dolson letter. It is reprinted for the first time since it appeared in the *Detroit Democratic Free Press* in 1836.

1961

Walter Lord, *A Time to Stand* (New York: Harper & Row Publishers, 1961).

Lord addresses the question "Did David Crockett Surrender?" in his chapter "Riddles of the Alamo."

1963

John H. Jenkins, "Did Davy Crockett Survive the Alamo?" *Texana*, Summer 1963.

1968

J. Hefter, "Some Comments on the Battle," in Gen. Miguel A. Sanchez Lamego, *The Siege and Taking of the Alamo* (Santa Fe, New Mexico: Press of the Territorian, 1968).

Hefter includes the section "The Death of Colonel Crockett" in his appendix to Lamego's book. He gives examples of three versions of Crockett's fate: Crockett went down fighting; Crockett was captured and executed; and Crockett survived and turned up alive later.

1975

Carmen Perry, editor and translator, *With Santa Anna in Texas: A Personal Narrative of the Revolution by José Enrique de la Peña* (College Station, Texas: Texas A&M University Press, 1975).

Perry's English translation of the Peña narrative.

"Did Davy Crockett Die at the Alamo? Historian Carmen Perry Says No" *People Weekly*, 13 October 1975.

Texas Jim Cooper, "Peña's Diary: How Did David Crockett Die?" *Carrollton (Texas) Star*, 6 November 1975.

1976

Bill Groneman, "The Death of Davy Crockett," *The Defender*, January 1976 and February 1976.

Groneman's first foray into the Crockett death controversy in a small "Alamo buff" newsletter.

1977

Charles Grosvenor, annotator, Reuben M. Potter, *The Fall of the Alamo* (Hillsdale, New Jersey: The Otterden Press, 1977).

Grosvenor published and annotated the 1878 version of Potter's *The Fall of the Alamo*. Grosvenor discusses Crockett's death in note #35 and determines that Crockett's execution remains only a possibility.

1978

Dan Kilgore, *How Did Davy Die?* (College Station, Texas and London: Texas A&M University Press, 1978).

Kilgore's volume in which he defends Crockett's execution by comparing it to other similar accounts.

"Take That, John Wayne" *Texas Monthly,* August 1978.

A short article on Dan Kilgore and *How Did Davy Die?*

1980

Francisco Becerra, *A Mexican Sergeant's Recollections of the Alamo & San Jacinto* with an introduction by Dan Kilgore (Austin: Jenkins Publishing Co., 1980).

The Becerra account.

1981

Robert F. Palmquist, "High Private—David Crockett at the Alamo" *Real West,* December 1981.

Palmquist devotes a good portion of this article to the question surrounding Crockett's death.

1982

Richard Boyd Hauck, *Crockett: A Bio-Bibliography* (Westport, Connecticut and London: Greenwood Press, 1982).

Hauck's book contains a section "The Many Deaths of Crockett."

David Lyons, "The Death of David Crockett" *Alamo Lore and Myth Organization Newsletter,* September 1982.

Bill Groneman, "Crockett's Last Stand" *Alamo Lore and Myth Organization Newsletter,* December 1982.

1985

Bill Groneman, "The Death of Davy Crockett" a chapter in Bill Groneman and Phil Rosenthal, *Roll Call at the Alamo* (Fort Collins, Colorado: Old Army Press, 1985).

Felton West, "How Crockett Died Still Stirs Furor" *Houston Post*, 22 November 1985.

1986

Gary L. Foreman, *Crockett: The Gentleman from the Cane* (Dallas: Taylor Publishing Co., 1986).

In this highly illustrated magazine-type publication, Foreman includes two pages devoted to "Crockett's Death: The Unending Controversy."

William Whitaker, "Alamo battle is 'racist myth,' according to university prof" *Del Rio (Texas) News-Herald*, 19 March 1986.

A short article on Paul A. Hutton and his beliefs concerning Crockett's death.

John Helyar, "Davy Crockett was no Great Shakes, The Debunkers Say" *Wall Street Journal*, 10 July 1986.

Barbara Paulsen, "Say It Ain't So, Davy" a sidebar to Paul Andrew Hutton, "Davy Crockett—Still King of the Wild Frontier" *Texas Monthly*, November 1986.

1987

Paul Andrew Hutton, Introduction to *A Narrative of the Life of David Crockett*, Written by Himself (Philadelphia: E.L. Carey and A. Hart, 1834; reprint, Lincoln, Nebraska and London: University of Nebraska Press, 1987).

David Lawrence Robbins, "David Crockett at the Alamo: An Analysis of His Death," 1987.

An unpublished manuscript that concludes that the evidence is in favor of Crockett's having died fighting at the Alamo.

1988

C.D. Huneycutt, *At The Alamo: The Memoirs of Capt. Navarro* (New London, North Carolina: Gold Star Press, 1988).

Huneycutt's translation of the Sanchez-Navarro account.

George A. McAlister, *Alamo: The Price of Freedom* (San Antonio: Docutex, Inc., 1988).

McAlister devoted twelve pages to the subject of "Crockett's Death by Various Authors."

1989

Paul Andrew Hutton, "An Exposition on Hero Worship" a chapter in Michael A. Lofaro, and Joe Cummings, eds. *Crockett at Two Hundred* (Knoxville, Tennessee: University of Tennessee Press, 1989).

Dan Kilgore, "Why Davy Didn't Die" a chapter in Michael A. Lofaro, and Joe Cummings, eds. *Crockett at Two Hundred* (Knoxville, Tennessee: University of Tennessee Press, 1989).

Nigel Hawkins, "How Did Davy Die? He Died Fighting!" *Alamo Journal*, December 1989.

1990

Stephen L. Hardin, "The Felix Nuñez Account and Siege of the Alamo: A Critical Appraisal" *Southwestern Historical Quarterly*, July 1990.

This is the first time the Nuñez account was published in its entirety since it first appeared in 1889.

Wallace O. Chariton, *Exploring the Alamo Legends* (Plano, Texas: Wordware Publishing, Inc., 1990).

Chariton includes a chapter, "Crockett vs. Kilgore, Santos, et al.: Davy's Last Fight"

Geoff Sutton, "Davy, Davy Crockett coward of the Wild Frontier" *Daily Mirror*, 23 August 1990.

Hyped-up tabloid article on Jeff Long's *Duel of Eagles*.

"Davee, Davy Crockett: Coward of the Wild Frontier—and Jim Bowie had a yellow streak, too" *The Star*, 11 September 1990.

Another hyped-up tabloid article concerning Long's book. This one describes Crockett and Bowie as "two cowboy legends."

1991

Dr. Todd E. Harburn, "The Crockett Death Controversy" *Alamo Journal*, April 1991.

Richard A. Davidson, "How Did Davy Really Die? *Alamo Journal*, October 1991.

1992

Chris Anderson, "How did Davy die? Does the cap tell the tale?" *Blackpowder Annual*, 1992.

Albert A. Nofi, *The Alamo and the Texas War of Independence, September 30, 1835 to April 21, 1836* (Conshohocken, Pennsylvania: Combined Books, 1992).

Nofi offers a small sidebar "The Death of Crockett," generally favoring Peña.

1993

Bill Groneman, "De La Peña and the Alamo Mystery Victim" *Alamo Journal*, February 1993.

Bill Groneman, "Some Problems with the Urriza Account" *Alamo Journal*, July 1993.

Bill Groneman, "A Witness to the Executions?" *Alamo Journal*, October 1993.

1994

Bill Groneman, *Defense of a Legend: Crockett and the de la Peña Diary* (Plano, Texas: Republic of Texas Press, 1994).

Bill Groneman, "The Diary of José Enrique de la Peña" *Journal of South Texas*, 1994.

Bill Groneman, "Some Problems with the Almonte Account" *Alamo Journal*, February 1994.

Charley Eckhardt, "Is the Alamo diary authentic or fake?" *Seguin (Texas) Gazette-Enterprise*, 31 March 1994.

Bruce Dettman, "Davy's Death: A Common Sense Approach" *Alamo Journal*, April 1994.

Charley Eckhardt, "Expert says de la Pena diary nothing but a fake" *Seguin (Texas) Gazette-Enterprise*, 6 April 1994.

Bill Groneman, "Some Comparisons to the de la Peña 'Diary'" *Alamo Journal*, July 1994.

James E. Crisp, "The Little Book That Wasn't There: The Myth and Mystery of the de la Peña Diary" *Southwestern Historical Quarterly*, October 1994.

1995

James E. Crisp, "Texas History—Texas Mystery" *Sallyport: The Magazine of Rice University*, February /March 1995.

Dan Goddard, "The Death of Davy Crockett—Rice Filmmaker Documents the Debate over Alamo Hero's Death" *San Antonio Express-News*, 5 March 1995.

Jan Reid, "Davy Crock?" *Texas Monthly*, May 1995.

Reid covers the controversy and Groneman's talk before the Texas State Historical Association in March of 1995.

Thomas Ricks Lindley, "Killing Crockett—It's All In The Execution" *Alamo Journal*, May 1995.

Thomas Ricks Lindley, "Killing Crockett—Theory Paraded as Fact" *Alamo Journal*, July 1995.

James Crisp, "Davy in Freeze-Frame: Methodology or Madness?" *Alamo Journal*, October 1995.

Thomas Ricks Lindley, "Killing Crockett—Lindley's Opinion" *Alamo Journal*, October 1995.

Bill Groneman, "The Controversial Alleged Account of José Enrique de la Peña" *Military History of the West*, Fall 1995.

This article was the text of the paper that Groneman gave before the Texas State Historical Association meeting in March of 1995.

James Crisp "When Revision Becomes Obsession: Bill Groneman and the de la Peña Diary" *Military History of the West*, Fall 1995.

This article was Crisp's response to Groneman's article.

Bill Groneman, "Publish or Perish—Regardless: Jim Crisp and the de la Peña 'Diary'" *Military History of the West*, Fall 1995.

This was Groneman's rejoinder to Crisp's response.

James Crisp, "Trashing Dolson: The Perils of Tendentious Interpretation" *Alamo Journal*, December 1995.

1996

James E. Crisp, "Back to Basics: Conspiracies, Common Sense, and Occam's Razor" *Alamo Journal*, March 1996.

Bill Groneman, "Crockett at the Alamo" [Letter to the Editor] *Wild West*, June 1996.

Dr. Todd E. Harburn, "If You Can Tolerate One More Comment On..." *Alamo Journal*, June 1996.

Bill Groneman, *Eyewitness to the Alamo* (Plano, Texas: Republic of Texas Press, 1996).

Groneman publishes all of the alleged eyewitness accounts of Crockett's death along with other accounts of the fall of the Alamo.

James Crisp [Letter to the Editor] *Alamo Journal*, September 1996.

Dean Musser, "Executions at the Alamo: Corroboration, Identification, and Speculation" *Alamo Journal*, December 1996.

Thomas Ricks Lindley, "Documents of the Texas Revolution" *Alamo Journal*, December 1996.

A letter from Peña to a friend, dated June 11, 1838.

James E. Crisp, "Truth, Confusion, and the de la Peña Controversy—A Final Reply" *Military History of the West*, Spring 1996.

A last word by Crisp that appeared in the journal's letters to the editor section.

Bill Groneman, "A Last Final Reply or, How I Learned to Stop Worrying and Love Jim Crisp" *Military History of the West*, Spring 1996.

A last word by Groneman in the same section as Crisp's above.

1997

Michael Lind, *The Alamo: An Epic* (Boston and New York: Houghton-Mifflin Company, 1997).

Lind includes three pages of information on Crockett's death as part of the appendix "On Epic" to his epic poem.

Garry Wills, "Remember the Alamo?" *New York Times Book Review*, 9 March 1997.

A review of Michael Lind's poem in which Wills accuses Lind of accepting "...the desperate claim of forgery [of the Peña account] though it has been definitively refuted by James Crisp."

Dan Rather, "Defending 'The Alamo'" [Letter to the Editor] *New York Times Book Review*, 30 March 1997.

Although this article really does not go into Crockett's death, it is an example of how the controversy continues to draw others into the fray.

Robert L. Durham, "*Where* Did Davy Die?" *Alamo Journal*, March 1997.

"How Did Davy Die?" BBC Radio 4, in London, 6 March 1997.

A radio interview concerning Crockett's death.

Rod Timanus, "Alamo Executions and David Crockett" *Alamo Journal*, September 1997.

Richard Davidson [Letter to the Editor] *Alamo Journal*, September 1997.

William C. Davis, "How Davy Probably Didn't Die" *Journal of the Alamo Battlefield Association*, Fall 1997.

"Crockett executed at Alamo: researcher" *Jackson Sun*, 16 November 1997.

This article focuses on Jim Crisp and his beliefs concerning Crockett's death.

Thomas Ricks Lindley, "José Enrique de la Peña's Petard" *Alamo Journal*, December 1997.

Allen Wiener [Letter to the Editor] *Alamo Journal*, December 1997.

James Crisp, Introduction to *With Santa Anna in Texas*, by Carmen Perry (College Station, Texas: Texas A&M University Press, 1997).

A new edition of *With Santa Anna in Texas* with Crisp's introduction replacing Llerena Friend's original. This version also includes the details of a "missing week" allegedly recorded by Peña but left out of Perry's original translation.

Paul Aron, *Unsolved Mysteries of American History* (New York: John Wiley & Sons, Inc., 1997).

Aron includes a chapter "How Did Davy Crockett Die?" the gist of which is that there is a Peña account and that Crockett died by execution according to the Peña account.

Dale Walker, *Legends and Lies: Great Mysteries of the American West* (New York: A Tom Doherty Associates Book, 1997).

Walker's first chapter is "The Day Davy Died—A Rendezvous at the Alamo."

1998

Michael Lind, "The Death of David Crockett" *Wilson Quarterly*, Winter 1998.

Bill Groneman, "De la Peña—the Man and The Myth" *Alamo Journal*, March 1998.

Bob Tutt, "Crockett's death mystery lives on" *Houston Chronicle*, 8 March 1998.

James Crisp, Bill Groneman, and Michael Lind, "Letters to the Editor" *Wilson Quarterly*, Spring 1998.

Dr. Todd E. Harburn, D.O., "The Crockett Death Controversy—A Brief Commentary and Opinion Regarding the Same," in Tim J. & Terry S. Todish, *Alamo Sourcebook 1836* (Austin: Eakin Press, 1998).

An updated version of Harburn's articles that appeared in *The Bexar Dispatch*, the newsletter of the San Antonio Living History Association (April 1990), and in the *Alamo Journal* (April 1991).

William C. Davis, *Three Roads to the Alamo* (New York: HarperCollins Publishers, 1998).

Davis includes a one and one-half page footnote on Crockett's death.

Bill Chemerka (William R.), "De La Peña Papers Sold for $350,000—Crockett Death Account Part of Collection" *Alamo Journal*, December 1998.

APPENDIX D

A Word About Forgeries

$\cdots\, \blacklozenge\, \cdots$

The idea of forgery is ludicrous.
—Gregory Shaw

IN HIS ARTICLE "The Little Book That Wasn't There" published in the *Southwestern Historical Quarterly*, Jim Crisp voiced many complaints about *Defense of a Legend*. One of these was that two chapters, "Texas Forgeries" and "Suspect Documents," were, in his opinion, irrelevant to the book and that they "...seemed to have been included for no more reason than to convince the reader that forgeries do take place and that suspicious documents do exist." Although I disagree with him about the relevancy of including chapters about forgeries in a book about a suspected forgery, I agree with him completely in his opinion as to why they were included. Forgeries do exist and have existed since ancient times. The legendary events and people of Texas history and the eagerness of people to buy documents about them have made Texas a lively field for forgeries in recent years. In 1989 a conference of scholars and documentary experts was convened at the University of Houston to address the question of forgeries and its impact on the academic and bibliographic world. A report of the Houston conference was published in Pat Bozeman's *Forged Documents: Proceedings of the 1989 Houston Conference*.

Forgeries, fakes, hoaxes, or whatever you wish to call them are not restricted to Texas. Nor are they restricted to documents. There need not be some great sinister purpose or criminal intent behind all forgeries, fakes, and hoaxes. Some have been launched with the best of intentions. All that is needed is a general willingness to play with the truth a little and a few people to believe. Sophisticated, well-educated, and intelligent people are often taken in by these scams. In fact, their cooperation is almost required in order for a good fake or forgery to take root.

What follows has nothing to do with the death of Davy Crockett, except that much of what we believe about the death of Crockett is based on the Peña account. My contention is that it is a fake. Most people are not that familiar with the subject of forgeries or fakes. In order to make a case for the Peña "diary" to be a forgery, you must show that such a possibility is not that far out. There are many interesting stories of forgeries, fakes, and hoaxes. With apologies to Jim Crisp, these are a few of my favorites.

$$\bullet \ \bullet \ \bullet \ \blacklozenge \ \bullet \ \bullet \ \bullet$$

Denis Vrain-Lucas
1860s

Vrain-Lucas forged a fabulous collection of letters and documents such as letters by: Alexander the Great; Attila the Hun; Herod; Judas Iscariot; Lazarus; Mary Magdalene; Pontius Pilate; Roger Bacon; Caligula; Nostrodamus; Pythagoras; Pliny the Younger; Plutarch; Dante; Cervantes; Shakespeare; Pompey; Archimedes; El Cid; Juvenal; Cicero; Ovid; De Vinci; Columbus; Charlemagne; and even love letters between Caesar and Cleopatra, to name just a few. The best part of these works were that they were written in modern French.

Motive:

Probably to make money. Maybe to change history.

True believer:

Michael Chasles, a member of the French Academy of Science and a professor of geometry at the Imperial Polytechnic of

Paris, bought 27,300 of these documents from Vrain-Lucas over the years.

Nice try:

Vrain-Lucas' attorney mounted a defense at his trial that an educated man like Chasles could not possibly have believed the documents he bought were intended as real.

See:

Kenneth W. Rendell, *Forging History: The Detection of Fake Letters and Documents* (Norman, Oklahoma, and London: University of Oklahoma Press, 1994), 57-58; and Charles Hamilton, *The Hitler Diaries: Fakes that Fooled the World* (Lexington, Kentucky: University Press of Kentucky, 1991), 115-122.

• • • ◆ • • •

The Piltdown Man
1912

Martin A.C. Hinton, later keeper of zoology at the British Museum from 1936 to 1945, attached an orangutan jaw to a human cranium, dipped it in acid, stained it with manganese and iron oxide, planted it in a gravel bed in Piltdown Common in England, and provided the world with fossil evidence of the "missing link" between ape and human.

Motive:

Possibly to embarrass the keeper of paleontology at the British Museum at the time who refused to put Hinton, a museum volunteer, on salary.

True believer:

Pierre Teilhard de Chardin, Jesuit priest, paleontologist, geologist, and philosopher.

Great quote:

> At the time in England we were hoping to find the earliest man. We didn't want the goddamn French or Germans [What, no Yankees?] to have it, we wanted it. People wanted to believe it.

—Brian Gardiner, Paleontologist of King's College, London, who along with his colleague, Andrew Currant, solved the mystery of who faked the skull

See:

Shanti Menon, "The piltdown perp.," *Discover*, January 1997, 18; and Frank Spencer, *Piltdown—A Scientific Forgery* (London, Oxford & New York: Natural History Museum Publications Oxford University Press, 1990).

• • • ◆ • • •

The Cottingly Fairies
1917

Two cousins, Elsie Wright and Francis Griffiths, cut out pictures of fairies from children's books, propped them up with hatpins, and posed with them in the woods of Cottingly in Yorkshire, England. With a borrowed camera the girls photographed one another with the cutouts, bringing proof of fairies to the world.

Motive:

Girls just want to have fun.

True believer:

Arthur Conan Doyle wrote about the incident in a 1922 book *The Coming of the Fairies*, but he admitted that the photos might be hoaxes.

Great quote:

... with fuller knowledge and with fresh means of vision these people [the fairies] are destined to become just as solid as the Eskimoes.
—Arthur Conan Doyle

See:

Vicki Goldberg, "Of Fairies, Free Spirits and Outright Frauds," *New York Times*, 1 February 1998, 48.

• • • ◆ • • •

The Horn Papers
1932

These papers detail the exploration and settlement of Washington and Greene Counties in western Pennsylvania. The information supposedly came from diaries written on birch bark and old linen and hidden away in a family chest of W.F. Horn. The diaries were reported destroyed shortly after their discovery, but luckily, Horn had already reproduced them by hand. These papers have been described as unique due to the quantity of "collateral artifacts advanced to substantiate them." The papers later were proven to be fakes.

Motive:

No one knows.

True believers:

A.L. Moredock, president of the Greene County Historical Society; the members of the Greene County Historical Society, which published the papers; and the *Waynesburg (Pennsylvania) Democrat Messenger*, and the *Washington (Pennsylvania) Observer*, which published excerpts from them.

Great touch:

The papers mentioned metal plates that had been buried by the French to mark territorial claims in 1751. If the plates were discovered, it would have verified the papers. An archaeological dig was conducted using a Horn map. Besides the archaeologist and WPA diggers, W.F. Horn also was on hand. The plates were discovered, by Horn, during a two-hour period while the director of the dig was absent. Horn rushed to a creek to wash the plates clean, thus destroying any archeological evidence that would have been on them had they really been buried. When the director returned and wanted to take photos of the spot, it developed that Horn could not quite remember where he had found them. No one chided Horn, because he was "skipping and dancing about like a kid."

See:

Arthur Pierce Middleton and Douglass Adair, "The Mystery of the Horn Papers," *William and Mary Quarterly* IV (October 1947): 409-445; and Dave Molten, "How the little man from Kansas staged 'The Great Hornswoggle.'" Unidentified newspaper 7 May 1989.

· · · ◆ · · ·

The Howard Hughes Autobiography
1972

Clifford Irving attempted one of the more daring forgeries in history by faking a 230,000-word autobiography of someone who was still living. Irving included forged Hughes authorization letters and verifications to support the autobiography. After the hoax was exposed, Irving spent seventeen months in prison.

Motive:

Possibly the $750,000 advance he and his wife received for the manuscript.

True believers:

McGraw-Hill publishers, which paid the $750,000.

Great quote:

... once you do a page, you can do 20. Once you do 20, you can do a book.

—Clifford Irving (commenting on the Hitler diaries)

· · · ◆ · · ·

Roots
1972

Alex Haley's landmark book traces his family's roots back to Africa. The book is a novel but Doubleday Books published it as nonfiction. As it turned out, Haley "borrowed" much of the plot from one, possibly two, other novels, *The African* by Harold Courlander and *Jubilee* by Margaret Walker. Haley paid Courlander an out-of-court settlement of $650,000, but Walker's copyright suit was dismissed by the court.

Motive:

Possibly to produce a more interesting book when the facts just did not do the job.

True believers:

Doubleday Books, the Pulitzer Prize Committee, and everyone who enjoyed the book or the television miniseries upon which it was based.

Great quote:

> *Roots* is a book that has had tremendous impact on its readers. Whether the book is fiction or nonfiction is not a concern of the greater world. Its impact is emotional rather than factual, which is why the book remains enduring.
>
> —Stuart Applebaum (Doubleday Books, senior vice president and director of public relations)

See:

Calvin Reid, "Fact or Fiction? Hoax Charges Still Dog 'Roots' 20 Years On," *Publishers Weekly*, 6 October 1997; Stanley Crouch, "The Roots of Alex Haley's Fraud," *New York Daily News*, 12 April 1998.

$$\cdots \blacklozenge \cdots$$

The Hitler Diaries
1983

Petty criminal and authenticator of World War II memorabilia Konrad Kujau perpetrated one of the most well-known cases of forgery in recent times. His sixty-two volumes of Adolph Hitler's personal diaries caught the attention of the world. At one point he was producing three of these volumes per month. The sheer volume of the material caused some experts to believe they were authentic. He also forged material to authenticate the forged material. The cheap journal books, replete with official-looking red wax seals and black ribbons, were soon exposed as fakes, and Kujau was eventually sentenced to four and a half years in prison.

Motive:

Possibly the equivalent of 4.1 million dollars that was paid for the diaries.

True believers:

Many, but most notably Peter Koch, editor of *Stern Magazine*, journalist Gerd Heidemann, who also was sentenced to prison, and Hitler scholar Hugh Trevor-Roper.

Great quote:

> I expected the uproar and expected that many incompetent people would denounce the diaries as fakes. This is because everybody is jealous of us and every historian will envy us.
>
> —Peter Koch, editor of *Stern*

See:

Charles Hamilton, *The Hitler Diaries: Fakes that Fooled the World* (Lexington, Kentucky: University Press of Kentucky, 1991), and Walter Goodman, "The Forger and the Führer," *New York Times Book Review*, 7 July 1991, 3.

• • • ◆ • • •

The Liberators
1992

This is the inspiring story of the all-black 761st Tank Battalion of the U.S. Army liberating the prisoners of the Dachau and Buchenwald concentration camps at the end of World War II. The story was told in a documentary that premiered at the famed Apollo Theater in Harlem in 1992. The story is also recounted in a book by the same name. The only problem was that although the 761st battalion had a distinguished combat record, they had nothing to do with the liberation of Dachau and Buchenwald and were miles away from the camps when they were liberated. The truth only came out when veterans of the 761st, proud of their real combat record and not feeling the need for fiction to enhance it, began to speak out.

Motive:

At the time of its premier the story was seen as a spiritual link between the Black and Jewish communities of New York City, whose relationship was at an all-time low.

True believers:

The glitterati of the New York City political and ethnic communities and just about everyone else, except, of course, the veterans of the 761st Tank Battalion and the survivors of the Dachau and Buchenwald concentration camps.

Great quote:

There are a lot of truths that are very necessary.
This is not a truth that's necessary.

- Peggy Tishman, a co host of the documentary's premier at the Apollo

See:

Eric Breindel "Concocting History," *New York Post*, 6 February 1993; and Stephen J. Dubner, "Massaging History," *New York Magazine*, 8 March 1993, 46-51

$$\cdots \blacklozenge \cdots$$

Jack the Ripper's Diary
1993

Scrap dealer Mike Barrett presented the world with the diary of the most infamous serial killer of all time in 1992. His story was that he received the diary from a friend, Tony Devereux, who had since died and never revealed where he had gotten it. The Ripper was identified as James Maybrick. All handwriting and forensic experts, including Kenneth Rendell, who examined the diary declared it to be a fake or expressed their belief in that possibility. Barrett later confessed to forging it.

Motive:

Probably for financial gain and possibly for the fun of tampering with history.

True believers:

Robert Smith, head of Smith Gryphon, who published the "diary" in Great Britian; Shirley Harrison, who wrote the narrative portion of the book; and Hyperion Books, which published it in the United States.

Great quote:

> Kenneth Rendell's report on the diary of Jack the Ripper is fundamentally flawed, inaccurate, and unreliable.
>
> —Robert Smith of Smith Gryphon Publishers

See:

Rendell, *Forging History*, 141-154; Shirley Harrison, *The Diary of Jack the Ripper* (New York: Hyperion, 1993); and Hamilton, *Great Forgers*, xiii.

· · · ◆ · · ·

Noah's Ark
1993

A Sun International Pictures production aired on CBS. It showed George Jammal claiming that he visited Mount Ararat. He displayed a weathered piece of wood, purported to be from Noah's ark, and proclaimed it a "gift from God." It was later determined that Jammal was a part-time actor, he had never been to Mount Ararat, and the wood was a piece of modern pine "soaked with various juices and baked in an oven."

Motive:

Probably the money to be made from having a television show air on CBS.

True believers:

CBS for a time and possibly any of the 20 million people who watched the show.

Great quotes:

> When we bought the special, it was as an entertainment special, not a documentary.
>
> —Unidentified CBS spokeswoman

...the show never purported the wood was from the ark, only that this person on the show said it was.

—Susan Tich, identified CBS spokeswoman

See:

Howard Rosenberg, "'Ark' Special sinks CBS' Reputation," *New York Post*, 8 July 1993; "CBS won't air 'Noah' correction," *New York Post*; Eric Mink, "How CBS bought into Noah's malarkey," *New York Daily News*, 7 December 1993.

Notes

The following abbreviations will be used in these notes and sources:

BRBML   Bieneke Rare Book and Manuscript Library, Yale University, New Haven, Connecticut

CAH   Center for American History, University of Texas at Austin

DRTL   Daughters of the Republic of Texas Library at the Alamo, San Antonio

GLO   Texas General Land Office

NLB   Nettie Lee Benson Latin American Collection, University of Texas at Austin

TSA   Texas State Archives

UTA   University of Texas at Austin

· · · ◆ · · ·

Chapter 1—Davy Crockett and the Alamo

1   Mark Derr, *The Frontiersman: The Real Life and the Many Legends of Davy Crockett* (New York: William Morrow and Co., Inc., 1993).

2   "The Alamo by Dr. Sutherland," John S. Ford Papers, CAH. For other versions of Sutherland's account, see *Dallas Morning News*, 5 and 12 February 1911; James T. DeShields, *Tall Men with Long Rifles* (San Antonio: The Naylor Co., 1935), 150-168; Dr. John Sutherland, *The Fall of the Alamo*, ed. by Annie B. Sutherland (San Antonio: The Naylor Co., 1936); and Howard R. Driggs and Sarah S. King, *Rise of the Lone Star* (New York: Frederick A. Stokes Co., 1936), 199-212.

3   Thomas Ricks Lindley, "The revealing of Dr. John Sutherland," DRTL, San Antonio, Texas.

4   James M. Morphis, *History of Texas from its Discovery and Settlement* (New York: United States Publishing Company, 1875),

174-177; William Corner, editor and compiler, *San Antonio de Bexar: A Guide and History* (San Antonio: Bainbridge & Corner, 1890), 117-119.

5 William B. Travis to Sam Houston, 25 February 1836, printed in the *Arkansas Gazette* April 12, 1836.

6 Thomas Ricks Lindley, "Davy Crockett: The Alamo's High Private," *Alamo Journal* 64 (December 1988): 3-11.

7 "Testimony of Mrs. Hannig Touching on the Alamo Massacre," 23 September 1876, TSA.

8 Morphis, *History of Texas*, 174-175.

9 Ibid., 175.

10 "Story of Enrique Esparza," *San Antonio Express*, 22 November 1902.

11 Charles Merritt Barnes, "Alamo's Only Survivor," *San Antonio Express*, 12 and 19 May 1907.

12 "Alamo Massacre—as told by the Late Madam Candaleria [sic]," *San Antonio Light*, 22 February 1899.

13 "Children of the Alamo," *Houston Chronicle*, 9 November 1901; Barnes, "The Alamo's Only Survivor"; and "Memoirs of John S. Ford—1815-1836," CAH.

14 DeShields, *Tall Men*, 184.

15 John Gadsby Chapman, *David Crockett*, oil on canvas, date unknown, Harry Ransom Humanities Research Center, UTA. This painting appears on the cover of *Southwestern Historical Quarterly* 98 (October 1994).

16 Juan Valentine Amador to the Generals, Chiefs of sections, and commanding officers, 5 March 1836, Archivo General de Mexico Papers, CAH, printed in John H. Jenkins, ed., *Papers of the Texas Revolution 1835-1836* Vol. 4 (Austin: Presidial Press, 1973), 518-519; and Antonio Lopez de Santa Anna to Jose Maria Tornel, 6 March 1836, printed in Jenkins, *Papers* Vol. 5, 11-12.

17 Antonio Lopez de Santa Anna to General Urrea, Commander, &c., 3 March 1836, in Jenkins, ed., *Papers* Vol. 4, 501; Santa Anna to General Joaquin Ramirez y Sesma, 29 February 1836, in *Papers* Vol. 4, 469; and William B. Travis To the People of Texas & All Americans in the World, 24 February 1836, TSA.

18 John A. Keegan, *A History of Warfare* (New York: Alfred A. Knopf, 1993), 322-323.

19 Thomas Ricks Lindley, "James Butler Bonham—October 17, 1835-March 6, 1836," *Alamo Journal* 62 (August 1988): 3-11; and Joe's account in Correspondence of the Fredericksburg Arena, "Letter from Texas," *Frankfort (Kentucky) Commonwealth*, 25 May 1836.

20 Thomas Ricks Lindley, "Alamo Artillery—Number, Type, Caliber and Concussion," *Alamo Journal* 82 (July 1992): 3-10.

21 Joe's account in "Letter from Texas."

22 Santa Anna to Tornel, 6 March 1836, in Jenkins, *Papers* Vol. 5, 11-12.

23 Ford, "Memoirs of John S. Ford."

24 "Extract of a Letter from a Friend to the Editor," *New Orleans Commercial Bulletin*, 11 April 1836, printed in the *Portland (Maine) Advertiser*, 3 May 1836; and Correspondence of the Fredericksburg Arena, "Letter from Texas."

25 Barnes, "Alamo's Only Survivor."

26 *San Antonio Express*, 22 November 1902.

27 See Bill Groneman, *Eyewitness to the Alamo* (Plano, Texas: Republic of Texas Press, 1996), 52.

28 There are a variety of spellings for the names of these two men. I use the spellings as they appear on a list of names of Tejanos who took part in one or more of the actions in the Texas Revolution. This list appears in Daughters of the Republic of Texas, *The Alamo: Long Barrack Museum* (Dallas: Taylor Publishing Co., 1986), 11. In other sources their names are spelled Anselmo Borgara, Ansolma Bergara, Anselmo Bergara, Anselmo Vergara, Andres Barcena, Andrew Barsena, Andrew Bagara, Andres Barcinas, and Andres Barsena.

29 Barcena et al Deposition, 11 March 1836; Letter by E.N. Gray, 11 March 1836; Sam Houston, Gonzales, Texas, to James W. Fannin, 11 March 1836, printed in Jenkins, *Papers* Vol. 5, 45, 48, 52, and 53.

30 "Witnessed Last Struggle of the Alamo Patriots," *San Antonio Express*, 19 July 1907.

31 Benjamin Briggs Goodrich, Washington, Texas, to Edmund Goodrich, Nashville, Tennessee, March 15, 1836, printed in Jenkins, *Papers* Vol. 5, 81. This theory was first developed by Alamo researchers Craig Covner and Nina Rosenstand of California.

32 Jerry J. Gaddy, *Texas in Revolt* (Fort Collins, Colorado: Old Army Press, 1973), 47.

33 Ibid., 49.

34 William Parker to the Editor of the *Free Trader*, printed in Jenkins, *Papers* Vol. 6, 122.

35 *Morning Courier and New York Enquirer*, 26 March 1836; *Stamford (Connecticut) Sentinel*, 28 March 1836; and *Monroe (New York) Democrat*, 5 April 1836.

36 Gaddy, *Texas in Revolt*, 52.

37 John H. Jenkins, "Did Davy Crockett Survive the Alamo?," *Texana* 1 (Summer 1963): 284-87.

38 *Denver Times*, 15 April 1912; *Brooklyn Daily Eagle*, 15 April 1912; and *New York Herald*, 15 April 1912.

39 Joseph Gustaitis, "There's No Mistake in Sam Patch," *American History Illustrated*, January/February 1991, 74; Brian McGinty, "They Never Found His Bones," *American History Illustrated*, January/February 1990, 57; Walter Lord, *A Night To Remember* (New York: Bantam Books, 1988), 78, 102-103; and Marc Shapiro, *Total Titanic* (New York: Pocket Books, 1998), 101.

40 For examples of some of these legendary departures and/or reappearances, see Dale L. Walker, *Legends and Lies: Great Mysteries of the American West* (New York: A Tom Doherty Associates Book, 1997); W.C. Jameson, *Return of Assassin John Wilkes Booth* (Plano, Texas: Republic of Texas Press, 1998); *Unsolved Mysteries of the Old West* (Plano, Texas: Republic of Texas Press, 1999); and W.C. Jameson and Frederic Bean, *The Return of the Outlaw Billy the Kid* (Plano, Texas: Republic of Texas Press, 1997).

Chapter 2—Execution

1   See Bill Groneman, *Eyewitness to the Alamo*, 25-28.

2 "Extract of a Letter from a Friend to the Editor," *New Orleans Commercial Bulletin*, 11 April 1836, printed in the *Portland (Maine) Advertiser*, 3 May 1836; and Correspondence of the Fredericksburg Arena, "Letter from Texas," *Frankfort (Kentucky) Commonwealth*, 25 May 1836.

3 Morphis, *History of Texas*, 177; "Another Story of the Alamo—The Battle Described by an Alleged Eyewitness," *San Antonio Express*, 12 April 1896.

4 "More Particulars Respecting the Fall of the Alamo," *Telegraph and Texas Register*, 24 March 1836.

5 See Bill Groneman, *Defense of a Legend: Crockett and the de la Peña Diary* (Plano, Texas: Republic of Texas Press, 1994), 77-84.

6 Paul Andrew Hutton, "Davy Crockett—An Exposition on Hero Worship," in Michael A. Lofaro and Joe Cummings, eds. *Crockett at Two Hundred* (Knoxville, Tennessee: University of Tennessee Press, 1989), 35.

7 Richard Boyd Hauck, *Crockett: A Bio-Bibliography* (Westport, Connecticut and London: Greenwood Press, 1982), 52. Richard Boyd Hauck is Abe Levin, Professor of Humanities at the University of West Florida at Pensacola; Stephen L. Hardin, "David Crockett," *Military Illustrated: Past & Present*, February/March 1990, 35; Paul A. Hutton, "Davy Crockett—Still King of the Wild Frontier," *Texas Monthly*, November 1986, 122, 246; "An Exposition on Hero Worship," in *Crockett at Two Hundred*, 34, 39 (footnote); Introduction to *A Narrative of the Life of David Crockett*, Written by Himself, (Philadelphia: E.L. Carey and A. Hart, 1834; reprint, Lincoln, Nebraska and London: University of Nebraska Press, 1987), xxxiii (page reference is to reprint edition).

8 Dan Kilgore, *How Did Davy Die?* (College Station, Texas and London: Texas A&M University Press, 1978), 16, 35, and 47.

9 Ibid., 22

10 *Morning Courier and New York Enquirer*, 9 July 1836.

11 Billings Hayward, New York to David G. Burnet Esq., Texas, 4 March 1836, printed in Jenkins, *Papers* Vol. 4, 511-12.

12 Oliver Carlson, *The Man Who Made News: James Gordon Bennett* (New York: Duell, Sloan and Pearce, 1942), 179.

13 Ramón Martinez Caro, *Verdadera Idea de la Primera Campaña de Tejas y Sucesos Ocurridos después de la accion de San Jacinto*

(Mexico: Imprenta de Santiago Perez, 1837), printed in Carlos E. Castañeda, *The Mexican Side of the Texas Revolution* (Dallas: P.L. Turner Co., 1928; reprint, New York: Arno Press, 1976), 101-104.

14 Samuel Swartwout, New York to Colonel James Morgan, New Washington, Texas, 20 April 1837, in Feris A. Bass Jr., and B.R. Brunson, eds., *Fragile Empires: The Texas Correspondence of Samuel Swartwout and James Morgan 1836-1856* (Austin: Shoal Creek Publishers, Inc., 1978).

15 Thomas Ricks Lindley, "Killing Crockett: Lindley's Opinion," *Alamo Journal* 98 (October 1995): 9-24; and James E. Crisp, "Back to Basics: Conspiracies, Common Sense, and Occam's Razor," *Alamo Journal* 100 (March 1996): 17-18. I do not know what carries more weight in Jim's argument—the idea of government employment in Washington, D.C., as proof of reliability and accuracy, or his use of three exclamation marks in three sentences. One can almost hear the mad scientist laughter: "Ha! Ha Ha! Ha Ha Ha!"

16 George M. Dolson, Galveston Island to his brother, Detroit, 19 July 1836, printed in the *Detroit Democratic Free Press*, 7 September 1836.

17 Kilgore, *How Did Davy Die?*, 37, footnote 36; and James E. Crisp, "The Little Book That Wasn't There: The Myth and Mystery of the de la Peña Diary" *Southwestern Historical Quarterly* 98 (October 1994): 287-88.

18 James E. Crisp, "Trashing Dolson: The Perils of Tendentious Interpretation," *Alamo Journal* 99 (December 1995): 8-9; and "Little Book That Wasn't There," 291.

19 Crisp, "Trashing Dolson," 3-6.

20 Samuel Swartwout, New York to James Morgan, Galveston Island, 29 June 1836, James Morgan Papers, Rosenburg Library, Galveston, Texas, printed in Jenkins, *Papers* Vol. 7, 311; Walter Lord, *A Time to Stand* (New York: Harper & Row Publishers, 1961), 209; Katherine W. Ellison and Robert Buckhout, *Psychology and Criminal Justice* (New York: Harper & Row Publishers, 1981), 111-112; Margaret Swett Henson, "Politics and the Treatment of the Mexican Prisoners after the Battle of San Jacinto," *Southwestern Historical Quarterly* 94 (October 1990): 190; and Walter Prescott Webb, ed., *The Handbook of Texas* Vol. II (Austin: Texas State Historical Assoc., 1952), 234.

21 Henson, "Treatment of Mexican Prisoners," 189-230.

22 *Detroit Democratic Free Press*, 9 November 1836, printed in Tim J. and Terry S. Todish, *Alamo Sourcebook 1836: A Comprehensive Guide to the Alamo and the Texas Revolution* (Austin: Eakin Press, 1998), 145.

23 Casey Edward Green CA, Archivist, Rosenburg Library, Galveston, to Bill Groneman, New York, 23 August 1991, original in possession of the author.

24 Labadie, "San Jacinto Campaign" in James M. Day, compiler, *The Texas Almanac 1857-1873: A Compendium of Texas History* (Waco, Texas: Texian Press, 1967), 175; Groneman, *Defense of a Legend*, 51-54; and Bill Groneman, "Some Problems with the Urriza Account," *Alamo Journal* 87 (July 1993): 6-7.

25 Hutton, introduction to *A Narrative of the Life of David Crockett*, liii.

26 Sylvia Van Voast Ferris and Eleanor Sellers Hoppe, *Scalpels and Sabers: Nineteenth Century Medicine in Texas* (Austin: Eakin Press, 1985), 76, 94, and 95.

27 Ferris and Hoppe, *Scalpels and Sabers*, 145; and Webb, ed., *Handbook of Texas*, Vol. II, 1.

28 [John S. Ford], "The Fall of the Alamo," *Texas Mute Ranger*, April 1882, 168-172.

29 Lord, *A Time to Stand*, 119; Kilgore, *How Did Davy Die?*, 24, 25 31; and Dan Kilgore, introduction to Francisco Becerra, *A Mexican Sergeant's Recollections of the Alamo & San Jacinto* (Austin: Jenkins Publishing Co., 1980), 8.

30 Francisco Becerra, *A Mexican Sergeant's Recollections of the Alamo & San Jacinto*, 13.

31 John S. Ford, *Origins and Fall of the Alamo* (San Antonio: Johnson Brothers Printing Co., 1900; reprint, Austin: Shelly Publishers, n.d.), 21 (page reference is to reprint edition); Ellison and Buckhout, *Psychology and Criminal Justice*, 106-110.

32 W.P. Zuber, Iola, Texas, to Charlie Jeffries, Winkler, Texas, 17 August 1904, printed in Charlie Jeffries, "Inventing Stories About the Alamo," in J. Frank Dobie, et al, eds., *In the Shadow of History* (Austin: Texas Folklore Society, 1939, reprint, Detroit: Folklore Associates, 1971), 42-47.

33 Carlos Sanchez-Navarro [y Peón], *La Guerra de Tejas: Memorias de un Soldado* (Mexico: Editorial Polis, 1938), 151-152. Translation by Bill Groneman.

34 José Juan Sanchez-Navarro, "Ayudantia de Inspeccion de Nuevo León y Tamaulipas," NLB; Carlos Sanchez-Navarro y Peón, *La Guerra de Tejas: Memorias de un Soldado* (Mexico: Editorial Polis, 1938); Lon Tinkle, *13 Days to Glory: The Siege of the Alamo* (New York, Toronto & London: McGraw-Hill Book Co., Inc., 1958), 249; Helen Hunnicutt, "A Mexican View of the Texas War: Memoirs of a Veteran of the Two Battles of the Alamo," *Library Chronicle of the University of Texas* 4 (Summer 1951): 59-74; and Charles H. Harris, *A Mexican Family Empire: The Latifundio of the Sanchez-Navarros, 1765-1867* (Austin & London: University of Texas Press, 1975), xxviii.

35 Groneman, *Defense*, 63, 95-98, 101-106, and 146; *Eyewitness*, 19-21, 188-191; and Jane Garner, Archivist, UTA to Bill Groneman, New York, 15 July 1991; Ralph L. Elder, Barker Texas History Center to Bill Groneman, New York, 15 July, 26 October 1991, originals in possession of the author; and A. Moffit, Librarian of the UTA to Dr. T.S. Painter, President of the UTA, 15 November 1950, original in the University of Texas President's Office Records, Austin.

36 J. Sanchez Garza, *La Rebelion de Texas: Manuscrito Inedito de 1836 por un Oficial de Santa Anna* (Mexico: A. Frank de Sanchez, 1955), 58-71. Translation by Bill Groneman. In translating this I have tried to keep the translation as literal as possible. For a variation on this translation, see Carmen Perry, trans. and ed., *With Santa Anna in Texas—A Personal Narrative of the Revolution by José Enrique de la Peña* Expanded Edition (College Station, Texas: Texas A&M University Press, 1997), 43-56.

37 The account of Antonio Cruz y Arocha, box SM-2, Gentilz Collection, DRTL.

• • • ◆ • • •

Chapter 3—Died Fighting

1 Corner, *San Antonio de Bexar*, 117-119.

2 James A. Shackford, *David Crockett: The Man and the Legend* (Chapel Hill, North Carolina: University of North Carolina Press, 1956; reprint, Westport, Connecticut: Greenwood Press, 1981),

229; and Lowell H. Harrison, "David Crockett," *American History Illustrated* 6 (July 1971), 30.

3   "Alamo Massacre" *San Antonio Light*, 22 February 1899.

4   Felix Nuñez, "Fall of the Alamo," *Fort Worth Gazette*, 23 June 1889.

5   Jeff Long, *Duel of Eagles: The Mexican and U.S. Fight for the Alamo* (New York: William Morrow and Co., Inc., 1990), 105; and Alex Shoumatoff, *Legends of the American Desert: Sojourns in the Greater Southwest* (New York: Alfred A. Knopf, 1997), 287.

6   Joseph Milton Nance, *Attack and Counterattack* (Austin: University of Texas Press, 1964), 174.

7   DeShields, *Tall Men*, 184-185.

8   Ibid., 180.

9   Barnes, "Alamo's Only Survivor."

10 Francis Antonio Ruiz, "Fall of the Alamo and Massacre of Travis and His Brave Associates," *Texas Almanac* (1860), 80-81.

11 William C. Davis, "How Davy Probably Didn't Die," *Journal of the Alamo Battlefield Association*, 2 (Fall 1997): 31. For a pricey membership fee the Alamo Battlefield Association's "president" provides an occasional newsletter and a sometimes annual journal.

12 Davis cites the Ramirez y Sesma report, Expediente XI/481.3/1149, Archivo Historico Mexicano Militar, Mexico City, in William C. Davis, *Three Roads to the Alamo* (New York: HarperCollins Publishers, Inc., 1998), 562-563.

13 Davis, "How Davy Probably Didn't Die," 35.

• • • ◆ • • •

Chapter 4—Other Deaths—Other Mysteries

1   Jenkins, *Papers*, Vol. 5, 48.

2   Ibid., 71.

3   Ibid., 81.

4   Richard G. Santos, "Alamo Countdown," *San Antonio Express-News*, 8 March 1989.

5   *El Mosquito Mexicano*, 5 April 1836. For a slight variation in this translation, see John F. Rios, compiler and editor, *Readings on the Alamo* (New York: Vantage Press, Inc., 1987), 116.

6   "Extract of a Letter from a Friend to the Editor," *New Orleans Commercial Bulletin*, 11 April 1836, printed in the *Portland (Maine) Advertiser*, 3 May 1836.

7   Correspondent of the Fredericksburg Arena, "Letter from Texas," *Frankfort (Kentucky) Commonwealth*, 25 May 1836.

8   Ruiz, "Fall of the Alamo and Massacre of Travis and His Brave Associates," 80-81.

9   Morphis, *History of Texas*, 177.

10 [Ford], "The Fall of the Alamo," 170.

11 "Santa Anna's Last Effort," *San Antonio Express*, 23 June 1878.

12 Felix Nuñez, "Fall of the Alamo," *Fort Worth Gazette*, 23 June 1889.

13 "Alamo Massacre," *San Antonio Light*, 22 February 1899.

14 Carlos Sanchez-Navarro [y Peón], *La Guerra de Tejas: Memorias de un Soldado* (Mexico: Editorial Polis, 1938), 151. Translation by Bill Groneman.

15 Garza, *La Rebelion*, 67. Translation by Bill Groneman.

16 Jenkins, *Papers*, Vol. 5, 48.

17 Ibid., 53.

18 Ibid., 71.

19 Ibid., 81.

20 A. Briscoe to Editor of the *Red River Herald*, 16 March 1836, DRTL.

21 *El Mosquito Mexicano*, 5 April 1836.

22 Ruiz, "Fall of the Alamo."

23 Morphis, *History of Texas*, 177.

24 "Santa Anna's Last Effort," *San Antonio Express*.

25 *Houston Daily Post*, 1 March 1882, printed in Andrew Jackson Sowell, *Rangers and Pioneers of Texas* (San Antonio: n.p., 1884), 146-149; and in Edward G. Rohrbough, "How Jim Bowie Died," in Dobie, *In the Shadow of History*, 48-52.

26 Corner, *San Antonio de Bexar*, 117.

27 "Fall of the Alamo—Historical Reminiscences of the Aged Madam Candelaria," *San Antonio Express*, 6 March 1892.

28 Mary A. Maverick, *The Fall of the Alamo* (n.p.: n.p., 1898).

29 "Alamo Massacre," *San Antonio Light*.

30 Barnes, "Alamo's Only Survivor."

31 Sanchez-Navarro [y Peón], *La Guerra de Tejas*, 151.

32 Jenkins, *Papers* Vol. 5, 52-54.

33 Reuben M. Potter, *The Fall of the Alamo: A Reminiscence of the Revolution of Texas* (San Antonio: Herald Steam Press, 1860), 11-12.

34 Morphis, *History of Texas*, 176.

35 Reuben M. Potter, "The Fall of the Alamo," *Magazine of American History*, January 1878; reprinted in book form (Hillsdale: New Jersey: The Otterden Press, 1977), 35 and 38.

36 "Dusty Attic Brings Forth Epic Story of Mrs. Dickinson. Her Photo Found by History Professor," *San Antonio Express* (n.d.) 1929.

37 "The Survivor of the Alamo," *San Antonio Express*, 28 April 1881.

38 Nuñez, "Fall of the Alamo," *Fort Worth Gazette*.

39 Corner, *San Antonio de Bexar*, 117.

40 Rena Maverick Green, ed., *Memoirs of Mary A. Maverick* (San Antonio: Alamo Printing Co., 1921), 135.

41 Driggs and King, *Rise of the Lone Star*, 223.

42 Garza, *La Rebelion*, 69.

43 Parker to Editor of the *Free Trader*.

44 Morphis, *History of Texas*, 176.

45 "Testimony of Mrs. Hannig touching on the Alamo Massacre," 23 September 1876, TSA.

46 "Dusty Attic Brings Forth Epic Story of Mrs. Dickinson," *San Antonio Express*.

47 "The Survivor of the Alamo," *San Antonio Express*.

48 Green, ed., *Memoirs of Mary A. Maverick*, 136.

49 Potter, *Fall of the Alamo*, 12.

50 *El Mosquito Mexicano*, 5 April 1836.

51 [Ford] "Fall of the Alamo," 170.

52 John Myers Myers, *The Alamo* (New York: E.P. Dutton & Co., Inc., 1948); Tinkle, *13 Days to Glory*, 221; and Lord, *A Time to Stand*, 174.

53 Hutton, "Davy Crockett—Still King of the Wild Frontier," 245-46.

54 Shoumatoff, *Legends of the American Desert*, 287.

• • • ◆ • • •

Chapter 5—José Enrique de la Peña and His Diary

1 "¡Recuerda el Alamo!," *American Heritage Magazine*, October 1975, 57; and Jeff Long, *Duel of Eagles*, 135.

2 Perry, *With Santa Anna*, xiii; and Long, *Duel of Eagles*, 135.

3 Garza, *La Rebelion*, xxv.

4 Ibid., 240-46.

5 José Enrique de la Peña, *Una Víctima del Despotismo* (Mexico: Imprenta del Iris, 1839), Manuscripts and Archives Department, Sterling Memorial Library, Yale University, New Haven, Connecticut.

6 James Presley, "Santa Anna in Texas: A Mexican Viewpoint," *Southwestern Historical Quarterly* 62 (April 1959): 489-512; Lord, *A Time to Stand*, 66, 150, 151, 162, 164, 165, 206; Tinkle, *13 Days to Glory*, 249; and "Crockett's Death at the Alamo Doubted," *New York Times*, 21 September 1975. For an example of how the Peña account is used for dramatic effect, see Stephen L. Hardin, *Texian Iliad: A Military History of the Texas Revolution* (Austin: University of Texas Press, 1994), 95, 101, 103, 104, 115, 129, 136, 148-49, 201-202, 216, 277.

7 Dora Guerra, San Antonio, to Bill Groneman, New York, 14 May 1991, original in possession of the author.

8 Clyde Hubbard, Cuernavaca, Mexico, to Bill Groneman, New York, 18 January 1992 and 17 March 1992, originals in possession of the author.

9 Hubbard to Groneman, 18 January 1992 and 20 April 1992, originals in possession of the author; and *Sociedad Numismatica de Mexico Boletin* Vol. 1 (October 1952).

10 Hubbard to Groneman, 10 February 1993, original in possession of the author. In bringing out this information I was accused of slandering Garza and told that the "...presentation of

anonymous, hearsay evidence...has no place in this process." It was not my purpose to slander Garza, but I believe that this information is relevant in the evaluation of the Peña account as authentic, or at least in evaluating its murky past. See James E. Crisp, "When Revision Becomes Obsession: Bill Groneman and the de la Peña Diary," *Military History of the West* 25 (Fall 1995), 151.

11 Charlette Phelan, "Carmen Perry—The Davy Crockett Affray," *Houston Post* 4 April 1976; and "Crockett furor simmers," *San Antonio Express-News*, 26 October 1975.

· · · ◆ · · ·

Chapter 6—The Peña Account as a Fake

1   Kenneth W. Rendell, *Forging History: The Detection of Fake Letters and Documents* (Norman, Oklahoma, and London: University of Oklahoma Press, 1994), i; and Charles Hamilton, *Great Forgers and Famous Fakes: The Manuscript Forgers of America and How They Duped the Experts* (New York: Crown Publishers, Inc., 1980; reprint, Lakewood, Colorado: Glenbridge Publishing Ltd., 1996), 257 (page reference is to reprint edition).

2   Garza, *La Rebelion*, xxxi.

3   Charles Hamilton, *The Hitler Diaries: Fakes that Fooled the World* (Lexington, Kentucky: University Press of Kentucky, 1991), 73-74; William L. Joyce, "The Scholarly Implications of Documentary Forgeries," in Pat Bozeman, ed., *Forged Documents: Proceedings of the 1989 Houston Conference* (New Castle, Delaware: Oak Knoll Books, 1990), 43-44.

4   Perry, *With Santa Anna*, 50.

5   Perry, *With Santa Anna*, footnote 39, footnote 54; See Bill Groneman, *Alamo Defenders: A Geneology of the People and their Words* (Austin: Eakin Press, 1990), 22-23, 47-48, and 86.

6   Perry, *With Santa Anna*, 54-55; and Charles Merritt Barnes, "Aged Citizen Describes Alamo Fight and Fire," *San Antonio Express*, 1 July 1906; and "Bullet-Ridden and Tomahawk-Scarred San Antonio Home is Being Demolished," *San Antonio Express*, 19 April 1914.

7   Hamilton, *Great Forgers*, 287.

8   Perry, *With Santa Anna*, 45; and Hunnicutt, "A Mexican View of the Texas War," 63.

9   Perry, *With Santa Anna*, 54-55; and [Ford], "Fall of the Alamo," 170, printed in Groneman, *Eyewitness*, 92-93.

10 Perry, *With Santa Anna*, 53; and Dobie, *In the Shadow of History*, 45-46.

11 Perry, *With Santa Anna*, 26-33; Wallace Woolsey, translator and editor, *Memoirs for the History of the War in Texas* by Don Vincente Filisola, Vol. II (Austin: Eakin Press, 1987), 157-164; and Presley, "Santa Anna in Texas," 502, (footnote 54).

12 This story itself is very likely one of the enduring fictions of the Alamo. In one version of the letter from Houston to Fannin the source of this story is identified as Anselmo Borgara, who, in the Barsena et al Deposition states that he had already arrived at the Flores ranch from Bexar on Saturday night [the night before the Alamo fell]. Perry, *With Santa Anna*, 52; "Dusty Attic Brings Forth Epic Story of Mrs. Dickinson," *San Antonio Express*; and Jenkins, *Papers*, 43-46, 52-54; Thomas Ricks Lindley, Texian Army Investigations, Austin, to Bill Groneman, New York, August 26, 1994. Original in possession of the author; Amelia M. Williams, "A Critical Study of the Siege of the Alamo and of the Personnel of its Defenders," Ph.D. diss., University of Texas, 1931. Published in abridged form, *Southwestern Historical Quarterly* 37 (July 1933): 18; and Lindley, "Alamo Artillery," 9 (footnote 2).

13 Garza, *La Rebelion de Texas*, 79, 116; Perry, *With Santa Anna*, 60, 91; Telford Taylor, *The Anatomy of the Nuremberg Trials* (New York: Alfred A. Knopf, 1992), 13, 56-78, 84, 648; and James F. Willis, *Prologue to Nuremberg: The Politics and Diplomacy of Punishing War Criminals of the First World War* (Westport, Connecticut and London: Greenwood Press, 1982), 27, 157, 175.

14 Compare John Laffite [John A. Laflin], ed., *The Journal of Jean Laffite* (New York: Vantage Press, 1958), 9 and Perry, *With Santa Anna*, xxviii; Laffite, 9 and Perry, xxiv; Laffite, 14 and Perry, xxvii; Laffite, 32 and Perry, xxvii; Laffite, 153 and Perry, 190-191; Laffite, 62 and Perry 52.

15 Joseph Musso, Santa Monica, California, to Bernard Osher, Butterfield & Butterfield, San Francisco, California, 29 October 1998, copy in possession of the author.

16 Hamilton, *Great Forgers*, 123; and Audrey Lloyd to John Laffite (Laflin) 10 June 1967, Laffite Collection, Sam Houston Regional Library and Research Center, Liberty, Texas. Ms. Lloyd wrote to

Laflin, "What fascinating old paper on which you wrote your letter of June 8. Imagine paper of today lasting that long. Impossible! They just made it better in those days."

17 Perry, *With Santa Anna*, 57, 69, and 131.

18 Michael Lind, *The Alamo: An Epic* (New York: Houghton-Mifflin Company, 1997), 233-34, 313-14.

19 Garry Wills, "Remember the Alamo?" *New York Times Book Review*, 9 March 1997; and "Texas Pride" from Universal Press Syndicate press release, 20 June 1997.

20 Crisp, "When Revision Becomes Obsession," 143.

21 James E. Crisp, introduction to *With Santa Anna in Texas: A Personal Narrative of the Revolution*, Expanded Edition, trans., and ed., Carmen Perry (College Station, Texas: Texas A&M University Press, 1997), xxii, xiv; and Vickie Davidson, "Diary says Crockett died by execution," *San Antonio Express*, 10 September 1975.

22 William B. Travis to The People of Texas, 24 February 1836, original copy in the TSA, Austin; and Groneman, *Defense*, 29-35.

23 Chester Newell, *History of the Revolution in Texas* (New York: Wiley & Putnam, 1838; reprint, Arno Press, 1973), 82, 91 (page references are to reprint edition); and Frederick C. Chabot, *The Alamo: Mission Fortress and Shrine* (San Antonio: priv. pub., 1936), 38-39, 45. Chabot includes a transcription of the original version of the Travis letter in the beginning of his book. In the text, he gives the edited version, written in the third person and omitting the sentences in question.

24 Bill Groneman, "The Controversial Alleged Account of José Enrique de la Peña," *Military History of the West* 25 (Fall 1995), 134-35; Crisp, "When Revision Becomes Obsession," 148-151; and Crisp, introduction to *With Santa Anna*, xxi-xxii.

25 James E. Crisp, Dora Guerra, and Kent Lioret, "La Semana Perdida," in Perry, *With Santa Anna* Expanded Edition, 193-196.

26 Crisp, introduction to *With Santa Anna* Expanded Edition, xiv. It is impossible to capture the gleeful relish with which Jim relates this information in public appearances and interviews. He must feel that this adds an air of realism to the account because, obviously, a forger would never do this.

27 Groneman, *Defense*, 28-29; Crisp, "Little Book," 266-68; and introduction to *With Santa Anna* Expanded Edition, xvii-xviii.

28 Crisp, "Little Book," 274.

29 Ibid., 286. Translation by James E. Crisp.

30 For Crisp's discovery of the pamphlet see James E. Crisp, "Texas History, Texas Mystery," *Sallyport: The Magazine of Rice University*, (February/March 1995), 13-21.

31 Hamilton, *Hitler Diaries*, 72.

32 Perry, *With Santa Anna*, xxvi-xxxi; and Garza, *La Rebelion*, 3-8.

33 James Ernest Crisp, "Anglo-Texan Attitudes toward the Mexicans, 1821-1845" (Ph.D. diss., Yale University, 1976), 468.

$$\bullet \; \bullet \; \bullet \; \blacklozenge \; \bullet \; \bullet \; \bullet$$

Chapter 7—History for Sale

1 Carmina Danini, "A Piece of History for Sale," *San Antonio Express-News*, 23 May 1998, 9A.

2 Barry Shlachter, "Texas may lose Alamo diary," *Fort Worth Star-Telegram*, 7 September 1998, A14; and Don McLeese, "Account of Davy Crockett execution up for auction," *Austin American-Statesman*, 15 November 1998, A1, A14-A15.

3 Shlachter, "Texas may lose Alamo diary;" Barry Shlachter, "Texans may lose their historic Alamo diary," *Star-Banner*, 15 September 1998, 6A; Carmina Danini, "Alamo diary rescuer hunted," *San Antonio Express-News*, 18 November 1998. Steve Hardin stated that he told the interviewer he was concerned about having to *travel* to the Bancroft library or to Yale to be able to study the document. The interviewer stated that Steve did not want the Yankees to have it, and Steve said yes.

4 Rick Lyman, "Mexican's Memoir of Alamo a Rage: Story of Davy Crockett's Execution is Going on Auction Block," *New York Times*, 18 November 1998, A20. Despite a number of misquotes in this article, at least it did refer to the Peña account as a Mexican's memoir.

5 Gregory Shaw and Stephen L. Hardin, interview by Ann Curry, 6 October 1998, NBC's *Today Show*.

6 David McLemore, "What really happened at the Alamo?" *Dallas Morning News*, 22 November 1998, 10J.

7 Rendell, *Forging History*, 23; and Hamilton, *Great Forgers*, 123.

8 Steve Wiegand, "Alamo fight: Just how did Crockett die?" *Sacramento Bee*, 17 October 1998, A21.

9 Danini, "Alamo diary rescuer hunted," 2B.

10 McLeese, "Account of Davy Crockett execution up for auction," *Austin American-Statesman*, 15 November 1998, A1.

11 Ibid., A14.

12 Barry Shlachter, "Alamo Diary set for sale despite claim it's fake," *Fort Worth Star-Telegram*, 17 November, 1998, 3B, *Fort Worth Star-Telegram*, 17 November 1998; and Hamilton, *Great Forgers*, xxii-xxiii.

13 Shlachter, "Alamo Diary set for sale," 3B; and *Fine Books & Manuscripts—Featuring the Memoirs of José Enrique de la Peña* (San Francisco, Los Angeles, and Elgin, Illinois: Butterfield & Butterfield Auctioneers Corp., 1998), 58 and 62.

14 Carmina Danini and Laura Tolley, "Alamo diary owners donate historic buy to UT-Austin," *San Antonio Express News*, 16 December 1998, 1A.

15 Carmina Danini, "Texans buy Alamo diary," *San Antonio Express-News*, 19 November 1998, 1A.

16 "Accessions," *Southwestern Historical Quarterly* 102 (January 1999): 392.

• • • ◆ • • •

Chapter Eight—Conclusions

1 Carmina Danini, "Diary of attack at Alamo up for Sale," *San Antonio Express-News*, 24 May 1998, 9A; and "DRT wants Alamo to house de la Peña diary," *San Antonio Express-News*, 21 November 1998, 1B.

Sources

Archival Material

Amador, Juan Valentine, to the Generals, Chiefs of sections, and commanding officers, 5 March 1836. Archivo General de Mexico Papers, UTA.

Ayudantia De Inspeccion De Nuevo León y Tamaulipas. NLB, UTA.

Berlandier Papers. BRBML.

Bowie, James, to commander of the invading forces below Bejar, 23 February 1836. Yale Collection of Western Americana, BRBML.

Briscoe, A. to the Editor of the *Red River Herald*, 16 March 1836. DRTL.

Chapman, John Gadsby. *David Crockett*, oil on canvas, date unknown. Harry Ransom Humanities Research Center, UTA.

"Diary of José Enrique De La Peña." CAH.

Ford, John S. "The Alamo by Dr. Sutherland." John S. Ford Papers. CAH.

_____. "Memoirs of John S. Ford—1815-1836." John S. Ford Papers. CAH.

Gentilz Collection. DRTL.

Hannig, Susanna. "Testimony of Mrs. Hannig touching on the Alamo Massacre," 23 September 1876. TSA.

Jean Laffite Collection. Sam Houston Regional Library and Research Center, Liberty, Texas.

Millsaps, Isaac, the Alamo, San Antonio de Bexar, to [Mary Millsaps, Gonzales], 3 March 1836. University of Houston, Houston, Texas.

Peña, José Enrique de la. *Una Victima del Despotismo*. Mexico: Imprenta del Iris, 1839. Manuscripts and Archives Department, Sterling Memorial Library, Yale University, New Haven, Connecticut.

Sanchez-Navarro, José Juan. "Ayudantia de Inspeccion de Nuevo León y Tamaulipas. NLB, UTA.

Swartwout, Samuel, New York to James Morgan, Galveston Island, 29 June 1836. James Morgan Papers, Rosenburg Library, Galveston, Texas.

Travis, William B. "To the People of Texas & All Americans in the World," 24 February 1836. TSA.

Articles

Almonte, Juan N. "The Private Journal of Juan Nepomuceno Almonte." *Southwestern Historical Quarterly* 48 (July 1944): 10-32.

Anderson, Chris. "How did Davy die? Does the cap tell the tale?" *Blackpowder Annual*, 1992: 30.

"Accessions." *Southwestern Historical Quarterly* 102 (January 1999): 391-94.

Belkin, Lisa. "Lone Star Fakes." *New York Times Magazine*, 10 December 1989, 66-76.

Castro, Janice. "Judging the Hoax that Failed." *Time*, 25 February 1985, 60.

Chemerka, Bill (William R.). "De La Peña Papers Sold for $350,000—Crockett Death Account Part of Collection." *Alamo Journal*, December 1998.

Connelly, Thomas Lawrence. "Did David Crockett Surrender at the Alamo? A Contemporary Letter." *Journal of Southern History* 26 (1960): 368-76.

Costeloe, Michael P. "The Mexican Press of 1836 and the Battle of the Alamo." *Southwestern Historical Quarterly* 91 (April 1988): 533-43.

Covner, Craig R. "Before 1850: A New Look at the Alamo Through Art and Imagery." *Alamo Journal* 70 (March 1990): 3-10.

Crisp, James E. "Back to Basics: Conspiracies, Common Sense, and Occam's Razor." *Alamo Journal* 100 (March 1996): 15-23.

_____. "Davy in Freeze-Frame: Methodology or Madness?" *Alamo Journal* (October 1995).

_____. [Letter to the Editor]. *Alamo Journal* (September 1996).

_____. "The Little Book That Wasn't There: The Myth and Mystery of the de la Peña Diary." *Southwestern Historical Quarterly* 98 (October 1994): 260-296.

_____. "Texas History—Texas Mystery." *Sallyport: The Magazine of Rice University*, February/March 1995, 13-21.

_____. "Trashing Dolson: The Perils of Tendentious Interpretation." *Alamo Journal* 99 (December 1995): 3-14.

_____. "Truth, Confusion, and the de la Peña Controversy—A Final Reply." *Military History of the West* (Spring 1996).

_____. "When Revision Becomes Obsession: Bill Groneman and the de la Peña Diary." *Military History of the West* (Fall 1995).

Curtis, Gregory. "Forgery Texas Style." *Texas Monthly*, March 1989, 105.

Davidson, Richard A. "How Did Davy Really Die?" *Alamo Journal* 78 (October 1991): 3.

_____. [Letter to the Editor]. *Alamo Journal* (September 1997).

Davis, William C. "The Alamo Remembered." *American History Illustrated*, October 1967, Vol. 2, no. 6, 5.

————. "How Davy Probably Didn't Die." *Journal of the Alamo Battlefield Association* (Fall 1997): 11-37.

Dettman, Bruce. "Davy's Death: A Common Sense Approach." *Alamo Journal* (April 1994).

"Did Davy Crockett Die at the Alamo? Historian Carmen Perry Says No." *People Weekly* (13 October 1975).

Durham, Robert L. "Where Did Davy Die?" *Alamo Journal* (March 1997).

[Ford, John S.]. "The Fall of the Alamo." *Texas Mute Ranger*, April 1882.

Gray, Paul. "Fakes that have Skewed History." *Time*, 16 May 1983, 48-49.

Green, Michael R. "To the People of Texas & All Americans in the World." *Southwestern Historical Quarterly* 41 (April 1988): 483-508.

————. "Two Contemporary Views of Texas Revolutionaries." *Military History of Texas and the Southwest* 14 no. 4, 197-202.

Groneman, Bill. "Crockett at the Alamo" [Letter to the Editor]. *Wild West* (June 1996).

————. "Crockett's Last Stand." *Alamo Lore and Myth Organization Newsletter* 4 (December 1982): 1-8.

————. "The Controversial Alleged Account of José Enrique de la Peña." *Military History of the West* (Fall 1995).

————. "Crossing the Border—Writing Western History as a Non-academic Historian." *Roundup Magazine*, December 1995.

————. "The Death of Davy Crockett." *The Defender*, January 1976 and February 1976.

————. "De la Peña and the Alamo Mystery Victim." *Alamo Journal* 85 (February 1993): 6-8.

————. "De la Peña—The Man and the Myth." *Alamo Journal* (March 1998).

————. "The Diary of José Enrique de la Peña." *Journal of South Texas* 7 (1994): 28-51.

————. "A Last Final Reply or, How I Learned to Stop Worrying and Love Jim Crisp." *Military History of the West* (Spring 1996).

————. "Publish or Perish—Regardless: Jim Crisp and the de la Peña 'Diary.'" *Military History of the West* (Fall 1995).

————. "Some Comparisons to the de la Peña 'Diary.'" *Alamo Journal* 92 (July 1994): 8-9.

————. "Some Problems with the Almonte Account." *Alamo Journal* 90 (February 1994): 3-5.

————. "Some Problems with the Urriza Account." *Alamo Journal* 87 (July 1993): 6-7.

_____. "A Witness to the Executions?" *Alamo Journal* 88 (October 1993): 3-6.

Gustaitis Joseph. "There's No Mistake in Sam Patch." *American History Illustrated*, January/February 1991, 38.

Hammer, Joshua. "For the Hughes Hoaxers, Notoriety Lingers." *People Weekly*, 23 May 1983, 30.

Harburn, Dr. Todd E. "The Crockett Death Controversy." *Alamo Journal* 76 (April 1991): 5-8.

_____. "If You Can Tolerate One More Comment On . . ." *Alamo Journal* (June 1996).

Hardin, Stephen L. "David Crockett." *Military Illustrated: Past & Present*, February/March 1990, 28-35.

_____. "The Felix Nuñez Account and the Siege of the Alamo: A Critical Appraisal." *Southwestern Historical Quarterly* 94 (July 1990): 65-84.

Harrison, Lowell H. "David Crockett." *American History Illustrated*, Vol. 6 no. 4 (July 1971), 22-30.

Hawkins, Nigel. "How Did Davy Die? He Died Fighting!" *Alamo Journal* 69 (December 1989): 11.

Henry, William A., III. "Burdens of Bad Judgment." *Time*, 16 May 1983, 50-52.

_____. "Hitler's Diaries: Real or Fake?" *Time*, 9 May 1983, 92-94.

Henson, Margaret Swett. "Politics and the Treatment of the Mexican Prisoners after the Battle of San Jacinto." *Southwestern Historical Quarterly* 94 (October 1990): 189-230.

Horn, Miriam. "How the West Was Really Won." *U.S. News & World Report*, 21 May 1990.

Hunnicutt, Helen. "A Mexican View of the Texas War: Memoirs of a Veteran of the Two Battles of the Alamo." *Library Chronicle of the University of Texas* 4 (Summer 1951): 59-74.

Hutton, Paul Andrew. "The Alamo: An American Epic." *American History Illustrated*, March 1986, 12.

_____ and Bill Groneman. "Did Davy Crockett Die Fighting, or was He Captured and then Executed at the Alamo?" Interview by Candy Moulton, *Wild West*, February 1998, 62-64.

_____. "Frontier Hero Davy Crockett." *Wild West*, February 1999, 38-44.

_____. "Davy Crockett—He was Hardly King of the Wild Frontier." *TV Guide*, 4 February 1989, 24-25.

_____. "Davy Crockett—Still King of the Wild Frontier." *Texas Monthly*, November 1986, 122.

Jenkins, John H. "Did Davy Crockett Survive the Alamo?" *Texana* 1 (Summer 1963): 284-287.

Labadie, Nicholas. "San Jacinto Campaign." *Texas Almanac*, 1859.

Lind, Michael. "The Death of David Crockett." *Wilson Quarterly* (Winter 1998): 50-57.

Lindley, Thomas Ricks. "Alamo Artillery—Number, Type, Caliber and Concussion," *Alamo Journal* 82 (July 1992): 3-10.

_____. "Alamo Sources." *Alamo Journal* 74 (December 1990): 3-13.

_____. "Davy Crockett: The Alamo's High Private." *Alamo Journal* 64 (December 1988): 3-11.

_____. "Documents of the Texas Revolution." *Alamo Journal* (December 1996).

_____. "James Butler Bonham—October 17, 1835-March 6, 1836." *Alamo Journal* 62 (August 1988): 3-11.

_____. "José Enrique de la Peña's Petard. *Alamo Journal* (December 1997).

_____. "Killing Crockett—It's All In the Execution." *Alamo Journal* (May 1995).

_____. "Killing Crockett—Lindley's Opinion." *Alamo Journal* 98 (October 1995): 9-24.

_____. "Killing Crockett—Theory Paraded as Fact." *Alamo Journal* (July 1995).

Lord, Walter. "Myths and Realities of the Alamo." In *The Republic of Texas*, Stephen B. Oates, ed. 18-25. Palo Alto, California: American West Publishing Co., 1968.

Lyons, David. "The Death of David Crockett." *Alamo Lore and Myth Organization Newsletter* 4 (September 1982): 1-4.

Magnuson, Ed. "Hitler's Forged Diaries." *Time*, 16 May 1983, 36-47.

McGinty Brian. "They Never Found His Bones." *American History Illustrated*, January/February 1990, 52-57.

Musser, Dean. "Executions at the Alamo: Corroboration, Identification, and Speculation." *Alamo Journal* (December 1996).

Palmquist, Robert F. "High Private—David Crockett at the Alamo." *Real West*, December 1981, 12.

Paulsen, Barbara. "Say It Ain't So, Davy." *Texas Monthly*, November 1986.

Presley, James. "Santa Anna in Texas: A Mexican Viewpoint." *Southwestern Historical Quarterly* 62 (April 1959): 489-512.

Randle, Kevin D. "Santa Anna's Signal." *Military History*, April 1985, 35-41.

"¡Recuerda El Alamo!" *American Heritage Magazine*, October 1975, 57.

Reid, Jan. "Davy Crock?" *Texas Monthly*, May 1995.

Ruiz, Francis Antonio. "Fall of the Alamo and Massacre of Travis and His Brave Associates." *Texas Almanac* (1860).

Saar, John and Joshua Hammer. "The Fuhrer Follies." *People Weekly*, 23 May 1983, 26-29.

Schoelwer, Susan P. "The Artists' Alamo: A Reappraisal of Pictorial Evidence, 1836-1850." *Southwestern Historical Quarterly* 41 (April 1988): 411-56.

"Take That, John Wayne." *Texas Monthly*, August 1978, 76.

Timanus, Rod. "Alamo Executions and David Crockett." *Alamo Journal* (September 1997).

Von Schmidt, Eric. "The Alamo Remembered—From a Painter's Point of View." *Smithsonian*, March 1986, 54-66.

Voss, Frederick S. "Portraying an American Original: The Likenesses of Davy Crockett." *Southwestern Historical Quarterly* 91 (April 1988): 456-82.

Wheelwright, William Bond. "Watermarks." *Papermaker* 17 (1948): 1-6.

Wiener, Allen. [Letter to the Editor.] *Alamo Journal* (December 1997).

Williams, Amelia M. "A Critical Study of the Siege of the Alamo and of the Personnel of its Defenders" Ph.D. diss., University of Texas 1931. Published in abridged form. *Southwestern Historical Quarterly* 36 and 37 (1933-1934).

• • • ◆ • • •

Books

Aron, Paul. *Unsolved Mysteries of American History*. New York: John Wiley & Sons, Inc., 1997.

Bass Jr., Feris A., and B.R. Brunson, eds. *Fragile Empires: The Texas Correspondence of Samuel Swartwout and James Morgan 1836-1856*. Austin: Shoal Creek Publishers, Inc., 1978.

Baugh, Virgil E. *Rendezvous at the Alamo*. New York: Pageant Press, 1960; reprint, Lincoln, Nebraska: University of Nebraska Press, 1985.

Becerra, Francisco. *A Mexican Sergeant's Recollections of the Alamo & San Jacinto*. With an introduction by Dan Kilgore. Austin: Jenkins Publishing Co., 1980.

Bennett, Leonora. *Historical Sketch and Guide to the Alamo*. San Antonio: priv. printed, 1904.

Boyd, Bob. *The Texas Revolution: A Day-By-Day Account*. Soren W. Nielsen, ed. San Angelo, Texas: San Angelo Standard, Inc., 1986.

Bozeman, Pat, ed. *Forged Documents: Proceedings of the 1989 Houston Conference*. New Castle, Delaware: Oak Knoll Books, 1990.

Callcott, Wilfrid Hardy. *Santa Anna: The Story of an Enigma Who Once Was Mexico*. n.p.: University of Oklahoma Press, 1936; reprint, Hamden, Connecticut: Archon Books, 1964.

Carlson, Oliver. *The Man Who Made News: James Gordon Bennett*. New York: Duell, Sloan and Pearce, 1942.

Caro, Ramón Martinez. *Verdadera Idea de la Primera Campaña de Tejas y Susesos Ocurridos después de la accion de San Jacinto*. Mexico: Imprenta de Santiago Perez, 1837.

Castañeda, Carlos E. *The Mexican Side of the Texas Revolution*. Dallas: P.L. Turner Co., 1928; reprint, New York: Arno Press, 1976.

Chabot, Frederick C. *The Alamo: Mission Fortress and Shrine*. San Antonio: priv. printed, 1936.

Chariton, Wallace O. *Exploring the Alamo Legends*. Plano, Texas: Wordware Publishing, Inc., 1990.

_____. *100 Days in Texas: The Alamo Letters*. Plano, Texas: Wordware Publishing, Inc., 1990.

Connell, Evan S. *Son of the Morning Star*. San Francisco: North Point Press, 1984.

Corner, William, ed. and comp. *San Antonio de Bexar: A Guide and History*. San Antonio: Bainbridge & Corner, 1890.

Daughters of the Republic of Texas. *Muster Rolls of the Texas Revolution*. Austin: priv. printed, 1986.

_____. *The Alamo: Long Barrack Museum*. Dallas: Taylor Publishing Co., 1986.

Davis, Robert E., ed. *Diary of William Barret Travis*. Waco, Texas: Texian Press, 1966.

Davis, William C. *Three Roads to the Alamo*. New York: HarperCollins Publishers, 1998.

Day, James M., compiler. *The Texas Almanac 1857-1873: A Compendium of Texas History*. Waco, Texas: Texian Press, 1967.

Derr, Mark. *The Frontiersman: The Real Life and the Many Legends of Davy Crockett*. New York: William Morrow and Co., Inc., 1993.

DeShields, James T. *Tall Men with Long Rifles*. San Antonio: The Naylor Co., 1935; reprint, 1971.

Dobie, J. Frank, et al, eds. *In the Shadow of History*. Austin: Texas Folklore Society, 1939; reprint, Detroit: Folklore Associates, 1971.

Driggs, Howard R., and Sarah S. King. *Rise of the Lone Star*. New York: Frederick A. Stokes Co., 1936.

Ellis, Edward S. *The Life of Colonel David Crockett*. Philadelphia: Porter & Coates, 1884.

Ellison, Katherine W. and Robert Buckhout. *Psychology and Criminal Justice*. New York: Harper & Row Publishers, 1981.

Ferris, Sylvia Van Voast and Eleanor Sellers Hoppe. *Scalpels and Sabers: Nineteenth Century Medicine in Texas*. Austin: Eakin Press, 1985.

Filisola, Vincente. *Memoirs for the History of the War in Texas*, Vol. II, Edited and translated by Wallace Woolsey. Austin: Eakin Press, 1987.

Fine Books & Manuscripts—Featuring the Memoirs of José Enrique de la Peña. San Francisco, Los Angeles, and Elgin, Illinois: Butterfield & Butterfield Auctioneers Corp., 1998.

Fisher, Leonard E. *The Alamo*. New York: Holiday House, 1987.

Ford, John S. *Origins and Fall of the Alamo*. San Antonio: Johnson Brothers Printing Co., 1900; reprint, Austin: Shelly Publishers, n.d.

Foreman, Gary L. *Crockett: The Gentleman from the Cane*. Dallas: Taylor Publishing Co., 1986.

Frantz, Joe B. *Texas: A Bicentennial History*. New York: W.W. Norton & Co., 1976.

Gaddy, Jerry J. *Texas in Revolt*. Fort Collins, Colorado: Old Army Press, 1973.

Gravell, Thomas L. and George Miller. *A Catalogue of Foreign Watermarks Found on Paper Used in America*. New York & London: Garland Publishing, Inc., 1983.

Gray, William F. *From Virginia to Texas, 1835-'36*. Houston: Gray, Dillaye & Co., 1909; reprint, Houston: Fletcher Young Publishing Co., 1965.

Green, Rena Maverick, ed. *Memoirs of Mary A. Maverick*. San Antonio: Alamo Printing Co., 1921.

Groneman, Bill. *Alamo Defenders: A Geneology of the People and their Words*. Austin: Eakin Press, 1990.

_____. *Battlefields of Texas*. Plano, Texas: Republic of Texas Press, 1998.

_____. *Defense of a Legend: Crockett and the de la Peña Diary*. Plano, Texas: Republic of Texas Press, 1994.

_____. *Eyewitness to the Alamo*. Plano, Texas: Republic of Texas Press, 1996.

_____ and Phil Rosenthal. *Roll Call at the Alamo*. Vol. 1, Sources Texana Series. Fort Collins, Colorado: Old Army Press, 1985.

Guerra, Mary Ann. *An Alamo Album*. San Antonio: priv. printed, 1979.

_____. *San Antonio*. San Antonio: priv. printed, 1980.

Hamilton, Charles. *American Autographs*. Vols. I & II. Norman, Oklahoma: University of Oklahoma Press, 1983.

_____. *Collecting Autographs and Manuscripts.* Norman, Oklahoma: University of Oklahoma Press, 1961.

_____. *Great Forgers and Famous Fakes: The Manuscript Forgers of America and How They Duped the Experts.* New York: Crown Publishers, Inc., 1980, reprint, Lakewood, Colorado: Glenbridge Publishing Ltd., 1996.

_____. *The Hitler Diaries: Fakes that Fooled the World.* Lexington, Kentucky: University Press of Kentucky, 1991.

_____. *Scribblers and Scoundrels.* New York: Paul S. Eriksson, Inc., 1968.

Hardin, Stephen L. *Texian Iliad: A Military History of the Texas Revolution.* Austin: University of Texas Press, 1994.

Harris, Charles H. *A Mexican Family Empire: The Latifundio of the Sanchez-Navarros, 1765-1867.* Austin & London: University of Texas Press, 1975.

Harrison, Shirley. *The Diary of Jack the Ripper.* New York: Hyperion, 1993.

Harrison, Wilson R. *Forgery Detection: A Practical Guide.* New York: Frederick A. Praeger Publisher, 1964.

_____. *Suspect Documents: Their Scientific Examination.* New York: Frederick A. Praeger Publisher, 1958.

Hauck, Richard Boyd. *Crockett: A Bio-Bibliography.* Westport, Connecticut and London: Greenwood Press, 1982.

Huneycutt, C.D., trans. *At The Alamo: The Memoirs of Capt. Navarro.* New London, North Carolina: Gold Star Press, 1988.

Hutton, Paul Andrew. Introduction to *A Narrative of the Life of David Crockett,* Written by Himself. Philadelphia: E.L. Carey and A. Hart, 1834; reprint, Lincoln, Nebraska and London: University of Nebraska Press, 1987.

Irving, Clifford. *Hoax.* Sagaponack, New York: Permanent Press, 1981; reprint of *Project Octavio.* Great Britain: Allison & Busby Ltd., 1977.

Jameson, W.C. *Unsolved Mysteries of the Old West.* Plano, Texas: Republic of Texas Press, 1999.

_____. *Return of Assassin John Wilkes Booth.* Plano, Texas: Republic of Texas Press, 1998.

_____ and Frederick Bean. *Return of the Outlaw Billy the Kid.* Plano, Texas: Republic of Texas Press, 1998.

Jenkins, John H. ed. *Papers of the Texas Revolution 1835-1836.* 10 Volumes. Austin: Presidial Press, 1973.

Johnson, Leah Carter. *San Antonio: St. Anthony's Town.* San Antonio: The Naylor Co., 1976.

Johnson, William Weber. *The Birth of Texas*. Boston: Houghton-Mifflin, North Star Books, 1960.

Keegan, John A. *A History of Warfare*. New York: Alfred A. Knopf, 1993.

Kilgore, Dan. *How Did Davy Die?*. College Station, Texas and London: Texas A&M University Press, 1978.

King, C. Richard. *Susanna Dickinson: Messenger of the Alamo*. Austin: Shoal Creek Publishing Co., 1976.

Laffite, John A. [John Laflin]. *The Journal of Jean Laffite*. New York: Vantage Press, 1958.

Lenz, Hans. *Historia del Papel en México y Cosas Relacionadas (1525-1950)*. Mexico: Miguel Angel Porrúa, 1990.

Lind, Michael. *The Alamo: An Epic*. Boston and New York: Houghton-Mifflin Company, 1997.

Lofaro, Michael A., and Joe Cummings, eds. *Crockett at Two Hundred*. Knoxville, Tennessee: University of Tennessee Press, 1989.

Long, Jeff. *Duel of Eagles: The Mexican and U.S. Fight for the Alamo*. New York: William Morrow and Co., Inc., 1990.

Lord, Walter. *A Night To Remember*. New York: Bantam Books, 1988.

_____. *A Time to Stand*. New York: Harper & Row Publishers, 1961.

_____. *The Night Lives On*. New York: Jove Books, 1987.

Maverick, Mary A. *The Fall of the Alamo*. n.p.: n.p., 1898.

McAlister, George A. *Alamo: The Price of Freedom*. San Antonio: Docutex, Inc., 1988.

McDonald, Archie P. *Travis*. Austin: The Pemberton Press, 1976.

McGuire, E. Patrick. *The Forgers*. Bernardsville, New Jersey: Padric Publishing Co., 1969.

McHenry, J. Patrick. *A Short History of Mexico*. Garden City, New York: Dolphin Books, Doubleday & Co., Inc., 1962.

Mills, John Fitzmaurice and John M. Mansfield. *The Genuine Article*. New York: Universe Books, 1979.

Morphis, James M. *History of Texas from Its Discovery and Settlement*. New York: United States Publishing Co., 1875.

Myers, John Myers. *The Alamo*. New York: E.P. Dutton & Co., Inc., 1948.

Naifeh, Steven and Gregory White Smith. *The Mormon Murders*. New York: Weidenfeld & Nicolson, 1988.

Nance, Joseph Milton. *Attack and Counterattack*. Austin: University of Texas Press, 1964.

Nesbitt, Alexander. *The History and Technique of Lettering*. New York: Dover Publications, Inc., 1957.

Nevin, David. *The Texans*. The Old West Series. New York: Time-Life Books, 1975.

Newell, Chester. *History of the Revolution in Texas*. New York: Wiley & Putnam, 1838; reprint, New York: Arno Press, 1973.

Nofi, Albert A. *The Alamo and the Texas War of Independence*, September 30, 1835, to April 21, 1836. Conshohocken, Pennsylvania: Combined Books, 1992.

Perry, Carmen, trans., and ed. *With Santa Anna in Texas: A Personal Narrative of the Revolution by José Enrique de la Peña*. Expanded Edition. With an Introduction by James E. Crisp. College Station, Texas: Texas A&M University Press, 1997.

Potter, Reuben M. *The Fall of the Alamo: A Reminiscence of the Revolution of Texas*. San Antonio: Herald Steam Press, 1860.

_____. "The Fall of the Alamo." *Magazine of American History*. January 1878; reprint in book form, Hillsdale, New Jersey: The Otterden Press, 1977.

Potter, Lou, with William Miles and Nina Rosenblum. *Liberators: Fighting on Two Fronts in World War II*. New York, San Diego, and London: Harcourt Brace Jovanovich, 1992.

Proctor, Ben H. *The Battle of the Alamo*. Austin: Texas State Historical Assc., 1986.

Rendell, Kenneth W. *Forging History: The Detection of Fake Letters and Documents*. Norman, Oklahoma and London: University of Oklahoma Press, 1994.

_____. *History Comes to Life: Collecting Historical Letters and Documents*. Norman, Oklahoma and London: University of Oklahoma Press, 1995.

Rios, John F., ed. and comp. *Readings on the Alamo*. New York: Vantage Press, Inc., 1987.

Ryder-Taylor, Henry. *History of the Alamo and of the Local Franciscan Missions*. San Antonio: Nic Tengg, 1900.

Sanchez Garza, J. *La Rebelion de Texas: Manuscrito Inedito de 1836 por un Oficial de Santa Anna*. Mexico: A. Frank de Sanchez, 1955.

Sanchez Lamego, Miguel A. *Apuntes Para La Historia del Arma de Ingenieros en Mexico: Historia del Batallón de Zapadores*. Tomo 1. Mexico, D.F.: Secretaria de la Defensa Nacional Taller Autografico, 1943.

_____. *The Siege and Taking of the Alamo*. Santa Fe: Press of the Territorian, 1968.

Sanchez-Navarro y Peón, Carlos. *La Guerra de Tejas: Memorias de un Soldado*. Mexico: Editorial Polis, 1938.

Santos, Richard G. *Santa Anna's Campaign Against Texas*. n.p.: Texian Press, 1968; reprint, Salisbury, North Carolina: Documentary Publications, n.d.

Schoelwer, Susan Prendergast, with Tom Glasser. *Alamo Images: Changing Perceptions of a Texas Experience*. With an introduction by Paul Andrew Hutton. Dallas: DeGolyer Library and Southern Methodist University Press, 1985.

Shackford, James Atkins. *David Crockett: The Man and the Legend*. Chapel Hill, North Carolina: University of North Carolina Press, 1956; reprint, Westport, Connecticut: Greenwood Press, 1981.

Shapiro, Marc. *Total Titanic*. New York: Pocket Books, 1998.

Shoumatoff, Alex. *Legends of the American Desert: Sojourns in the Greater Southwest*. New York: Alfred A. Knopf, 1997.

Sillitoe, Linda and Allen Roberts. *Salamander*. Salt Lake City, Utah: Signature Books, 1988.

Sowell, Andrew Jackson. *Rangers and Pioneers of Texas*. San Antonio: n.p., 1884.

Spencer, Frank. *Piltdown: A Scientific Forgery*. London, Oxford, and New York: Natural History Museum Publications, Oxford University Press, 1990.

Streeter, Thomas W. *Bibliography of Texas 1795-1845*. Portland, Maine: Anthoensen Press, 1955; reprint, Woodbridge, Connecticut: Research Publications, Inc., 1983.

Sutherland, Dr. John. *The Fall of the Alamo*. Edited by Annie B. Sutherland. San Antonio: The Naylor Co., 1936.

Taylor, Telford. *The Anatomy of the Nuremberg Trials*. New York: Alfred A. Knopf, 1992.

Taylor, Tom. *Texfake: an Account of the Theft and Forgery of Early Texas Printed Documents*. Austin: W. Thomas Taylor, 1991.

Thompson, Frank. *Alamo Movies*. Plano, Texas: Republic of Texas Press, 1994.

Tinkle, Lon. *13 Days to Glory: The Siege of the Alamo*. New York, Toronto & London: McGraw-Hill Book Co., Inc., 1958.

_____. *The Valiant Few: Crisis at the Alamo*. New York: Macmillan Co., 1964.

Todish, Tim J. & Terry S. Todish. *Alamo Sourcebook 1836: A Comprehensive Guide to the Alamo and the Texas Revolution*. Austin: Eakin Press, 1998.

Turner, Martha Anne. *William Barret Travis: His Sword and His Pen*. Waco, Texas: Texian Press, 1972.

Tyler, Ron, Douglas E. Barnett, Roy R. Barkley, Penelope C. Anderson, Mark F. Odintz, eds. *The New Handbook of Texas*, 6 Vols. Austin: The TSHA, 1996.

Walker, Dale L. *Legends and Lies: Great Mysteries of the American West*. New York: A Tom Doherty Associates Book, 1997.

Warren, Robert Penn. *Remember the Alamo*. New York: Random House Inc., 1958.

Webb, Walter Prescott, ed. *The Handbook of Texas*, Vols. I & II. Austin: Texas State Historical Assoc., 1952.

Willis, James F. *Prologue to Nuremberg: The Politics and Diplomacy of Punishing War Criminals of the First World War*. Westport, Connecticut and London: Greenwood Press, 1982.

· · · ◆ · · ·

Correspondence

Crisp, James E., William Groneman, and Michael Lind. "Correspondence." *Wilson Quarterly*. (Spring 1998): 7-11.

Elder, Ralph L., Barker Texas History Center, Austin, to Bill Groneman, New York, 15 July, 21 August, 26 October 1991.

Gannon, Gerald R., John R. Knaggs, Jim Dumas, and Jean Mangano. "The Roar of the Crowd." *Texas Monthly*, January 1987.

Garner, Jane, UTA, to Bill Groneman, New York, 15 July 1991.

Green, Casey Edward CA, Archivist, Rosenburg Library, Galveston, to Bill Groneman, New York, 23 August 1991.

Green, Michael R., Austin, to Bill Groneman, New York, 25 April, 24 May 1991.

Guerra, Dora, University of Texas, San Antonio, to Bill Groneman, New York, 14 May, 4 June, 13 August 1991.

Hubbard, Clyde, Cuernavaca, Mexico, to Bill Groneman, New York, 18 January, 17 March, 20 April 1992, 10 February, 21 July 1993.

Hutton, Paul Andrew, Alburquerque, New Mexico, to Bill Groneman, New York, July 1989.

Lindley, Thomas Ricks, Austin, to Bill Groneman, New York, 26 August 1994.

Lloyd, Audrey, Texas, to John Laffite [Laflin], South Carolina, 10 June 1967, Sam Houston Regional Library and Research Center.

Marchado, Manuel A., Missoula, Montana, to Ed Eakin, Austin, 1 November 1990, (including a translation of Peña document: Caja 534/C/111, 122 224-42).

Moffit, A. UTA to Dr. T.S. Painter, president, University of Texas, 15 November 1950.

Musso, Joseph, Santa Monica, California, to Bernard Osher, Butterfield & Butterfield, San Francisco, California, 29 October 1998.

Perry, Carmen, San Antonio, to Bill Groneman, New York, 18 March, 6 April, 10 May 1991.

Rager, Kay, DRTL, to Bill Groneman, New York, 25 June 1991.

Velasco, Sergio, TSA, Austin, to Bill Groneman, New York, 20 June 1991.

• • • ◆ • • •

Newspapers

"Alamo Massacre—as told by the Late Madam Candalearia [sic]." *San Antonio Light*, 22 February 1899.

"Another Story of the Alamo—The Battle Described by an Alleged Eyewitness." *San Antonio Express*, 12 April 1896.

Barnes, Charles Merritt. "Aged Citizen Describes Alamo Fight and Fire." *San Antonio Express*, 1 July 1906.

_____. "Alamo's Only Survivor." *San Antonio Express*, 12, 19 May 1907.

_____. "Story of the Massacre of the Alamo Heroes." *San Antonio Express*, 7 March 1905.

Brooklyn Daily Eagle, 15 April 1912.

"Bullet-Ridden and Tomahawk-Scarred San Antonio Home is Being Demolished." *San Antonio Express*, 19 April 1914.

"Children of the Alamo." *Houston Chronicle*, 8 and 9 November 1901.

Cooper, Texas Jim. "Peña's Diary: How Did David Crockett Die?" *Carrollton (Texas) Star*, 6 November 1975.

"Crockett executed at Alamo: researcher" *Jackson Sun*, 16 November 1997.

"Crockett furor simmers." *San Antonio Express-News*, 26 October 1975.

"Crockett's Death at the Alamo Doubted." *New York Times*, 21 September 1975, 45: 1.

Danini, Carmina. "Alamo diary rescuer hunted." *San Antonio Express-News*, 18 November 1998.

_____. "A Piece of History for Sale." *San Antonio Express-News*, 23 May 1998, 9A.

_____. "Diary of attack at Alamo up for Sale." *San Antonio Express-News*, 24 May 1998, 9A

_____. "DRT wants Alamo to house de la Peña diary." *San Antonio Express-News*, 21 November 1998, 1B.

_____. "Texans buy Alamo diary." *San Antonio Express-News*, 19 November 1998, 1A.

_____, and Laura Tolley. "Alamo diary owners donate historic buy to UT-Austin." *San Antonio Express-News*, 16 December 1998, 1A.

"Davee, Davy Crockett: Coward of the Wild Frontier—and Jim Bowie had a yellow streak, too." *The Star*, 11 September 1990.

Davidson, Vickie. "Diary says Crockett died by execution." *San Antonio Express*, 10 September 1975.

"Davy Crockett probably surrendered at Alamo, history professor says." *Austin Star-Telegram*, 14 November 1997.

Denver Times, 15 April 1912.

DeShields, James T. "[Dr. John Sutherland]." *Dallas Morning News*, 5 and 12 February 1911.

Detroit Democratic Free Press, 9 November 1836.

Dolson, George M. "Texas—Extract from a letter written by Mr. George M. Dolson, an officer in the Texian army to his brother in this city: Dated Galveston Island, Camp Trevos [sic] July 19, 1836." *Detroit Democratic Free Press*, 7 September 1836.

"Dusty Attic Brings Forth Epic Story of Mrs. Dickinson. Her Photo Found by History Professor." *San Antonio Express*, n.d. 1929.

"1836 Paper Tells Story of Davy's Death." *Knoxville News-Sentinal*, 5 May 1955.

Eckhardt, Charley. "Is the Alamo diary authentic or fake?" *Seguin (Texas) Gazette-Enterprise*, 31 March 1994.

"Extract of a Letter from a Friend to the Editor." *New Orleans Commercial Bulletin*, 11 April 1836.

"Extract of a letter from a friend to the Editor." *Portland (Maine) Advertiser*, 3 May 1836.

"Fall of the Alamo—Historical Reminiscences of the Aged Madam Candelaria." *San Antonio Express*, 6 March 1892.

Goddard, Dan. "The Death of Davy Crockett—Rice Filmmaker Documents the Debate over Alamo Hero's Death." *San Antonio Express-News*, 5 March 1995.

[Gray, William F.] "Letter From Texas—Correspondence of the Fredricksburg Arena—Groce's Retreat, March 30th, 1836." *Frankfort (Kentucky) Commonwealth*, 25 May 1836.

Helyar, John. "Davy Crockett was no Great Shakes, The Debunkers Say." *Wall Street Journal*, 10 July 1986, 1 (W) and 1 (E).

Hinckley, David. "End of the innocence: Crockett debunked." *New York Daily News*, 11 December 1990.

_____. "The eyes of N.Y. are upon y'all." *New York Daily News*, 3 March 1992.

_____. "Phew! Davy Crockett survives another attack." *New York Daily News*, 12 March 1991.

"How the Alamo Really Looked: Earliest Pictures that tend to Clear up Mystery." *San Antonio Express*, 28 September 1913.

Lind, Michael. "Crockett's return pushes buttons left and right." *Arizona Daily Star*, 27 November 1998.

Loranca, Manuel. Interview, "Santa Anna's Last Effort." *San Antonio Express*, 28 June 1878.

Lyman, Rick. "Mexican's Memoir of Alamo a Rage: Story of Davy Crockett's Execution is Going on Auction Block." *New York Times*, 18 November 1998, A20.

"Many Valuable Lafitte Papers Lost in Blaze." *Spartanburg (South Carolina) Journal*, 10 December 1959.

Martínez, Rick. "'Missing Week' adds insight to Alamo battle." *San Antonio Express-News*, 12 November 1995, Sec. 1B.

May, Carl. "Laffite History—Relived." *Spartanburg (South Carolina) Journal*, 28 November 1966, Sec. 2.

McLeese, Don. "Account of Davy Crockett execution up for auction." *Austin American-Statesman*, 15 November 1998, A14.

McLemore, David. "What really happened at the Alamo?" *Dallas Morning News*, 22 November 1998, 10J.

Mitchell, Christie. "Story of Lafitte's Demise Discounted." *Galveston News*, 19 November 1967, 15B.

Monroe (New York) Democrat, 5 April 1836.

"More Particulars Respecting the Fall of the Alamo." *Telegraph and Texas Register*, 24 March 1836.

Morning Courier and New York Enquirer, 26 March 1836, 9 July 1936.

Mosquito Mexicano, 5 April 1836.

New York Herald, 15 April 1912.

Nuñez, Felix. "Fall of the Alamo." *Fort Worth Gazette*, 23 June 1889.

Phelan, Charlette. "Carmen Perry—The Davy Crockett Affray." *Houston Post*, 4 April 1976.

Rather, Dan. "Defending 'The Alamo' [Letter to the Editor]." *New York Times Book Review*, 30 March 1997.

Sancton, Thomas. "Says Jean LaFitte Died 'A Mild Old Man' in Alton, Ill." *New Orleans Times-Picayune*, 15 September 1950.

Santos, Richard G. "Alamo Countdown." *San Antonio Express-News*, 6, 7, 8 March 1989.

Shlachter, Barry. "Alamo Diary set for sale despite claim it's fake." *Fort Worth Star-Telegram*, 17 November, 1998, 1B.

_____. "Texans may lose their historic Alamo diary." *Star-Banner*, 15 September 1998, 6A.

_____. "Texas may lose Alamo diary." *Fort Worth Star-Telegram*, 7 September 1998, 7.

Stamford (Connecticut) Sentinel, 28 March 1836.

"Story of Enrique Esparza." *San Antonio Express*, 22 November 1902.

Sutton, Geoff. "Davy, Davy Crockett coward of the Wild Frontier." *Daily Mirror*, 23 August 1990.

"The Survivor of the Alamo." *San Antonio Express*, 28 April 1881.

"Texas." *Frankfort (Kentucky) Commonwealth*, 27 June 1836.

"Texas Pride." Universal Press Syndicate press release, 20 June 1997.

Travis, William B., to Sam Houston, 25 February 1836. *Arkansas Gazette*, 12 April 1836.

Tutt, Bob. "Crockett's death mystery lives on." *Houston Chronicle*, 8 March 1998, sec. 1E.

West, Felton. "How Crockett Died Still Stirs Furor." *Houston Post*, 22 November 1985.

Wiegand, Steve. "Alamo fight: Just how did Crockett die?" *Sacramento Bee*, 17 October 1998, A21.

Wills, Garry. "Remember the Alamo?" *New York Times Book Review*, 9 March 1997.

"Witnessed Last Struggle of the Alamo Patriots." *San Antonio Express*, 19 July 1907.

Whitaker, William. "Alamo battle is 'racist myth,' according to university prof." *Del Rio (Texas) News-Herald*, 19 March 1986, Sec. 10C.

· · · ◆ · · ·

Unpublished Material

Crisp, James Ernest. "Anglo-Texan Attitudes toward the Mexicans, 1821-1845." Ph.D diss., Yale University, 1976.

"How Did Davy Die?" BBC Radio 4, London, 6 March 1997.

Lindley, Thomas Ricks. "The revealing of Dr. John Sutherland." DRTL, San Antonio, Texas, n.d.

Robbins, David Lawrence. "David Crockett at the Alamo: An Analysis of His Death." Unpublished manuscript, 1987.

Shaw, Gregory, and Stephen L. Hardin. Interview by Ann Curry, NBC's *Today Show*, 6 October 1998.

Index